"This book is the answer to hundreds of CIOs who have asked me how IT can be used to disrupt their market and change the rules of competition. If you live in a hypercompetitive world, CIOs will find this book an invaluable resource."

Richard A. D'Aveni, author of *Hypercompetition*

"I wish Bernie Boar had written this book 20 years ago. And I wish every IT manager and architect had read it and placed his hand on it and sworn by it 20 years ago. Then we wouldn't be in the pickle we find ourselves in today!"

John A. Zachman

"The world of technology has architects that build structures that have been designed on the back of napkins. Novel as these designs are, there is an element of discipline and rigor that is missing. Bernie Boar's book sets the stage for a firm foundation for information systems across the enterprise."

Bill Inmon

"Boar, a pioneer in enterprise systems architecture, has finally filled a long-standing gap in our field. Now, we can design blueprints for the technology infrastructure using rigorous modeling techniques similar to those for data and applications.

I recommend this book for architects who want to plan and design integrated, flexible enterprise-wide systems."

Steven H. Spewak, PhD
Principal, Enterprise Architects, Inc.

"This book is a must read for both Senior Management and serious Enterprise Architecture practitioners committed to deliver information technology capabilities as a competitive advantage. This is much more than just a "how to" book on Architecture Blueprinting. Bernie Boar captures the essence of the REAL work Enterprise Architects should be doing."

Vinny Raineri
Information Technology Strategist
AT&T Consumer Markets

Constructing Blueprints for Enterprise IT Architectures

Constructing Blueprints for Enterprise IT Architectures

Bernard H. Boar

Director of Strategic Solutions
RCG Information Technology

WILEY COMPUTER PUBLISHING

John Wiley & Sons, Inc.
New York • Chichester • Weinheim • Brisbane • Singapore • Toronto

Publisher: Robert Ipsen
Editor: Theresa Hudson
Managing Editor: Angela Murphy
Electronic Products, Associate Editor: Mike Sosa
Text Design & Composition: Publishers' Design and Production Services

Designations used by companies to distinguish their products are often claimed as trademarks. In all instances where John Wiley & Sons, Inc., is aware of a claim, the product names appear in initial capital or ALL CAPITAL LETTERS. Readers, however, should contact the appropriate companies for more complete information regarding trademarks and registration.

This book is printed on acid-free paper. ∞

Published by John Wiley & Sons, Inc.

Published simultaneously in Canada.

This publication is designed to provide accurate and authoritative information in regard to the subject matter covered. It is sold with the understanding that the publisher is not engaged in professional services. If professional advice or other expert assistance is required, the services of a competent professional person should be sought.

Library of Congress Cataloging-in-Publication Data:

Boar, Bernard H.
   Constructing blueprints for enterprise IT architectures / Bernard
  Boar.
     p. cm.
   "Wiley Computer Publishing."
   Includes index.
   ISBN 0-471-29620-1 (alk. paper)
   1. Management information systems. 2. System design. I. Title.
  T58.6.B584 1998
  658.4′038.dc21   98-8272

Printed in the United States of America

10 9 8 7 6 5 4 3 2 1
Printed and bound by Malloy Lithographing, Inc.

For Diane, Jessica and Debbie
With Love Always

On Strategy

Go forth where they don't expect it; attack where they are unprepared.

—Sun Tzu, The Art of War

Contents

Foreword

It is no secret that the telecommunications industry has entered a state of hyper-competition. All of the industry drivers that propel a hyper-competitive business environment are present:

- Barriers to market entry are being eroded as the telecommunications industry experiences radical deregulation.
- The technology foundations of the industry are being destabilized by revolutionary technologies such as voice Internet.
- The power balance between customer and supplier has shifted to the customer who now has numerous choices of supplier and mode of supply such as PIC relationship, dial around alternatives, and prepaid cards.
- Globalization is motivating the need to form international alliances to deliver integrated services to global clients.
- Multiple deep pocketed and able competitors like Worldcomm, GTE, Sprint, SBC, Bell Atlantic, US West, and Ameritech are all eyeing each other's markets with envy.

It is a competitive business environment in which advantage becomes fleeting and one must continuously reinvent attractive value propositions at compelling price points to attract and retain ever more demanding customers.

I was therefore quite excited when recently my job responsibilities were extended to include IT architecture for the AT&T Consumer Markets Division. In this role, my staff of IT architects are responsible for the design and evolution of our IT architecture so that the Consumers Market Division can win in the marketplace everyday, with every customer, and with every transaction. It is our mission to order our IT assets so that in the hyper-competitive game of move and counter-move, we can continuously rearrange our IT assets to create the game winning moves.

This is not an easy mission. Our architecture supports the entire customer experience. It is an architecture characterized by enormous volumes of transactions, large quantities of data, demanding internal users, heterogeneous technologies, and subtle interoperability requirements. This would be an enormous challenge in a period of moderately intense competition but we have to do it, and do it extremely well, in a period of hyper-competitive instability.

The ideas Bernie Boar presents in this book deserve careful consideration. They offer specific ways to increase the clarity of architectural communication. I believe that such clarity greatly improves the likelihood that business needs will be appropriately translated into useful technical products. It is our experience that technological competence is necessary but not sufficient to do architecture well. Architecture has such an all-encompassing impact on the systems and business community that visualization is necessary to enable clear communication. One could neither build nor maintain an aircraft carrier from casual and ad-hoc sketches. IT systems are becoming as complicated and, proportionality, as important to the business as an aircraft carrier is to the defense of a country, yet our IT practices have not risen to the challenge. To meet the challenge of IT based hyper-competition, IT architecture must be done with the same blueprinting precision, formal representation, and discipline that all engineering professions have adopted.

It is an old adage that *a picture is worth 10 thousand words*. When you have an information systems community where thousands of people have to work in a coordinated but dispersed manner to create advantage, that picture has to communicate the exact same ten thousand words to each individual. That result is not a fortuitous accident, but the consequence of implementing a formal blueprinting system to represent IT architectures in a consistent and predictable manner. In that way, we position our IT assets so that we disrupt the status quo, so that we create favorable imbalances, so that we bring excitement and value to our customers, and so that we prevail over our competitors who have already lost.

Best of luck in all your efforts.

Phyllis L. Remolador
Strategy, Planning, and
  Integration Vice President
AT&T Consumer CIO

Acknowledgments

During the past year and a half, I have had the distinct pleasure of working on both IT strategy and IT architecture projects with the AT&T Database Marketing District. The members of that district have demonstrated, again and again, extended effort, zeal, and determination far beyond the norm. It was directly attributable to their team commitment that so much progress was made. So to Edward Pinner, Marianne Goldberg, Brian E. Smith, Robert Juliano, Mike Weaver, Joyce M. Jackson, Mary Lee M. Miller, Marvin Brander, Dennis M. Sitarik, and Janine Stoyko, I would like to publicly say thank you for your remarkable efforts.

In particular, I would like to acknowledge the visionary leadership of the Database Marketing District Manager, Vinny Raineri. Vinny has repeatedly demonstrated himself to be a person who sees what others do not see and knows what other do not know. Vinny is one of those rare individuals who sees the subtle and notices the hidden. His insight into architecture has been invaluable in making architecture blueprinting a reality.

Acknowledgments

Preface

In December 1997, I attended a major industry information technology (IT) architecture conference. I was very interested to discover the emerging best architectural practices and to ascertain the general state of the art. The marketing material advertised that the speakers represented the "who's who," or "gurus," on the subject and would provide actionable blueprints for architecture. This in particular attracted me, and I approached the conference with great anticipation.

I was quite disappointed. Though there were very interesting seminars on many aspects of IT architecture, and presentations on management support, architecture methodology, component selection, case studies, vendor tools, user involvement, lessons learned, as well as multiple panels of experts who discussed common shortcomings and took questions from the ever appreciative audience, there were good presentations on everything except blueprinting.

Perhaps I had it wrong. The word blueprint has various meanings. One common use of the word is to convey only imagery to communicate the likeness of a structured plan. Another possible meaning of blueprint is the literal one, to mean a rigorously constructed drawing of a subject, a drawing that follows a well-defined set of notations, pictorials, and rules that ensures that the resulting diagram is predictable, repeatable, and most important, can be read unambiguously by anybody who knows the drawing system. A rigorous blueprint is a communication system for complicated constructs.

I was interested in the latter meaning. A blueprint (an engineering drawing) is a document which, by means of pictorial graphics, textural presentations, and rules of notation, depicts the physical and functional end-product requirements of an item. I thought the presenters at the conference were going to explain how to draw rigorous blueprints of IT architectures. In fact, they only vaguely alluded to the subject.

A leading-edge conference on IT architecture that doesn't address the essence of architecture is most unsatisfactory. Architects perform a wide variety of tasks, but regardless of who they are, where they work, the kinds of IT technology they use, or the training and mentoring they have received, they intuitively know that they need to draw the architecture. Without any prompting, they know that the essence of communicating IT architecture is a visual depiction of the information technology elements that compose the architecture and, most important, the specification of the relationships between those components. Architecture and pictorial representation of architecture are two sides of the same coin, and are thus indivisible.

Having spent many years as a consultant involved in the subject of IT architecture, the reason for this is now pretty obvious to me: There is a serious deficiency in our industry, and that deficiency is the complete absence of a formal notational system for drawing and communicating IT architectures. All of the engineering disciplines—civil, mechanical, and electrical—as well as other fields as diverse as music, chess, and sports score keeping, have correctly concluded that a rigorous blueprinting system is necessary to eradicate ambiguity. An airplane manufacturer would never imagine constructing an airplane without a complete set of configuration-managed blueprints. Yet routinely, the same company would implement a collage of heterogeneous and distributed computing systems with only vague personal sketches to communicate the incredibly complicated and subtle relationships of the IT components.

This shortcoming, IT architecture as personal and ambiguous sketches, is reaching a critical juncture at which it can no longer be ignored or tolerated. The competitive fervor in many industries has escalated to a state called *hypercompetition* characterized by rapid competitive interactions. Competition becomes a war of swift and unpredictable movement. To be successful, companies have to be agile; they have to continually create an endless stream of overlapping and staggered temporary advantages to attract and retain customers. To win means to change incessantly.

At the same time, we have entered the so-called Information Age. With the convergence of three events—the digitization of information regardless of form, ubiquitous and cheap computing, and broadband communications—information technology is being elevated to the weaponry of competition. Business processes are information-intensive; business products are informated; information technologies run the business; and information technology is increasingly the means by which the business touches the customer. In the Information Age, it may be a little crude (but only a little) to say that you are your information systems.

The response to hypercompetition, necessary to remain competitive, is to become an information technology-based hypercompetitor predator. The war of hypercompetitive movement is a war of information systems. Those companies that can build, maintain, and extend their IT infrastructure with alacrity will have significant advantage. In a war of information systems, IT architecture is the foundation of advantage. If you are going to be as swift as lightning, you must begin with your IT architecture. You cannot create an agile IT environment bottom up; enterprise IT agility is a holistic problem. IT architecture is the essence of IT strategy for the hypercompetitive Information Age, and the essence of IT architecture is the way that you communicate it pictorially.

This book addresses this fundamental problem. It provides a formal notational system for drawing and maintaining IT architectures, which I call the Enterprise Information Technology Architecture Blueprinting (EAB for short). The methodology addresses the features required of any formal notational system. It defines:

- A set of drawings.
- A set of functional specifications and bill of materials.
- How to draw each type of diagram (vocabulary, rules, graphics icons, objects and notations).
- How the diagrams and functional specifications relate to each other.
- How to package the finished EAB.
- How to integrate multiple drawings.
- How to perform configuration management to evolve the drawings.
- How to design architectures to maximize maneuverability.

In short, EAB defines a communications system that allows a community of IT professionals to visualize architectures in a standard manner.

The structure of this book is as follows:

Chapter 1: Introduction: The Business Context. This chapter explains why the concurrence of hypercompetition and the Information Age makes a dramatic improvement in IT architecture blueprinting mandatory for competitive survival.

Chapter 2: IT Architecture. This chapter formally defines an IT architecture and explains why the absence of a rigorous architecture blueprinting system is a serious threat to business success.

Chapter 3: Enterprise IT Architecture Blueprinting. This chapter teaches the blueprinting methodology. It is the heart of the book.

Chapter 4: Configuration Management. This chapter addresses the problem of performing configuration management of an architecture blueprint as it is changed over time and how to manage distributed blueprints.

Chapter 5: Architecture Design for Extreme Maneuverability. This chapter prescribes a way to do design infrastructure and application architectures that will maximize the maneuverability of the IT assets.

Chapter 6: EAB Miscellany. This chapter offers guidelines on a number of topics that round out the implementation of EAB.

Epilogue. This chapter summarizes the key ideas of this book.

The appendices provide templates for the icons and page layouts that compose an EAB.

This book will be of interest to a wide and diverse audience. For senior IT management, the book explains the linkage between hypercompetition and IT architecture. Senior managers will learn how IT architecture can be positioned to enable the business to prevail in the Information Age. For IT architects, developers, planners, analysts, and designers, the book will explain how to draw and maintain rigorous blueprints that can transform the way architecture is performed within their business. By reading the whole book, both audiences will learn to better appreciate the entire strategic logic and mechanisms of IT architecture.

Sun Tzu, the greatest strategist who ever lived wrote, "The end of an army's form is formlessness." He did not mean that an army was to be literally formless; he meant, that to cope with hyperconflict and to win, an army must be able to rapidly change its form. Victory goes to those who can adapt to the situation with speed, agility, and the absence of friction.

In the hypercompetitive Information Age, the end of an IT architecture's form is formlessness. Only when the IT architecture can endlessly morph its shape will the business be able to adapt to relentless turbulence and uncertainty. It is not enough for the business to be able to change on a dime; it has to be able to spin on a dime. IT architecture is the source of Information Age advantage, and architecture blueprints are the means for visualization and communication of the weaponry of business success.

Bernard H. Boar
East Brunswick, New Jersey
September 1998

About the Author

Bernard (Bernie) Boar is an accomplished author and consultant in the field of information technology. He has six published books on the critical topics of IT strategy and architecture: *Strategic Thinking for Information Technology, Cost-Effective Strategies for Client/Server Systems, Practical Steps to Aligning Information Technology with Business Strategy, The Art of Strategic Planning for Information Technology: Crafting Strategy for the 90s, Implementing Client/Server Computing: A Strategic Perspective,* and *Application Prototyping: A Requirements Definition Strategy for the 80s.* The latter is now recognized as the seminal work on the subject.

Bernie's work has also been published in *CIO Journal, Computerworld, Journal of Systems Management, Journal of Business Strategy, DMR,* and *The Journal of Systems Development.* He has been a speaker at leading industry conferences on IT strategy, IT management, and distributed computing. He holds an MBA from the Baruch Graduate School of Business and a B.Sc. in Computer Science from the City College of NY. Bernie is a member of both the Strategic Planning Society and the Strategic Management Society. He has been a guest lecturer at American Graduate School for International Business, Sydney Technology University, West Indies University, University of Minnesota, Stevens Institute of Technology, and Cornell University. Bernie serves as Director of Strategic Solutions at RCG Information Technology in Iselin, New Jersey, and may be reached at bboar@rcgit.com.

Constructing Blueprints for Enterprise IT Architectures

CHAPTER 1

Introduction: The Business Context

This is a book about how to draw and maintain rigorous architectural blueprints for information technology (IT) systems. The need for these blueprints, while both obvious and compelling, has become critically important because IT architecture is rapidly becoming the foundation of competitive business advantage. Those who implement IT architecture well will win and those who don't will lose.

Strategy is about the perpetual struggle for advantage. The objective of strategizing is to take actions that build, sustain, and compound advantage. The acquisition and retention of customers is a function of your advantages; parrying competitors is a function of your advantages. Nothing is more important than taking actions that can create or extend advantage.

Advantage has three important attributes: persistence, size, and type. Advantage may be sustainable or temporary. Sustainable advantages are durable. Having struggled to create them, they deliver something highly valued by the customer and not easily duplicated by competitors. Temporary advantages deliver value to customers but have a short life span, because competitors find ways to mimic or leapfrog the advantage. Competing through a portfolio of temporary advantages requires the capability to continuously create overlapping and staggered advantages.

Advantages come in different sizes (size here is defined as the distance between your advantage and your competitor's). The greater the distance, the more compelling your product is to your customers. Advantages can be sustainable but of such small size that they don't hold customers or deter competitors. Advantage is, therefore, a relative as opposed to an absolute concept.

While there are limitless ways to build advantage, all advantages are classified into five generic types:

- **Cost.** Results in the ability to provide products/services cheaper.
- **Differentiation.** Creates a product or service that offers some highly desirable and unique feature or functionality.
- **Focus.** More tightly meets the explicit needs of a particular customer.
- **Execution.** Permits you to service customer needs *better* than others.
- **Maneuverability.** Permits you to adapt to changing requirements quicker than your competitors. Being able to maneuver more quickly enables you to constantly refresh the other types of advantage. It's the only advantage that your competitors can never take from you.

Consequently, business strategy must focus on how to: build new advantages that increase customer satisfaction and create distance from competitors; maintain existing advantages that increase customer satisfaction and create distance from competitors; and compress or eliminate the advantages of competitors. Creating an ever-evolving portfolio of advantages that mixes the suitable types and sizes of advantage with the appropriate persistence does this.

Our simple thesis is that, as we move through the hypercompetitive Information Age, IT architecture is becoming the linchpin of competitive advantage. The way that you perform, document, implement, communicate, visualize, and standardize IT architecture determines your ability to create, sustain, and compound advantage.

Why is this so? Why has IT architecture become so important? Why should you care if your architects draw casual sketches or formal architectural blueprints? Why should you care now? The answer is *hypercompetition*.

HYPERCOMPETITION

Most industries have entered or are at the brink of entering into a state of competition called hypercompetition,[1] a state that is marked by some very alarming characteristics:

Advantage. It's increasingly difficult, if not impossible, to create and maintain sustainable competitive advantages. From trying to defend a set of sustainable advantages, the war of advantage migrates to creating an endless stream of overlapping and staggered temporary advantages.

Innovation. There is rapid and dislocating innovation in the industry. All forms of know-how are subject to rapid devaluation, and continually have to be refreshed.

Competitive escalation. Competitors continually raise the ante to play the game. A state of market equilibrium is neither achieved nor desired by winner-takes-all competitors.

Customer power. Customers become extraordinarily demanding and have heightened expectations. These demands are made actionable by effortless substitution between supplier products and services.

Value proposition. There is a continuing market redefinition of what is valued by consumers. Competitors constantly search for new combinations of basic products and add-on features that entice customers. Nobody can either pause or rest on past laurels.

End of chivalry. Competitors have no respect for the status quo. Barriers to entry are viewed as challenges to circumvent. There is no tacit division of the marketplace pie with each supplier taking a share. Each competitor craves it all and acts relentlessly to satisfy that craving.

End of customer loyalty. Markets are characterized by excessive churn. Customer loyalty is fleeting and often needs to be bought. Dissatisfied, curious, and better-value-seeking customers vote quickly "with their feet," by taking their purchasing dollars elsewhere.

Market disruption as the rule. Competitors take actions to disrupt rather than to protect markets. The objective of competitive strategy shifts from protecting what one has to taking what one doesn't have. Explicit actions are designed and executed to devalue the opponent's advantages and renew one's own advantages before a competitor decreases in value your advantages.

Hypercompetition is a state of intense and often lethal competition caused by the concurrence of a number of market factors:

Shift of market power to customers. Customers perceive a wide selection of choices and become accustomed to exercising a wide selection of alternatives.

Rapid decline in barriers to market entry. Creative and ambitious competitors discover ways to circumvent barriers to entry. With ingenuity, a competitor can realize that a seemingly impenetrable barrier to entry is no barrier at all.

Accelerating technology/know-how change. The half-life of competencies is dramatically shortened by rapid innovation. The game of advantage through know-how is constantly being reset with all the players having to start over again.

Rise of multiple deep-pocket players. Multiple companies enter an industry with the financial resources to fight it out. One big company can no longer bully all the others into submission and make them stay in their place.

Deregulation. Government and regulatory authorities disassemble legal barriers to entry. Often, the deregulation also aggressively encourages intense competition.

Inability to sustain advantage. The durability of advantages dramatically declines. Dramatic innovation, shifts in technological know-how, and creativity in redefining the product value proposition conspire to reduce the resiliency of any advantage.

Globalization. Time and space barriers to market entry are overcome. Geographic strongholds become easily breached, and foreign competitors, often with deep pockets, no respect for the status quo, and rich resources can effectively invade markets.

Figure 1.1 illustrates the various states of competition that can exist within an industry as a continuum in which hypercompetition is the virulent state that precedes profitless perfect competition.

The four anchor states of competition are:

1. **Low competition.** A state enjoyed by monopolies. There is little or no competition, and because of the legally endorsed monopoly, the monopolist enjoys almost perfect advantage.

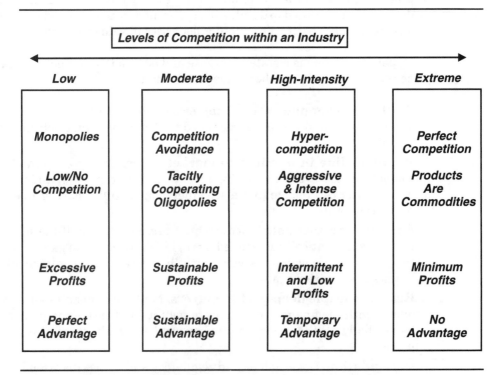

FIGURE 1.1   Levels of competition within an industry. Competition within an industry moves along a continuum with four distinct points.

2. **Moderate competition.** Competitors exist, but they tacitly cooperate to divide the market pie; they avoid intense direct rivalry, and competition is quite civil. Competitors respect each other's advantages and barriers to entry, and tend to defend rather than to attack. Moderate competition is characterized by competitors nourishing sustainable competitive advantages.
3. **High-intensity competition.** Aggressive, no-holds-barred, intense competition. Rather than defend, competition escalates to a war of movement with each competitor constantly shifting to improve its competitive position. Advantages are not sustainable, and successful competitors become adept at creating and managing an endless stream of short-lived and overlapping temporary advantages.
4. **Extreme competition.** Products and services are completely commoditized. Attempts at differentiation are instantly matched by the competition. There is little advantage, and consumers enjoy ultimate value, that is, the absolute maximum product at the absolute minimum cost.

One of the most important points to take away from Figure 1.1 is the change in the nature of advantage in each state. Most of us who have spent their careers in stable states of moderate competition understand strategy as the creation and maintenance of sustainable advantage. As highlighted in Figure 1.2, the mode

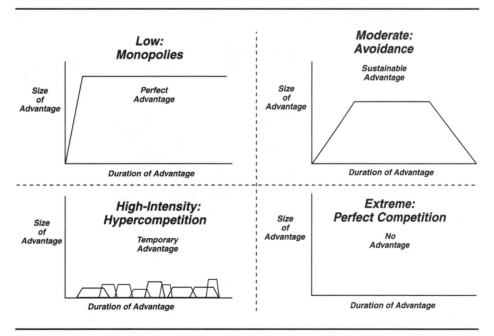

FIGURE 1.2 Models of advantage. Each state of competition requires a different primary form of advantage.

of advantage dramatically shifts in a hypercompetitive environment from sustainable advantage to temporary advantage.

This shift occurs for all the reasons previously discussed, and means that the tools used to build advantage must be designed to enable speed, flexibility, the elimination of friction, and agility. What matter most are not your current advantages, which are rapidly aging, but your advantages on the drawing boards. What matters most is not preserving what is but creating very rapidly what will be, and doing this over and over again.

Hypercompetition destroys *sustainable competitive advantage* (SCA). As shown in Figure 1.3, sustainable competitive advantage can be understood as a function of the variables of time and cost. The longer it takes to replicate an advantage, or the more money it costs to replicate an advantage, the more sustainable is the advantage. By its nature, hypercompetition either reduces the time and cost of replicating an advantage or permits bypassing an advantage altogether. Consequently, advantages are not sustainable, and competition shifts to creating a stream of overlapping temporary advantages.

Hypercompetition takes place in four primary arenas (Figure 1.4). While competition occurs in all these four arenas across the entire competition continuum (Figure 1.1), it is important to appreciate the rapid escalation and intensity of competition both within and between arenas that occurs with hypercompetition. The speed of competitive interaction continually increases

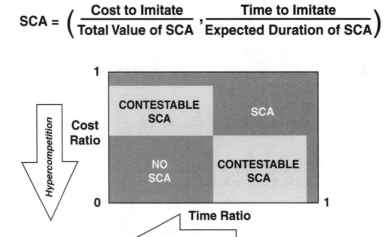

$$SCA = \left(\frac{\text{Cost to Imitate}}{\text{Total Value of SCA}} , \frac{\text{Time to Imitate}}{\text{Expected Duration of SCA}} \right)$$

FIGURE 1.3 Hypercompetition destroys sustainable competitive advantage by eroding the time and cost to replicate or bypass.

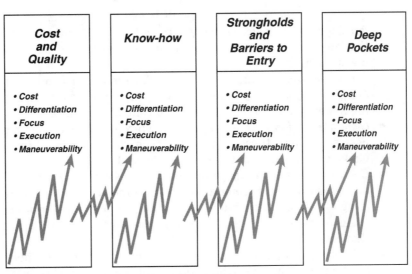

FIGURE 1.4 Arenas of hypercompetition. In a hypercompetitive environment, competition rapidly escalates within and between four arenas of competition.

and escalates within an arena; and, as opportunities depreciate within an arena, competitors rapidly jump to other arenas to continue the fray.

The four arenas of competition are:

1. **Cost and quality.** Competition focuses on the price and value proposition mix to be presented to the customer.
2. **Know-how.** Competition focuses on competencies and creating the skills required to create future value for the customer.
3. **Strongholds and barriers to entry.** Competition focuses on creating advantages that block competitors from entering the market.
4. **Deep pockets.** Competition focuses on the use of financial resources to fund and endure the competitive war.

Ultimately, competitors have no choice but to become hypercompetitive, or to exit the marketplace. Industry-dependent technological change, deregulation shift to customer power, globalization, multiple deep-pocketed players, and erosion of barriers to entry destabilize each arena. Either you learn to compete as a hypercompetitor or those who have leave you behind in the marketplace. Hypercompetitors leave others in their wake by continually redefining value for the customer. This renders your stable value proposition as a historically interesting but dated artifact.

Hypercompetitors demonstrate very aggressive market behaviors. Typically, they:

- *Quickly and purposely bring assets to a chosen point of opportunity that offers disproportionate returns for the effort.* When others belatedly turn to that opportunity, the hypercompetitor moves on to the next disproportionate opportunity.
- *Create menaces for their opponents.* They make their opponents turn their attention from their planned agenda to the hypercompetitor's agenda. Thus the hypercompetitor commands and controls the initiative.
- *Generate friction for their opponents.* They destabilize their opponents' business by making those opponents respond to them, and in so doing, alter plans, processes, initiatives, alliances, and so on.
- *Continually raise the tempo and occurrences of their marketplace maneuvers in all the arenas of competition.* Confronted with an increasingly deteriorating situation, and unable to respond, the opponent's internal processes begin to collapse under the strain and stress of rapid and unpredictable change.
- *Deliberately cause imbalances to destabilize the market.* There is no respect for the status quo; destabilization creates opportunities for exploitation.
- *Win by being the marketplace puppeteers.* They create a dynamic set of actions built upon opportunism to excite customers.
- *Continually redefine the value proposition offered to the customer.* By aggressive redefinition of value propositions, established and long-standing competitor advantages are devalued.
- *Show no respect for their competitors' advantages.* They view every advantage as having an innate disadvantage component. Hypercompetitors find the disadvantage element in an advantage and exploit it.
- *Rob their opponents of the ability to make choices.* If they can keep their opponents busy chasing them, the opponents don't have time or energy to develop plans of their own. Thus competitors are reduced to playing a perpetual game of catch-up.
- *Improvise to take advantage of opportunistic situations as they unfold.* Opportunities emerge as opposed to being planned.
- *Lure opponents out of their strongholds to fight on turf more favorable to the hypercompetitors.* This nullifies the stronghold and barrier to entry advantages.
- *Are experimenters.* They test opponents to learn where they are strong and where they are weak. From that information, initiatives can be manufactured with the maximum success potential.
- *Use deception, speed, and surprise to paralyze opponents into inaction.* The hypercompetitors get a long grace period before the shocked and numbed opponent regroups and mounts a counteroffensive. Hypercompetitors, there-

fore, often suffer no response to their thrusts or experience only severely delayed responses, which opens windows of distinct advantage.

- *Compete against time.* Through rapid innovation, the hypercompetitor contracts the anticipated duration of return that competitors expected on their advantages and thus mangles the opponents' business model.
- *Focus* on *satisfying the customer* while they make their opponents focus on them.

The competitive attitude of a hypercompetitor is best captured in the dictum of Sun Tzu to "Go forth where they do not expect it, attack where they are unprepared."[2]

Hypercompetitors see competition as a war of movement where market success goes to those who can move with purpose and alacrity. Even when wrong, speed and dexterity permit rapid corrections. As illustrated in Figure 1.5, the battle shifts from a slow Industrial Age war of attrition to an Information Age war of disruption and maneuver. One cannot make peace with a hypercompetitor. The hypercompetitor wants it all, and doesn't accept surrenders that consummate in peaceful coexistence.

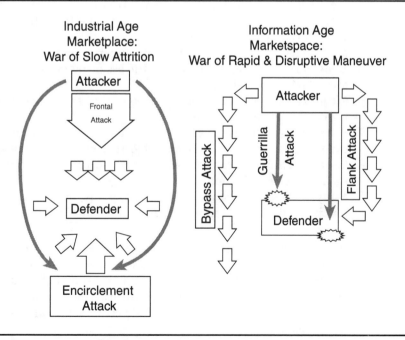

FIGURE 1.5 **Hypercompetition alters the rules of the battlefield from a slow war of attrition to a war of rapid and disruptive maneuver.**

THE STRATEGIC IMAGERY OF HYPERCOMPETITION

Hypercompetition, as a theory of competitive strategy, has its origin in other strategy frameworks. By examining those frameworks, one can better understand the nature of hypercompetition and, more important, plan how to respond to it. The antecedents of hypercompetitive theory can be found in the other frameworks of military strategy, Lanchester strategy, strategic paradox, and the teachings of Sun Tzu. Together, they provide strategic imagery of how a hypercompetitor thinks and behaves. With this imagery, one can design a favorable strategy to respond and successfully compete in a hypercompetitive environment.

Military Strategy

There are many schools of military strategy, but there is general agreement on nine basic principles, as follows:

1. **Objective.** The objective must be clear, conclusive, and obtainable.
2. **Offense.** Victory requires offensive action. Defensive actions only prevent defeat.
3. **Unity of command.** All military forces must be under one commander with full authority and responsibility. It is better to have one incompetent general than two good ones.
4. **Mass.** Victory goes to the army with superior forces at the point of contact.
5. **Economy of force.** Allocate only the essential minimum forces to areas of secondary responsibility.
6. **Maneuver.** Forces must be deployed so that they can come together in the right place at the right time.
7. **Surprise.** If you strike your enemy at a time or place or in a way that is not expected, you can often win your objective even before the enemy can react.
8. **Security.** Surprise cannot exist without security. An army must safeguard its intentions and plans.
9. **Simplicity.** All objectives, strategies, plans, and orders, should be clear, concise, and simple. Simplicity keeps forces motivated, focused, and unified.

Hypercompetition strongly embraces three of these principles. First, offense: Hypercompetitors are aggressive; they are conquerors, not defenders. Second, maneuver: Hypercompetitors fight a war of movement and disruption. Third, surprise: Hypercompetitors see surprise as a positive dual-edge sword. At the same time, while delighting their customers, surprise paralyzes their numbed opponents.

One of the most renowned military strategists is Captain B. H. Liddell-Hart. He offers eight principles of military strategy based on the theme of winning through indirection:

1. Adjust your end to your means.
2. Keep your object always in mind.
3. Choose the line of least expectation.
4. Choose the line of least resistance—indirection not confrontation.
5. Take a line of operation that offers alternative objectives.
6. Ensure that both dispositions are flexible/adaptable to circumstances (maneuverability).
7. Do not throw your weight into a stroke while your opponent is on guard.
8. Do not renew an attack along the same line or in the same form after it has once failed.

The relationship of Captain Liddell-Hart's strategic thinking to hypercompetition is summarized in his quote: "For success, two major problems must be solved: dislocation and exploitation. One precedes and one follows." As illustrated in Figure 1.6, his view of strategy involves three steps: self-preparation, battlefield (marketplace) disruption, and subsequent exploitation of the resulting instability based on one's prior preparation.

This is exactly the behavior of hypercompetitors. They prepare themselves by creating capabilities of speed, adaptability, and a culture that embraces rapid change. They take actions to destabilize the market by doing the unan-

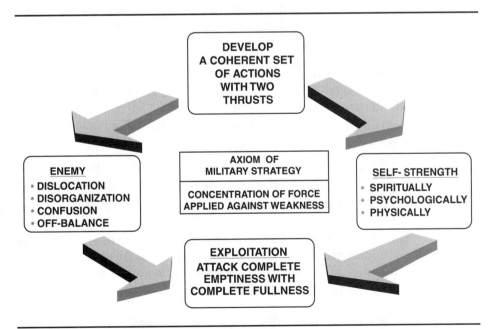

FIGURE 1.6 Liddell-Hart military strategy model. Hypercompetitors behave in the manner presented in this model. They prepare, they dislocate, and they exploit.

ticipated such as changing long-standing rules of the game, and finally, they exploit the resulting instability by bringing value to their customers while their dazed and less-competitive opponents try to figure out what happened. Hyper-competitors thus build their success on the Liddell-Hart teachings of preemption, dislocation, and disruption.

Lanchester Strategy

F.W. Lanchester was a British aeronautical engineer during Word War I. In 1916, he authored a book on air warfare called *Aircraft Warfare* in which he proposed mathematical models of warfare. Japanese management consultants have restructured and mapped Lanchester's theories into business marketing and sales strategies for mainstream markets. These strategies are called "the strategy for the weak" and "the strategy for the strong."[3]

The essence of Lanchester Strategy, which has enjoyed growing popularity in the computer industry, is that most companies, even the market leader, are the weak. They are the weak because they do not enjoy an insurmountable lead. Lanchester strategy calls this being in "shooting range." For the weak to become the strong, they need a strategy for the weak. Conversely, if you are the strong, enjoying a seemingly insurmountable lead, you need a strategy for the strong that maintains that lead. So the marketplace is a battle between the "haves" who execute the strategy for the strong against the "have-nots" who execute the strategy for the weak. Ultimate victory goes to those who execute better.

The principles of the strategy for the weak are as follows:

Avoid the strong and attack the weaker. Gain market share by beating up on those weaker than you until you are strong enough to turn your attention to the market leader.

Engage in duels. Choose battles where size is not the determining factor. Fight battles on limited fronts.

Focus. Concentrate your forces at a point of exceptional opportunity.

Differentiate yourself. Create unique value for the customer.

Keep moving; avoid strength. The strong will not be able to crush you if they can't catch you.

Speed is the essence of strategy. As illustrated in Figure 1.7, speed provides momentum. It enables surprise, is necessary to master the initiative, compensates for fewer resources, and is necessary for dislocation and exploitation.

The essence of Lanchester strategy for the weak is focus, maneuver, differentiation, and speed. These ideas are fully embraced by hypercompetitors.

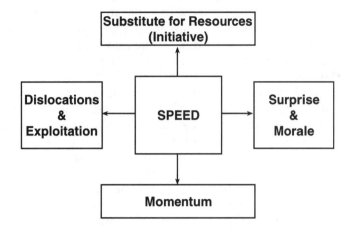

FIGURE 1.7   Speed is the essence of strategy. Speed is fundamental to engage in hypercompetitive strategy.

The principles for the strategy for the strong are as follows:

Quickly match the actions and movements of the weak. Diffuse any and all acts of differentiation. Do not let them acquire gains by their maneuvers.

Fight battles on huge fronts. Exploit your superior strength. Do not engage in duels that dilute your superior strength and make you but equal to the weaker competitor.

Provide full and comprehensive product lines. Do not leave the weak any niche markets.

Exploit your size; size matters. Use large and dispersed distribution channels. Advertise heavily.

Most of all, the strategy for the strong teaches, paradoxically, that if you wish to remain strong, behave as though weak. How can the weak defeat you if you beat them with their own strategy? So hypercompetitive firms, whether the strong or the weak, behave like the weak. They attack weak spots, they attack the weaker, they engage in speed and surprise, they continually differentiate, and they keep moving.

Strategic Paradox

In conducting our daily lives, purposeful opposition to our routine efforts does not exist. No one has the explicit goal to deliberately thwart our actions. We use what is called *linear logic* to solve our problems. Linear logic consists of using common sense, deductive/inductive reasoning, and concern for economies of time, cost, and effort to solve problems. One is routinely criticized for taking a circuitous route when a more direct one is available. Daily life applauds the logical, the economic, and the rich application of common sense.

Hypercompetitive business strategy, to the contrary, is executed against a background of intense conflict and intelligent countermeasures. Able and motivated competitors, purposefully and energetically, attempt to foil your ambition. Because of this excessive state of conflict, many strategic actions demonstrate a surprising and counterintuitive paradoxical logic.

There are two types of strategic paradox that are routinely encountered in hypercompetitive business situations: coming together of opposites, and reversal of opposites. Coming together of opposites is a linear logic action or state that evolves into a reversal of itself ("A" becomes "not A"), or "you can have too much of a good thing." An example is that an advantage, unrefreshed, becomes a disadvantage. This paradox occurs because conflict causes an inevitable reversal due to the complacency of the winner and the hunger of the loser. While the current winners gloat in their success, this same success lulls them into a false sense of permanent security while it paradoxically stimulates the current losers to tax their ingenuity to overcome it.

Reversal of opposites means that to accomplish your objectives, do the reverse of what linear logic would dictate. So, "If you wish peace, prepare for war"; to accomplish "A," do the set of actions to accomplish "not A." Or put another way, your primary competitor should be yourself. This occurs because the nature of conflict reverses normal linear logic. While taking a long, dangerous, and circuitous route is bad logic under daily circumstances, in a state of conflict (i.e., war), this bad logic is good logic exactly because it is bad logic (it is less likely to be defended). The logic of conflict is often in total opposition to the logic of daily life. Conflict causes strategic paradox to occur; bad logic becomes good logic exactly because it is bad logic, and the able strategist must learn to think and act paradoxically. Paradoxically, strategists often have to recommend, to an unbelieving and astonished audience, that they should take actions that are directly contrary to routine business sense. So, as previously stated, the best strategy for the strong is, paradoxically, the strategy for the weak.

An example of reversal of opposites thinking is illustrated by the Kano Methodology, an analytical method used to stimulate strategic thinking. As illustrated in Figure 1.8, the logic of Kano suggests that candidate strategic actions are divided into three types.

The first, *threshold action,* says that for every dollar invested in this type of action, customer satisfaction increases, but gradually reaches a point at which less than a dollar of satisfaction is achieved for each dollar of investment. It therefore doesn't make sense to invest beyond the break-even point. The second, *performance action,* says that for every dollar invested in this type of action, there is a constant positive increase in customer satisfaction in excess of

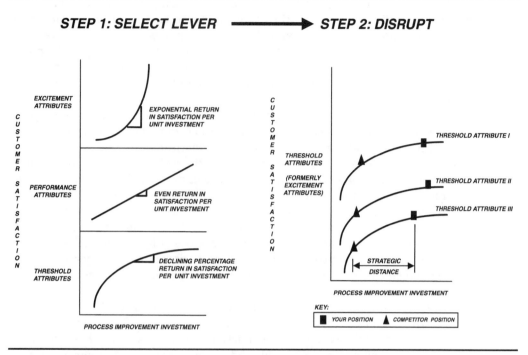

FIGURE 1.8   The Kano methodology illustrates the logic of strategic paradox.

your investment. It pays to continue to invest in these actions. The third, *excitement action*, which says that for every additional dollar invested in this type of action, there is an exponential increase in customer satisfaction. These are prized actions, the best to invest in.

While this is solid linear thinking, the true brilliance of the methodology occurs next through paradoxical thinking. The suggestion is that, after one has developed the excitement capability, it should be presented to the customer as a threshold attribute; paradoxically, the truly exceptional is most exceptional when it is the ordinary. What this does is position your capability as minimum ante to play the game. A customer may be willing to forgo the exceptional, but every customer will minimally expect and demand the ordinary. Since you can do it and your competitors can't, you create strategic distance between yourself and your competitors. While they struggle to do the exceptional as the norm, you raise the tempo of the game and work on converting another excitement attribute to threshold status ad infinitum. The great insight of the Kano Methodology is not the linear thinking of threshold to performance to excitement attributes, but the recognition that maximum value and market disruption occurs when excitement capabilities are presented, paradoxically, as the ordinary (reversal of opposites).

This kind of thinking is common among hypercompetitors, who act as their own most capable competitors; they replace their own advantages before their competitors can. They understand that when they position an excitement attribute as a threshold attribute, they totally disrupt the status quo. With one sweeping move, they turn their opponent's threshold and performance attributes into dissatisfier attributes, and radically redefine value in the marketplace.

Most important and paradoxical of all, however, is their view of a competitor's advantages. While traditional strategy and common sense tell you to avoid strength, paradoxical logic teaches that a competitor's greatest weakness lies in their greatest strength. By understanding their strengths, you understand what they will defend, leverage, and hold onto under any circumstances. When hypercompetitors develop a superior alternative, they are safe from being copied because opponents are committed to what has made them great rather than what will make them great. As they lovingly hold onto their advantage, the hypercompetitor, with immunity, changes the rules of the game, and develops a superior alternative. So in the ultimate paradox, the hypercompetitor is able to engage in strategic judo and turn his or her opponent's great strength into an even greater weakness.

Strategic paradox also explains the often difficult-to-accept logic of replacing sustainable advantages with temporary advantages. Hyperturbulent conflict results in the following self-contradiction: The most sustainable advantage is a series of overlapping, staggered, and contemporaneous temporary advantages. Hypercompetition causes paradox to apply to advantage, and the phenomenon of reversal of opposites causes sustainability and temporariness to dramatically swap roles. The ability to create a ceaseless stream of temporary advantages becomes sustainable advantage, and classical sustainable advantage becomes reversed into temporary advantage (it cannot be sustained). As initially difficult as this is to accept, it is perfect strategic logic under the framework of strategic paradox.

The Strategic Teachings of Sun Tzu

Sun Tzu's *Art of War* contains numerous aphorisms that provide the strategic imagery and foundation upon which hypercompetitive strategy is built. The following seven quotes are particularly informative to understand the attitude of hypercompetitors:

On psychological conflict:
Overcome your opponents by dispiriting them rather than by battling with them . . . overcome the opponent psychologically . . . cause them to lose spirit and direction so that even if the opponent's army is intact, it is useless.

On speed:
Use swiftness to wear them out. Get the upper hand through extra-ordinary swiftness. Be as fast as the lightning that flickers before your eyes.

On surprise:
In battle, confrontation is done directly, victory is gained by surprise.

On an endless procession of temporary advantages:
There are only five basic flavors, but the varieties are so many that they cannot all be tasted. There are only two basic charges in battle, the unorthodox surprise attack and the orthodox direct attack, but the variations of the orthodox and the unorthodox are endless. The orthodox and the unorthodox give rise to each other like a beginningless circle—who can exhaust them.

On maneuverability:
Adaptation means not clinging to fixed methods but changing appropriately to events. The ability to gain victory by changing and adapting to the enemy is called genius.

On initiative:
Wear enemies out by keeping them busy and not letting them rest. Make them rush about trying to cover themselves and they will not have time to formulate plans.

On opportunism:
When the front is prepared, the rear is lacking. Preparedness on the left means lack on the right. Preparedness everywhere means lack everywhere. Attack where there is no defense.

Military conflict is the ultimate hypercompetitive situation, and Sun Tzu was a hypercompetitor 2,500 years ago. His teachings become ever more relevant as hypercompetition replaces moderate competition.

You should now have the imagery of hypercompetition. It is, perhaps unfortunately, the imagery of war. Many commentators dismiss military strategy as being inappropriate to business strategy. They find the use of war as a metaphor to be morally offensive, and in any case, they view it as an inappropriate metaphor because the customer is unaccountably left out. This commentary misses four important points:

1. The essence of both problems is coping with psychological, political, economic, social, and physical (in the case of war) conflict.

2. The ultimate objective of both is the same. As Sun Tzu taught, the height of success is to win without fighting.
3. The objective of strategy is to satisfy customers, but the reason for strategy is competition. If there weren't any competition, strategy would reduce to a bureaucratic problem of administration. It is always prudent to attack a problem at its roots.
4. The simple truth is that, in general, military strategic thought is much deeper and far-reaching than business strategic thought. The reason is that it really matters. If you doubt this, read a typical business or IT strategy book and then read an excellent military strategy book. Which do you believe will provide a much more penetrating strategic analysis? If a business fails, everybody picks himself or herself up and gets another job. If a country loses a war, its entire way of life and freedom are compromised.

So in a period of hypercompetition, the marketplace is a battlefield, and war imagery accurately conveys the level of heightened competition. The booty of a hypercompetitive marketplace war is not land, cities, or natural resources; it is the customer.

How does one respond to hypercompetition? What do you do when confronted with competitors who don't play nicely? Before we answer that question, we need to take a brief detour to understand the opportunities and impact of the coincident emergence of the Information Age. The response to hypercompetition is grounded in information technology.

THE INFORMATION AGE

We are now living through an era called the Information Age. It has the following distinguishing characteristics:

- *The dominant technology of the era is the computer.* Computing intelligence is dispersed into anything and everything that can be improved by being smart. The computerization of anything and everything is called *mechatronics* (mechanical electronics).
- *The icon of the era is the microprocessor.* Inexpensive and programmable chips permit products to be customized and made dynamically and personally responsive to each user.
- *The output of the era is knowledge.* Making products information-rich results in products and services with a high attraction to consumers.
- *The basis of wealth of the era is information.* Information drives the creation of knowledge that drives agile strategic actions that create temporary competitive advantage for the business.
- *The defining work is the knowledge worker.* Greater than half the work force is involved with collecting, processing, and communicating information.
- *The means of moving things is communications networks.* Logistics is concerned with moving bits (electronic products) rather than atoms (physical products).

- *The marketplace becomes the marketspace.* The marketplace, where people gather to buy and sell products and services shifts from the physical marketplace (a mall or shopping center) to the marketspace (an electronic marketplace in cyberspace).
- *Information-based enhancements become the primary way to create new products and services and to embellish the value of existing products and services.* A broadly accessible information highway (currently personified as the Internet) permits global and interactive access to multimedia information.
- *People buy dynamic and variable nondiscrete combinations of information-based products.* Value is created at the time of purchase through digitized customization.
- *Customers are treated (marketed, sold, and serviced) as individuals, not as statistical averages.*
- *The convergence of information forms yields entirely new ways of working and living.* Time and space constraints on markets collapse, permitting people to live where they please, work with remote employers, and purchase products from local or distant providers as situation-desired.

The Information Age means, more than anything else, radical shifts in the basis of wealth. In the Industrial Age, products were physical; in the Information Age, products become virtual. In the Industrial Age, the focus of effort was the automation of labor; in the Information Age, the focus of effort is the creation and exploitation of knowledge. In the Industrial Age, information flow was physical and paper-based; in the Information Age, information flow is virtual and digitized. This results in the movement from manufacturing as the basis of societal wealth to knowledge as the linchpin of wealth. It results in the entire global economy becoming merged and information-centric.

Five Perspectives

In summary, the Information Age can be understood from five primary perspectives: technology, economics, employment, spatial, and cultural.

Technology

Continued innovation in information technologies results in information technology permeating all aspects of life. As the internal combustion engine permitted the automating of labor, the computer permits the "informating" of society.

Economics

The economy becomes information-centric. Wealth creation is closely tied to the ability to create new information-based products and amend existing products with information. Information technology permits entirely new ways of collaboration to create products and services with closer ties to all value-chain participants.

Employment

The density of employment shifts to knowledge workers. Most people make their living creating, moving, analyzing interpreting, or disseminating information.

Spatial

The networking of computers throughout the world results in a collapse of the traditional market constraints of time and space. The world becomes one global marketspace.

Cultural

Society becomes media-laden. Information is readily available in multimedia formats; it is customizable and interactive. We expect information in forms that are readily accessible and convenient to our needs. The social capabilities of computers and communications permit new social structures to emerge.

Three Concomitant Technological Changes

The Information Age is driven by three concomitant technological changes, as described here.

Digitization of Information

With the digitization of information, regardless of form, all information—audio, data, image, and video—becomes a series of bits. All information shares the same bit-based "DNA" and becomes interoperable, transportable, and subject to interactive manipulation by the consumer. This has the net effect of radically changing business value chains, dramatically altering products and services, and completing revising consumer expectations as they are presented with interactive multimedia.

Declining Cost of Computing

The physics of computing has had only one impact on its price/performance for the past 30 years, and the same impact is anticipated for the foreseeable future: It will continue to dramatically decline. This cost efficiency is critical because it enables computing to become ubiquitous and available with sufficient power at an enabling and attractive price point.

Availability of Broadband Communications

The emergence of broadband communications is critical because multimedia is both storage-intensive and time-sensitive. The availability of gigabit communications will enable Information Age companies to improve both the efficiency and effectiveness of work as follows:

- Individual personal productivity will be enhanced through wireless communications, fax, and personal digital assistants.
- Rather than people moving to work, work will move to people, through telecommuting and videoconferencing.
- Business organization structures can become more adaptive, to include virtual structures, remote employees, and part-time employees.
- Information can be made widely available to all employees through intranets.
- Electronic commerce can be used to interoperate with all value-chain partners (suppliers, distributors, customers, regulators, etc.).
- Bringing appropriate interactive multimedia, hypertext, or hypermedia to each task can enable work processes. The daily generic work activities of problem solving, decision making, creativity, process management, information exchange, relating, and influencing can all be enriched by informating them.

The key strategic implications of the Information Age are:

- All information becomes digitized and is subject to interactive manipulation. The interface to the user becomes multimedia-rich and is as much entertainment as it is instructive or transactional.
- The economy becomes digital. More frequently, products and services take on electronic personas. Employment is dominated by knowledge work.
- Information becomes available to all, anywhere, anytime, and in any form.
- Information exchange occurs on a global basis. The location of information and the people with whom you interact is virtual to you; their location makes no difference. There is just one all-encompassing cyberspace.
- The economy becomes very knowledge-centric. Creating and applying knowledge, rather than making things, creates value.
- Business, shopping, leisure time, games, socialization, and so on all take on an electronic character. It is often easier, more efficient, and convenient to conduct daily affairs through electronic media than through physical presence.
- People become more self-sufficient in satisfying their needs through electronic distribution channels. This is the phenomenon of disintermediation.
- Products and services undergo mass customization. Information Age products undergo final assembly at the point of purchase in response to the exact desires of the consumer.
- Computing is ubiquitous. Everything that can benefit from being "made smart" is made smart. Once made smart, it is necessary that it be connected to be able to relate its knowledge to others. Like the availability of electricity today, the universal presence of computers will be taken for granted.
- Information becomes democratized. The first 30-year tyranny of text data comes to an end as image, video, audio, animation, and so on are all equally accessible, and often, much more valuable.

- Speed is of the essence. A digital society is a society where things happen quickly. A business must have the capability to respond ever more quickly to rapidly changing consumer tastes. In the Industrial Age, the large companies devoured the small companies. In the Information Age, the fast and agile companies obsolete the slow and ponderous companies.
- Software agents that search, negotiate, and buy for you replace or complement human agents.
- Traditional barriers to market entry, as well as the historical market constraints of time and space, collapse. It becomes a war of all against all, as customers become free to choose from a global marketplace. Market power shifts to consumers, as information access creates a near perfect marketplace where consumers have unlimited ability to comparison shop.
- Commerce becomes continuous. Business is conducted around the world around the clock without respite. Neither your personal software agents nor the databases that they operate on ever need a vacation or time off.

The Information Age is built on information technology (IT), which comprises those technologies engaged in the operation, collection, transport, retrieval, storage, access presentation, and transformation of information in all its forms (voice, graphics, text, video, and image). Movement of information can take place between humans, between humans and information-processing machines, or between multiple information-processing machines. Management of IT ensures the proper selection, deployment, administration, operation, maintenance, and evolution of the IT assets consistent with organization goals and objectives.

The utility of information technology is built upon its architecture. The technologies that are deployed are transient. The business functions that they deliver offer only temporary advantage. Architecture, however, has persistence as the organizing framework for both technology and the derivative business function that is delivered. Herein lies the root of the response to hypercompetition.

RESPONDING TO HYPERCOMPETITION

The tempting response to hypercompetition is to retreat into your strongholds and try to keep the barbarians at the moat; that is, build bigger and better barriers to entry. This will not prove successful. The hypercompetitors will find a way to bypass your fortress and render your value proposition antiquated as customers abandon you. Paradoxically, your barrier to entry will motivate your opponents to tax their ingenuity to overcome it.

The only response that is viable is to transform your business into a hypercompetitor. This means you have to:

- Replace moderate competitive behaviors with hypercompetitive behaviors.
- Replace your devotion to sustainable advantages with an endless string of temporary advantages (Figure 1.9).

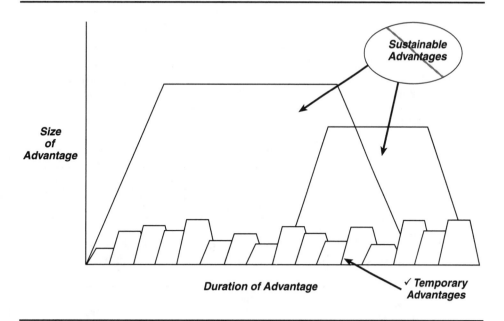

FIGURE 1.9 **Temporary competitive advantage. To cope with hypercompetition, you must become adept at creating an endless string of temporary competitive advantages.**

- Make speed, agility, surprise, and the ability to maneuver and disrupt the cornerstones of your strategy.
- Compete against time; time is of the essence.

Most of all it means that a war of rapid and disruptive movements must replace your traditional strategy of defending your strongholds. There is no safe harbor in retreat; either you surrender or you become a hypercompetitive predator. Those are your only choices.

You make yourself into a hypercompetitor by mastering and exploiting information technology. As illustrated in Figure 1.10, software is the fuel of Information Age advantage. Software is the critical mechanism to lower costs, compress time-to-market, provide value-added, and interact with customers and suppliers. Software, or software functionality, is increasingly the actual product that customers receive. Software is increasingly the vehicle of customer satisfaction and value-added innovation. Software is the primary vehicle for creating new advantages and parrying the advantages of competitors. It is through software, its associated information technologies, and the foundation of IT architecture that you engage in hypercompetition. In the Information Age, you engage in hypercompetition to dislocate, disrupt, exploit, surprise, and so on, through your information business systems.

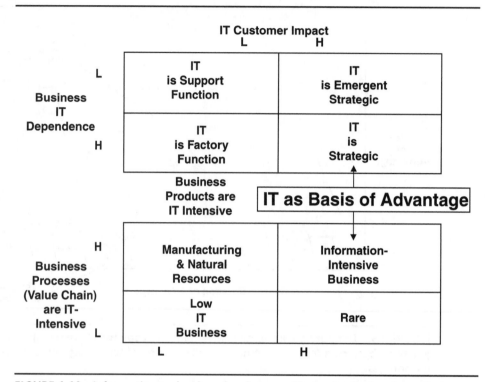

FIGURE 1.10 Information technology has become the basis of advantage. To be hypercompetitive, you must be outstanding in the use of software.

John Zachman, noted industry expert on information technology architecture, has stated: "We are now on the verge of IT architecture coming into its own. In the twenty-first century, IT architecture will be the determining factor—the factor that separates the winners from the losers, the successes from the failures, the acquiring from the acquired, the survivors from the rest." As illustrated in Figure 1.11, Zachman is on target because:

1. The business wins in the marketplace by virtue of a continuously evolving set of temporary advantages.
2. In a hypercompetitive business environment, the ability to continuously create temporary advantages is based on the ability to maneuver.
3. In the Information Age, the ability to maneuver is built upon the information technology architecture.

So the heart of the response to hypercompetition is the ability to maneuver, and the ability to maneuver in the Information Age is based on IT architecture. The all-compelling need to maneuver creates a solution junction between hy-

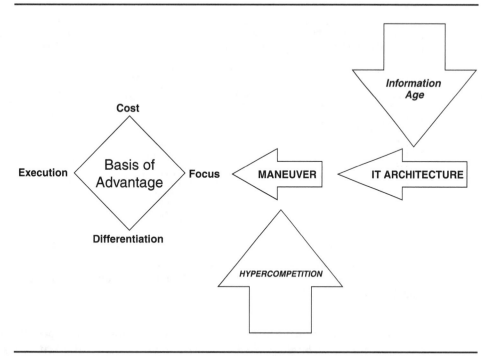

FIGURE 1.11   The importance of IT architecture. IT architecture provides the basis for maneuvering a business in the Information Age in response to hypercompetition.

percompetition and the Information Age. IT architecture emerges as critically important to any business that is information-based; and, of course, that is almost every business.

THE STRATEGIC LOGIC OF IT ARCHITECTURE

To an information technology strategist, businesses are no more than massively parallel information-processing factories. Numerous streams of information flow into it; the information is massaged; new information is created; and numerous streams of information flow out of it. IT has historically existed to make these information flows happen with maximum efficiency and effectiveness, to enable the noninformational business purpose. In the hypercompetitive Information Age environment, these information flows become the mechanism of maneuver.

Information flows within a business are exceedingly complex. To model that diversity, we use a "business diversity box" (Figure 1.12). Four dimensions define diversity: *work site diversity,* which defines the variable geography of where people work; *work unit diversity,* which defines the different types of work groups within which people work; *information diversity,* which defines the

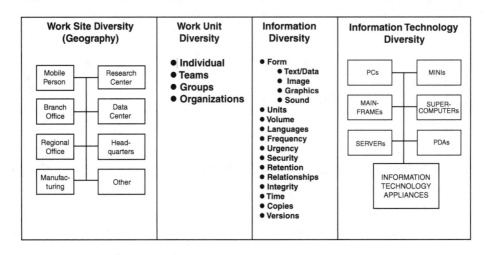

FIGURE 1.12   Business diversity box. The variety of information flows in a business is a function of four variables.

different forms of information with associated attributes that people require; and *information technology diversity,* which defines the different types of information-processing technologies that are used to create, present, move, store, and analyze information.

In a company of even small stature, the number of permutations and combinations of information flows across these four dimensions becomes astronomical. These flows, of course, do not remain constant. They are not a still-life picture, but undergo continuous revision, as required, by the business dynamic. The ability to efficiently revise information flows is a function of the IT architecture.

What happens to this maze when we add the value chain? A business does not exist as an isolated entity. It participates with other trading partners in a value chain. As shown in Figure 1.13, each partner, supplier, regulator, distributor, financier, insurer, consumer, and so on, first, has its own proprietary diversity box with all its private information flow complexities, and second, must interface diversity boxes across the value chain. The attempt to move information across the value chain with the information diversity boxes is difficult because of the proprietary nature of each one; the dynamic changes of information flow; the uncertainty of which flows will be needed next; the constant state of flux; the continuous shifting combinations and permutations of flows; and poorly designed IT architectures.

The hypercompetitive Information Age promotes this picture to center stage (Figure 1.13). The purposeful design of your IT architecture to maximize maneuverability is the mechanism to cope with this complexity.

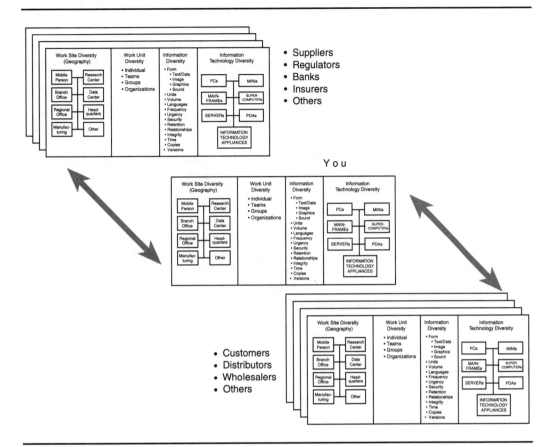

FIGURE 1.13   Business diversity box and the value chain. The ability of the information flows to cross the business diversity boxes of each trading partner is a function of the IT architecture.

Hypercompetition excites the level of turbulence and change and makes the information flows in Figure 1.13 more unpredictable, unstable, and chaotic than ever. So to be a hypercompetitor means to manage, in a superior and dynamic manner, the information flows both within and across information diversity boxes.

We are suggesting that you create advantage by building your business diversity value chain upon a foundation of IT architecture. By virtue of the IT architecture, which has been explicitly designed to support information-based adaptive maneuver, you are in a superior position to engage in hypercompetitive behaviors.

You exploit your IT architecture to make life miserable for your competitors while exciting your customers. You use it to deliberately disrupt the status quo to your advantage by:

- Changing information-based value propositions.
- Manipulating the tempo and rhythm of change.
- Rapidly attacking emerging but unexploited market niches.
- Preempting competitor moves with your own announcements, to which they must respond.
- Performing acts of mass customization.
- Being first to market.
- Surprising your competitors with acts of collaboration that they cannot duplicate.
- Attracting the best combination of value-chain partners by virtue of your superior methods of value-chain collaboration.
- Rolling out a continuous stream of temporary advantages.

You disrupt the environment by being able to *go forth where they don't expect it and attack where they are unprepared.* You fracture the cohesion of your opponent's processes and plans by creating a turbulent and deteriorating situation with which they cannot cope while, concurrently, satisfying your customers. Your prowess enables you to defeat your opponents psychologically. As they become discouraged and quarrelsome, they will begin to flail about and fall hopelessly behind you. This is how IT architecture becomes the weaponry of a hypercompetitor.

CONCLUSION

The logic for focusing on IT architecture as the mechanism to create hypercompetitive advantage is as follows:

- Industries are confronting hypercompetition on a global basis.
- An endless stream of temporary advantages must replace sustainable advantage as the means to marketplace success.
- The ability to build temporary advantages is a function of the ability of the business to maneuver.
- In the Information Age, the ability to maneuver the business is a function of the malleability of information technology. What must be maneuvered are your information systems.
- The malleability of your information technology is built upon your information technology architecture.

IT architecture is no longer an enabler of business success; it is the very essence (weaponry) of competing in the hypercompetitive Information Age. It is the essence of competing because it is *the* mechanism for creating and re-creating customer value.

There must be a dramatic change in how IT architecture work is carried out, in terms of:

- Defining what an architecture is.
- Architect training, skills, tools.
- Definition of outputs of architecture work.
- Ability for large audience to understand architecture.
- Ability to rapidly assess changes to architecture.
- Visibility of architecture.
- Currency of architecture.
- Clarity of architecture.
- Substantive documentation of architecture in a repeatable way.
- Professionalism of architecture.

Architecture must be positioned so that the business can use it to become a hypercompetitive predator. IT architecture must be positioned so that the business will prevail over its competitors, which have already lost by virtue of their inferior architectural prowess. When a predator in the wild prepares to strike, it doesn't call endless meetings; neither can you in the hypercompetitive Information Age. Your IT architecture must enable you to move swiftly and decisively.

ENDNOTES

1. The seminal work on hypercompetition is *Hyper-Competition: Managing the Dynamics of Strategic Maneuvering*, Richard A. D'Aveni, The Free Press, 1994. Professor D'Aveni's book, supplemented by his executive education course at Dartmouth University on hypercompetition, provides the basis for the description of hypercompetition included in this chapter. For more information on hypercompetition, also see:

    Special Issue on Hyper-Competition, *Organization Science*, Vol. 7, No. 3, May-June 1996; "Coping with Hyper-Competition: Utilizing the New 7S's Framework," Richard A. D'Aveni, *Academy of Management Executive*, Vol. 9. No. 3, 1995; "Toward the Flexible Form: How to Remain Vital in Hyper-Competitive Environments," H. W. Volberda, *Organization Science*, 5,4, pp. 479-482.

2. *The Art of War*, Sun Tzu, translated by Thomas Clearly, Shambhala Dragon Editions, 1988. *The Art of War* is generally recognized as the premier treatise on the strategy of conflict; mastery of *The Art of War* is mandatory for all aspiring strategists. There are numerous English translations of *The Art of War*. I prefer the one listed here but the quotations in this book are from multiple translations.

3. See *The Friction-Free Economy*, T.G. Lewis, HarperBusiness, 1997; *Lanchester Strategy*, Shinichi Yano, Lanchester Press, 1995; *New Lanchester Strategy*, Shinichi Yano, Lanchester Press, 1996.

CHAPTER 2

IT Architecture

An IT architecture is a series of principles, guidelines, drawings, standards, and rules that guide an organization through acquiring, building, modifying, and the interfacing of IT resources throughout the enterprise. IT resources include hardware equipment, software, communication protocols, application development methodologies, database systems, modeling tools, IT organizational structures, data, and more. With the migration to distributed-computing environments, an IT architecture most importantly defines and demonstrates the interoperability, scalability, and portability of applications and their subcomponents across the architecture. Architecture must preserve the IT investment as underlying technologies evolve.

ENTERPRISE ARCHITECTURE FRAMEWORKS

The overall definition for an architecture is preferably done by selecting an architectural framework to define the contents and boundaries of the architecture. Figures 2.1 (Zachman model), 2.2 (Gartner Group model), and 2.3 (Index model) are examples of popular architecture frameworks, which while broadly similar have clear, distinctive features. Each framework model defines the entities of an architecture as rows and the attributes of those rows as columns. We prefer—and therefore use throughout this book—the Index model, so we will explain it in more detail.

The rows of the Index model are as follows:

> **Infrastructure.** Denotes the technical infrastructure of IT assets. This includes communication networks, software, and hardware.

	DATA	FUNCTION	NETWORK	PEOPLE	TIME	MOTIVATION
SCOPE						
ENTERPRISE MODEL						
SYSTEM MODEL						
TECHNOLOGY MODEL						
COMPONENTS						

FIGURE 2.1   The Zachman model is a 30-cell definition of what embraces an enterprise IT architecture.

Data. Denotes the data assets of the business. This includes data and database definitions.

Applications. Denotes the business applications that are used to run the business. These applications are built on the infrastructure and use the data from the prior rows.

Organization. Denotes organization and people issues that enable the IT environment. This includes items such as the IT organizational structure, processes, core competencies, and human resource polices.

The columns of the Index model are as follows:

Inventory. Defines the IT assets you currently have, such as your as-is inventory.

Principles. Defines overarching rules and guidelines that are used to guide decision making and motivate collaboration across the IT community.

Models. Defines diagrams, blueprints, or other forms of schematics that are used to express and illustrate the contents of the row.

Standards. Defines agreed-upon standards and processes that are used in executing each row.

	VALUES	PRINCIPLES	PROCESSES	STANDARDS	BUY LIST
EXECUTIVE DIRECTION		N/A	N/A	N/A	N/A
ORGANIZATION ARCHITECTURE	N/A			N/A	N/A
APPLICATION ARCHITECTURE	N/A				
DATA ARCHITECTURE	N/A				
SERVICES LAYER	N/A				
FACILITIES LAYER	N/A				
PLATFORM	N/A				
NETWORK	N/A				

FIGURE 2.2 The Gartner Group model is a 40-cell definition of what embraces an enterprise IT architecture.

	INVENTORY	PRINCIPLES	MODELS	STANDARDS
INFRASTRUCTURE				
DATA				
APPLICATIONS				
ORGANIZATION				

FIGURE 2.3 The Index model is a 16-cell definition of what embraces an enterprise IT architecture.

The other architecture frameworks overlap with this framework definition but are also quite distinct. The Gartner Group framework, for example, breaks the Index infrastructure row into: Service, Facilities, Platform, and Network. The Zachman framework has Time and Motivation columns that are nonexistent in the others.

ARCHITECTURE GOVERNANCE

With this basic understanding of architectural frameworks and their distinctions, we can address the fundamental concept of *architecture governance*. Architecture governance consists of five steps:

1. **Architecture framework selection.** In this step, you decide which architecture framework to use to govern your community's understanding of what is meant by an IT architecture. The framework may be any of the three discussed, a cut-and-paste version of the three, or another that you prefer. In any case, you must precisely define, preferably as a matrix, what you mean when you say enterprise architecture.
2. **Cell contents.** During this step, you decide on the contents of each cell for the selected framework. The architecture framework is divided into definition cells. You must choose how each cell is completed. In some case, the answer is obvious or has been standardized; in other cases, you have to make choices; in still other cases, you need to develop a home-grown solution. Regardless, you must precisely define the contents of each cell.
3. **Cell completion responsibilities.** At this point, you select the organizational units responsible for completing each cell in its entirety; that is complete a vertical level of each cell, and/or complete a horizontal partition of each cell. Most organizations have multiple architecture groups. Though the groups are dispersed, the architecture coordinates the IT assets across the enterprise. It is therefore necessary to define how the cells are completed in a nonredundant, coherent, and integrated manner; this requires making careful decisions about the horizontal and vertical partitioning of the contents of each cell across responsible organizational entities. It is, in practice, analogous to the problem of distributing tables across distributed databases while maintaining a single logically integrated view to the users.
4. **Cell delivery coordination.** The goal for this step is to define how the delivery of cells is coordinated across architecture groups over time. Given a dispersed but integrated set of groups that are responsible for completing and maintaining the architecture, it is necessary to design how their work efforts are coordinated. It is not enough that each group does its part; each part must be coordinated with the others across time. This requires the utilization of a global configuration management process to permit periodic baselining of the architecture.

5. **Architecture governance evolution.** At this step, you address the problem of evolving steps 1–4 in synchronization with ever-changing times and circumstances. A responsive administrative procedure must be put in place to revise the definitions of each step as demanded by the dynamic business situation.

When you can explain your solution for performing the five steps, you have completed the foundation for doing architecture work. If you can't explain the steps, you probably have a lot of people running around engaging in architecture work without a mutual understanding or coordination of what they are doing. In this case, when things work together, it is a combination of heroic efforts, coincidence, and personal deals. Such an approach will not hold up against the turbulence of hypercompetition.

ARCHITECTURE STRATEGY

We can now go on to the next important idea: *architecture strategy*. As illustrated in Figure 2.4, architecture strategy is the planned change in the architecture cells over time. There is an existing architecture framework which is referred to as the "as-is-built" architecture or *architecture of record* (AOR). The AOR architecture models the state of each architecture cell as of a baseline period. There is also a "to-be-built" architecture that is the sum of architectural initiatives that are to be completed at time baseline $+t$. When this architecture is completed, it becomes the new AOR architecture; this cycle continues ad infinitum.

Finally, there is a *vision architecture* that serves as a strategic intent for all architectural work. The vision architecture defines a far-reaching goal that goes through periodic revision. The point is, it is never achieved; it keeps moving, and thus serves as a long-term ideal and collective target for all architectural work. If you ever achieved a vision architecture, it would result in complacency, and complacency is the worst strategy of all.

We assume that architecture-strategy execution is dispersed but integrated. As shown in Figure 2.4, three groups—corporate architects, business-unit (BU) architects, and application-family architects—are each responsible for selected portions of the architecture. Each group does its allocated responsibilities in compliance with the governance rules that have been established.

Further, we assert that the way you govern architecture and execute architecture strategy makes the difference in your ability to maneuver in the hypercompetitive Information Age that confronts you. Without governance and strategy, there is no way to design and coordinate your enterprise architecture to enable speed, flexibility, maneuverability, and agility. Many companies find themselves with an architectural mess because they have never instituted a clear and manageable definition of architecture. Instead, they have taken isolated actions under the rubric of architecture yet never put in place a managed governance and strategy process.

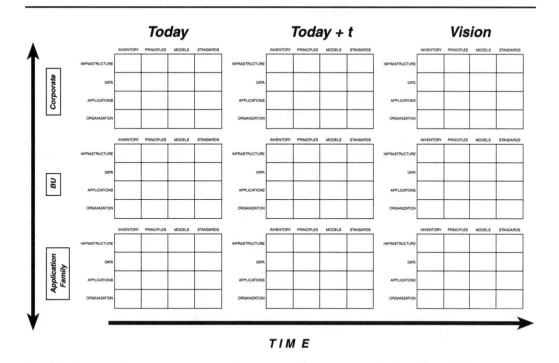

FIGURE 2.4 Architecture strategy is coordinated change in the cells of the selected architecture framework over time.

In the next section of this chapter, we give examples of how to complete sample cells for the Index framework model. This provides the next level of understanding, following architecture governance and strategy. To jump ahead, it is our contention that the two cells most critical to enabling maneuverability—infrastructure models and application models—do not currently enjoy a rigorous blueprinting system.[1] As a consequence, most of these models are poorly done, in the sense that they are ambiguous, have no persistence, and vary widely in content. The consequence is that a great deal of architecture work proceeds in confusion, gross misunderstandings, and the inevitable need for time-consuming and expensive rework when the former yields the inevitable results.

Confusion, misunderstandings and rework are not the attributes of a hypercompetitive predator. In Chapter 3, we propose an Enterprise IT Architecture Blueprinting (EAB) drawing system for completing those cells in a manner that is analogous to engineering drawings. This dramatically improves the ability of the IT organization to model its architecture and make rapid, broadly understood, and prudent changes that enable the business to alter its architecture in timely compliance to hypercompetitive movement requirements.

To restate and extend from Chapter 1, the logic for focusing on IT architecture as the mechanism to create hypercompetitive advantage is that:

- Industries are confronting global hypercompetition.
- An endless stream of temporary advantages must replace sustainable advantage as the means to winning.
- The ability to build temporary advantages is a function of the capability of the business to maneuver.
- In the Information Age, the ability to maneuver the business is a function of the malleability of information technology. What must be maneuvered are your information systems.
- The malleability of your information technology is built upon your information technology architecture.
- To be effective, an information technology architecture framework must be selected and deployed within a shared community understanding of architecture governance and architecture strategy.
- The key architecture framework cells to enable hypercompetitive behavior are the infrastructure and the application models.
- Infrastructure and application models are effective only if drawn using a rigorous blueprinting methodology and managed through structured configuration management.

The infrastructure and application models are the critical hypercompetitive enabling cells because they provide the unambiguous and complete visualization of the as-is-built and to-be-built IT infrastructure and application systems.

A blueprint (an engineering drawing) is a document that, by means of pictorial graphics, textural presentations, and rules of notation, rigorously depicts the physical and functional end-product requirements of an item. In general, a blueprint has four constituent components:

1. **Front matter.** Textural material that explains the problem and provides the context for all the other components
2. **Bill of materials.** A structured parts list.
3. **Diagrams.** Drawings (schematics) that illustrate the parts, their relationships to each other, and the attributes of those relationships.
4. **Functional specifications.** Detailed explanations of the functionality and behavior of entities defined within the diagrams.

If what you currently deliver under the guise of IT architecture blueprints does not meet these four definitions, it's not a blueprint.

As with all other engineering disciplines, infrastructure models and application models must be elevated in formality to the category of blueprints. Once promoted to the level of blueprints, the logic chain for IT architecture is complete, and the enterprise architecture is positioned to enable the company to defend or attack as dictated by the gyrating times and circumstances.

COMPLETING AN ARCHITECTURE FRAMEWORK

The examples given in this section illustrate how to complete samples cells in the Index framework. Figure 2.3 has been reproduced in Figure 2.5 with identification numbers to simplify relating the framework cells with the text that follows. (Note: These identification numbers are not part of the framework.) As shown in Figure 2.5, Enterprise Architecture Blueprinting (EAB) focuses on the application model and infrastructure model cells (cell identifier 8). It is not our intent to provide a detailed methodology for completing the entire framework, rather to provide perspective on the framework so that when we turn our attention to the focus of this book—the application and infrastructure model cells—you will have a complete understanding of the framework context in which they exist.

Principles Column

The Principles column contains community rules (laws or policies) that provide enduring overall direction and guidance for the long-term evolution of the IT assets (see cell identifier 1 in Figure 2.5). They provide a basis for dispersed but integrated decision making, and serve as the tiebreaker in settling disputes. They also establish the basis from which to make design decisions that cumulatively result in the development of a highly valued future (vision) architecture. Finally, principles are organization-dependent. Table 2.1 lists examples of a starter set of principles.

Principles are selected based on their efficacy to meet the strategic requirements of the business. In a period of hypercompetition, they enable the

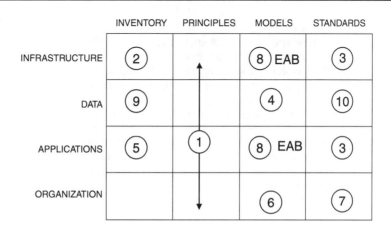

FIGURE 2.5 Index architecture framework revisited. The numbers on the illustrated matrix are for identification purposes only.

TABLE 2.1   Principles

Infrastructure Principles	Industry standards are preferable to internal standards. The vendor is as important as the product. We employ reusable parts. Systems must provide end-to-end management. Technologies must enable platform scalability. Technologies must enable platform portability. We leverage existing assets. We are an early adopter of new technology. The domain of our infrastructure and applications is global.
Data Principles	Data is captured at its source once, then electronically distributed. Data is a corporate resource. We propagate the unit-of-record concept. We promote data stewardship. An enterprise data model drives application architecture. Derivable data is not stored. Data is separated from applications. Data redundancy is actively managed. Data must be timely, accessible, and understandable. Data access is transparent to users of physical location and structure.
Application Principles	It is preferable to buy rather than to build. All production applications must have a disaster recovery plan. All systems must take into account appropriate security issues. Applications are designed to execute in a global environment. Applications are deployed in a layered architecture structure. Applications balance efficiency and maintainability. Whenever possible, applications start small and grow. Applications share a common application look and feel. We promote shared functionality. Applications are driven from the business model. All new applications adhere to the vision architecture. Application design must include testability. Human factors are considered in all designs. Applications are maintained under version control. Applications designs are modular. Applications permit electronic bonding with value-chain partners.
Organization Principles	We execute our work in a manner to prevent problems rathen than fix problems. There is corporate ownership of security definitions. Standard development methodologies are adhered to. There is periodic maintenance of architecture governance.

business to use IT to cope with the overarching hypercompetition business drivers, which include:

- The shift of market power to customers
- Rapid decline in barriers to market entry
- Accelerating change in technology/know-how
- Rise of multiple deep-pocketed players
- Deregulation
- Inability to sustain advantage
- Globalization

Principles address the perpetual management problem of influence at a distance. Though the decision maker cannot be everywhere, and neither can nor should make every decision, agreed-to principles provide influence without presence. This is very important if one hopes to promote coordinated but independent actions across a large and often quite opinionated organizational community over time.

The architecture governance team has to decide the organization-specific set and, most important, the degree of liberty and conformity that they will promote. There are three categories of principles: *overarching,* which establish broad rules for using the IT assets; *design*, which define rules that dictate design decisions; and *buy,* which are rules for how to make purchase decisions

Principles are normally the first cells completed because they draw the sandbox boundaries for completing the other cells. Appendix C provides a detailed methodology for developing a set of principles that directly link the principles to business drivers.

Infrastructure Inventory

The Infrastructure Inventory column is a detailed inventory of the IT assets that you currently have deployed (see cell identifier 2 in Figure 2.5). You must define the primary entities, such as computers by type, software by type, networks by type, and so on, as well as their associated attributes that you wish to manage. This cell answers the common management questions: What are my IT assets? How much of them do I have? How are they used?, and Where are they?

Infrastructure and Application Standards

Infrastructure and application standards are structured "parts lists" and assembly lists that itemize the elements that have been approved for use by the IT organization (Figure 2.5, cell identifier 3). They represent the elements of IT from which systems are assembled. Though in practice these are usually lengthy, wordy volumes, the specification of the standards reduces to a relation with the following attributes:

Class of components. A major classification of IT elements used to group and differentiate IT components. Examples of component classes are processors, database management systems (DBMS), networks, transaction managers, and testing tools.

Class of subcomponents. Defines a subclassification within a component class. For example, subcomponent classes for the database management systems class are hierarchical, network, relational, and object. The component and subcomponent model that you create defines a complete taxonomy of the IT resources that you use to build your information system environment. Like everything else about IT, this taxonomy has to be updated as new classes and subclasses of technology emerge.

Standard IT component. The specific selection, product, and vendor that you have made to fulfill the requirements of the component and subcomponent class. For example, Oracle may be your standard IT component for the component class for database management systems and subcomponent class of relational databases

IT component standards adherence. Defines the industry standards to which the standard IT component adheres. For example, if your standard IT component is the UNIX operating system, the adherence standard is Posix.

IT component application program interface (API). Defines how other IT components interface or invoke this component. For example, if your IT component is the Teradata database management system, the Teradata call-level interface is one of many possible APIs.

IT component status. Defines the currently approved usage level for the component, such as restricted, general, grandfathered, and so on.

IT component suitability. Defines the types of applications for which this component is suitable. For example, a multidimensional database management system is suitable for a departmental datamart, but not for large-scale transaction processing.

IT component dependencies. Defines which other components are prerequisites and corequisities to use this component. For example, an index pointer checker is usually database-management-system dependent.

IT component technology life cycle stage. A statement as to where in the technology life cycle this component is, such as emergent, growth, mainstream, mature, decline, or cobweb.

IT component technology road map. A statement as to what technologies may repalce this technology and when.

IT component principle linkage. A list of the principles that governed the selection of this component.

Experience indicates that many IT organizations confuse these cells with an IT architecture. They create a robust list of standards and believe they are finished with architecture. A parts list—even the world's best parts list—is not architecture; it is a *piece* of your architecture—a very important piece, but only a piece. Your architecture is the complete framework that you have chosen and the completion of all the cells. If you only have the time and energy to complete one cell, focus on the application models cell. It gives you the blueprints that you vitally need; by doing so, it requires you to specify the other components as a by-product of the blueprinting effort.

Data Architecture Cells

The Data Models cell (cell identifier 4 in Figure 2.5) defines the data architecture view of your architecture. The IT data community has developed a robust set of modeling techniques and methodologies to engineer data. These methods are generally predicated on separating data from specific applications, data administration, and rigorous modeling methodologies. The prescribed methods and modeling techniques include enterprise data modeling, subject database modeling, dual database designs, entity relationship modeling, relational normalization, and multidimensional database modeling. (Footnote 3 identifies resources that describe how to perform data engineering.) The enterprise architecture blueprints assume that rigorous data modeling has already been adopted. Although the blueprints point to such models, they don't include how to develop them.

Obviously, data models are also fundamental to maneuverability. Since we assume that data modeling has been adopted, there is not the same sense of urgency to implement them as suggested for the infrastructure and application models. However, if you have not implemented proper data modeling, *the implementation of this cell is equally urgent to the application and infrastructure model cells.*

The other data architecture cells—Data Inventory and Data Standard—support the data models (see cell identifiers 9 and 10 in Figure 2.5). The Data Inventory cell identifies all the operational and data warehouse databases of record; the Data Standards cell provides the definition for each data element under data administration and data naming standards.

Application Inventory

The Application Inventory cell (cell identifier 5 in Figure 2.5) provides a structured inventory of your business applications and the relationship of those applications to the business. How this cell is completed varies widely; although there are many competing views on how to represent this information effectively, the following two are common.

Business Function Model

A business function model as shown in Figure 2.6 is maintained for each major business process, and the model is related to the applications that deliver the atomic functions.[3]

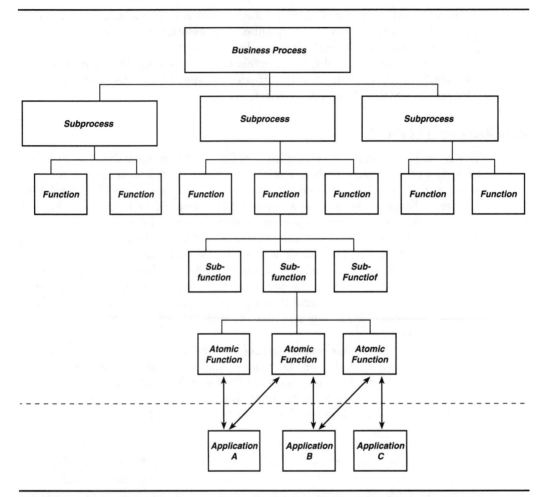

FIGURE 2.6   A business function model is a functional decomposition of a business process into its atomic functions.

Application Positioning

Each application is positioned within an application taxonomy. By positioned, we mean that its essential attributes from both a business and a technology perspective are itemized. Typical attributes for an application business position are:

Description. A short description of the application.

Functionality. The business functions that the application delivers.

User interface. How the user community interfaces with the application.

Utilization. The number of users and frequency of use.

Cost per user. The economics of the application.

Support. The ratio of support personnel to users and how support is provided.

Education. The training system used to educate users on how to implement the application.

Customer satisfaction. The measurement system used and the results obtained on customer satisfaction with the application.

Requirements gathering. The methodology used to gather and implement new functionality for the application.

Growth. Anticipated expansion (shrinkage) of the application.

Best-in-class comparison. Benchmark results that compare the application to best-in-class benchmarks.

Typical attributes of an application technology position are:

Technology inventory. The parts list for the application.

Technology life cycle. An assessment of where the application, as a whole, is from a technology life cycle perspective.

Cost. Operational and maintenance costs for the application.

Maintainability. The maintenance record for the application.

Relationships to other applications. A sketch of the application and its relationship to other applications.

Staff competence. The required technical competencies needed to support the application

Quality. Historical metrics of defect and productivity for the application.

Both business and technical positioning attributes are visually depicted using a technique such as KIVIAT charts to illustrate the positions (see Figure 2.7).

Another way to illustrate the application positions is though composite application position matrices as illustrated in Tables 2.2 and 2.3. In this case, you

TABLE 2.2   Function Matrix

| | *Business Functionality Assessment* | | | | | |
	Inferior	*Basic*	*Adequate*	*Competitive*	*Superior*	*Best in Class*
User Group 1				Application A		
User Group 2			Application B			
User Group 3						Application C
User Group n	Application D					

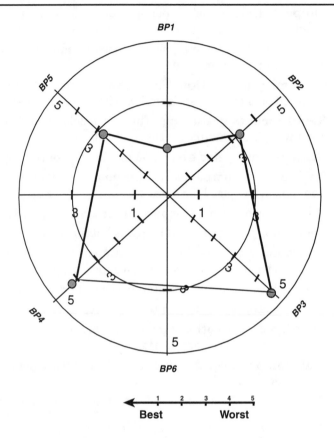

FIGURE 2.7   A KIVIAT chart can be used to visualize both the business and the technical positions of an application.

TABLE 2.3   Advantage Matrix

	Type of Advantage				
	Cost	Differentiation	Focus	Execution	Maneuverability
Sustainable Advantage	Application C			Application A	
Temporary Advantage		Application B			Application n

choose key attributes for all applications and then show their positions together on the matrices.

Organization Models

The Organization row is a repository for nontechnical business issues that directly impact the architecture (see cell identifier 6 in Figure 2.5). Examples of an organization row include IT processes, IT human resource management, IT organization structure, business location model, and organizational core competencies. Figure 2.8 shows a sample core competency model for those competencies needed to do architecture work. From a set of architecture core competencies, you develop a composite competency in architecture that enables you to effectively deliver multiple types of architectures.

Organization Standards

The Organizational Standards cell (number 7 in Figure 2.5) defines nondata, noninfrastructure, and nonapplication standards that influence architecture design and delivery. Processes that are typically subject to standardization are

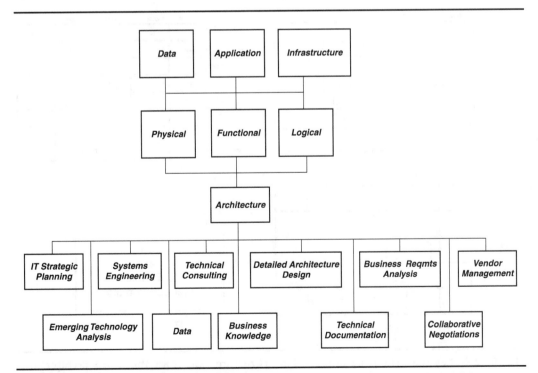

FIGURE 2.8   A core competency model illustrates the structural leverage relationship between root competencies and end products.

application development, project management, vendor management, production operations, user support, asset management, technology evaluation, architecture governance, configuration management, and problem resolution. For example, it's common to have standard software development methodologies, waterfall model, rapid application development, prototyping, and so on, to which developers are expected and required to adhere.

THE PROBLEM WITH IT ARCHITECTURE

With the cursory survey of the Index architecture framework complete, we can turn our attention to the cells of topical interest. Again, the intent was not to provide a total methodology for completing all the cells of the framework, but to give an overview so that the context is set for focusing attention on the EAB infrastructure and application model cells.

The cells critical to enabling the business to use IT to engage in hypercompetitive behavior are the application models and the infrastructure models (Figure 2.5 cell identifier 8 and Figure 2.9). If IT is to enable rapid and agile ma-

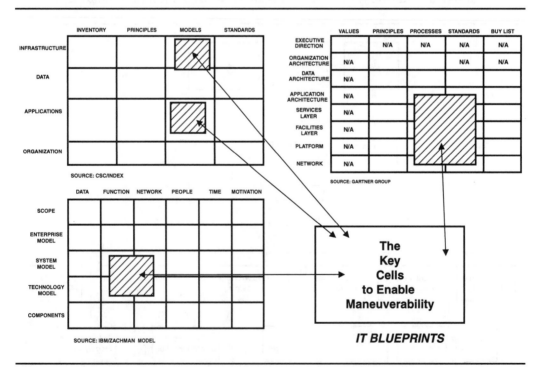

FIGURE 2.9   Key cells. The application and infrastructure models are the critical architecture components to facilitate business maneuverability.

neuvering, it must be carefully crafted for change. Extreme IT maneuverability is the consequence of purposeful and executable design. The blueprints provide the visualization and communication of that design; they are the focal point for understanding the relationships between IT assets and the ease of changing those IT-asset relationships. They illustrate to the blueprint reader all the architectural joints that provide the points of adaptability.

In Chapter 5, we develop the concept of an architecture adaptability (or change) space. Briefly, for our purposes here, the adaptability space defines an area across which applications, built on top of that architecture, can engage in rapid architectural transformation. The adaptability space prepositions applications that can alter their relationships with other applications with absolute minimum friction. This is what creates maneuverability; but it requires blueprinting to visualize and control. So blueprinting is critical to IT maneuverability because, as is true in all engineering disciplines, one has to know precisely what is built, what is desired to be built, and how the transformation can be made at minimum cost, with minimum disruption, yet at maximum speed. In Chapter 5, we also explain the integral role that blueprinting plays in establishing architecture adaptability spaces, which is the IT root capability necessary to support IT-based maneuverability.

Figures 2.10 through 2.14 show samples of common IT architecture drawings. Each conveys a message and has merit. When you review this typical set of unstructured, nonmethodological, ad hoc, and intuitive drawings found in these figures created by typical IT architecture staff, you cannot help but reach some collective and pessimistic conclusions about the industry state of IT blueprinting:

> **There is no meaningful or repetitive notation.** Every drawing is a personal expression without persistence of representation across drawings.
>
> **There are confused and intermixed levels of notation.** A drawing is at at once a logical drawing, a physical drawing, and a functional drawing; the same symbols are often used to mean different things on the same drawings.
>
> **The notational system is ad hoc.** It changes dynamically with each new drawing; it is never clear exactly what any drawing means.
>
> **There is no solid underlying concept of what the drawing is trying to explain.** No one has defined what the elements are that need to be represented on a drawing nor which attributes of those elements must to be itemized.
>
> **It is usually impossible to know whether a drawing is consistent or correct.** Since the drawing is inherently ambiguous, how can it be critiqued for validity or desirability?

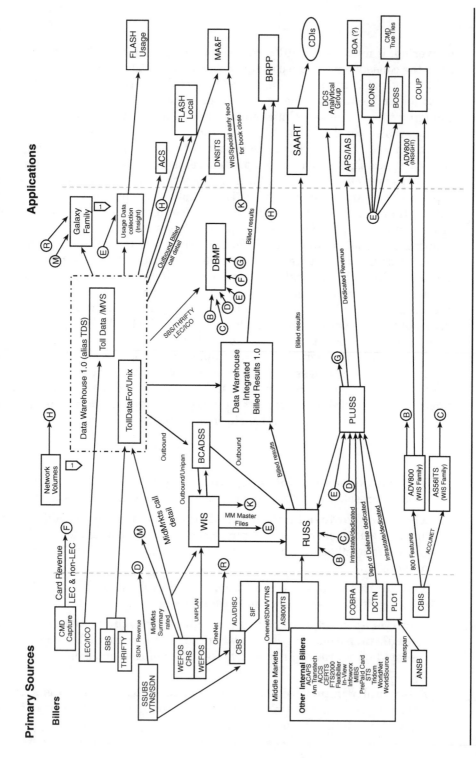

FIGURE 2.10 Intersystem data flows.

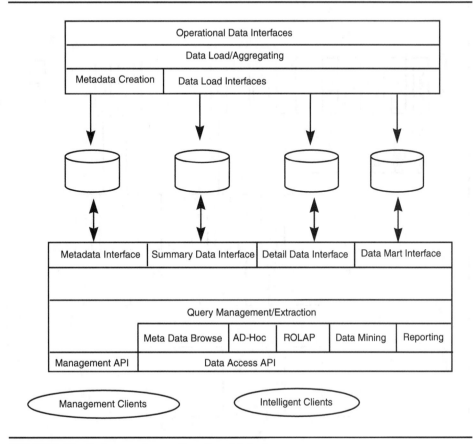

FIGURE 2.11   Data warehouse functional interface.

The drawings often do not communicate the essence of distributed and heterogeneous computing environments. One cannot substantively understand from the typical drawing interoperability, scalability, portability, service invocation, heterogeneity, or most important, the ability to reconfigure the architecture in response to dynamic business requirements.

The current and predominant individual approach to architecture diagramming makes purposeful architecture development, communication, adherence, and evolution extraordinarily difficult, if not impossible. It also makes the application and infrastructure models cells the most pressing problem with IT architecture, because, in truth, they are done extraordinarily poorly, without any semblance of blueprinting rigor; at the same time, these cells are the most critical for enabling IT hypercompetitive maneuverability.

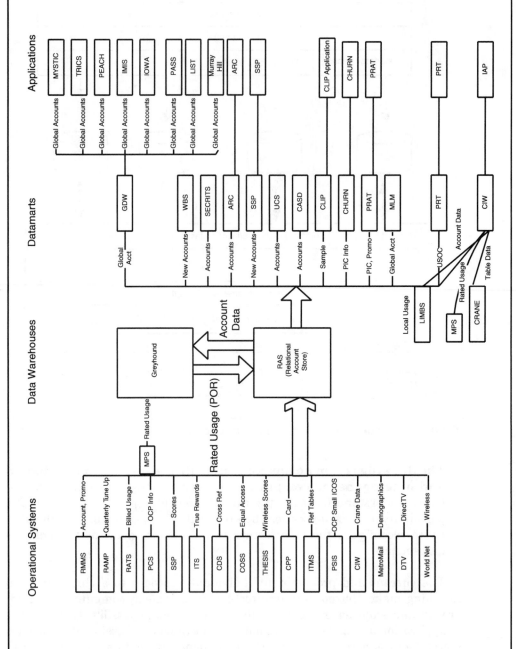

FIGURE 2.12 Composite of a data warehouse/datamart system.

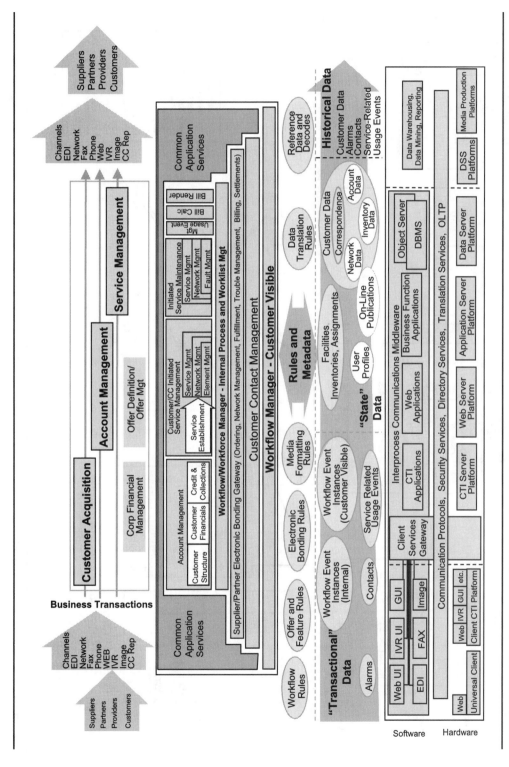

FIGURE 2.13 How business architecture, functional architecture, data architecture, and technical architecture relate to each other.

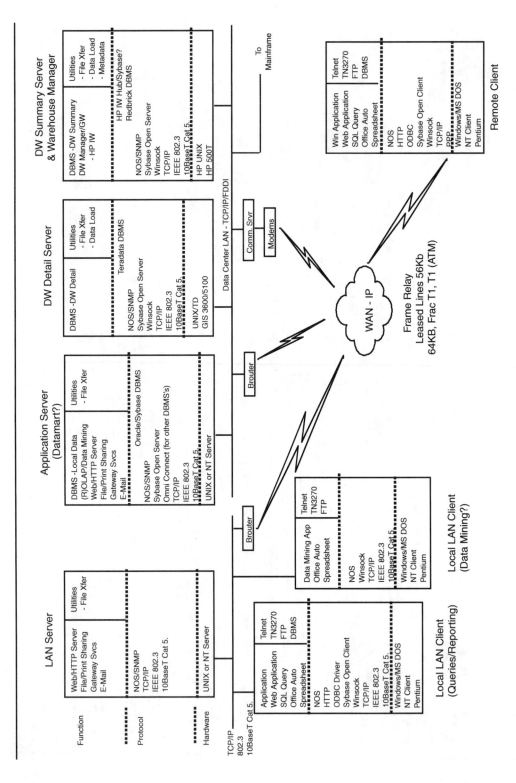

FIGURE 2.14 Decision support architecture.

TABLE 2.4 Drawing Comparisons

Blueprinting Issue	Engineering Drawings	Typical IT Architecture Drawing
Degree of specification of drawing rules	Formal notation system: Icons/graphics Formal text Precise meanings	Personal notation per drawing: Random icons/graphics Random text Ambiguous meanings
Representation of a given problem	Repeatable	Seldom Repeatable
Maintenance of model to reflect reality	Active model	One time model
User Expectation	Predictable presentation	Ad hoc presentation
Methodology	Managed methodology	No methodology
Education	Formal education and Certification	No education No certification
Community Use of Blueprinting System	Community practice	No community practice
Objects to Express	Defines minimum of what to communicate	Personal definition
Completeness of Blueprinting	Drawing system	Personal sketching
Knowledge Repository of Record	The blueprint	Individual's mind
Visibility of Designs	High visibility	Fog

Table 2.4 compares the typical IT drawing to engineering drawings. The differences are so evident that it is almost embarrassing to the IT profession. But it does point out a conundrum that must be resolved. IT architecture cannot become the arsenal of hypercompetitive maneuverability if it is built on a foundation of casual, superficial, flighty and personal sketches.

If you find yourself resistant to this situation analysis, do an experiment with your own internal architecture drawings. Choose some drawings and an audience of architects and developers as reviewers. Give out the drawings to this group and ask them to prepare a presentation on what the drawings mean. Chances are, you will observe some combination of the following:

The presentations are very short. The drawings convey very little substantive information.

The presentations vary widely in their interpretations of the drawings. Each person interprets the drawing in a personal manner and includes his or her own elaboration of what the drawing means to fill in all the blanks.

The presentations engender an extended debate of what the drawings mean. It is most interesting, of course, when a reviewer tells the creator, unknowingly, that the creator's interpretation of the drawing is completely wrong.

Under intensive review, the drawings deconstruct. As the reviewers carefully concentrate and focus on trying to understand the drawings, they discover the gross inconsistencies and incompleteness inherent in them.

How can anyone use IT architecture to be an Information Age predator if no one really has a clue as to the meaning of any architecture drawing?

Capability Maturity Model

Another tool for grasping the true current state of IT architecture modeling is the software capability maturity model (CMM). The CMM, supported by the Software Productivity Consortium and Carnegie-Mellon University Systems Engineering Institute (SEI), is a framework that assesses software process maturity. It defines five levels of process maturity: initial, repeatable, defined, managed, and optimizing. Table 2.5 describes the five CMM maturity levels. In accordance with this framework, architecture blueprinting is clearly at the initial level, meaning heroes do it; the process is sporadic; it is shrouded in mystery (i.e., it is a black art); and it rewards individual creativity as opposed to promoting an engineering discipline. To support a war of IT anchored movement, architecture diagramming must be repositioned to at least the defined level.

The essential questions you need to answer in regard to the state of architecture diagramming are:

- Does IT architecture require a consistent and repeatable notational drawing system (as in all other engineering disciplines), or are any and all personal and ad hoc blueprinting/drawing methods satisfactory?
- Given the backdrop painted for hypercompetition and the Information Age, can you win if you continue doing architecture the way you currently do?
- Are you content with your architecture being a CMM initial level process?

If you are satisfied with the architecture status quo, then your architects should continue their current mode of drawing IT architectures. In this case, however, you should ask why you are so complacent and self-satisfied. What is your alternative game plan?

If you are not satisfied with the architecture status quo, you need to adopt a formal graphical notational system for blueprinting IT architectures that is

TABLE 2.5   Capability Maturity Model

CMM Level	Description	Key Process Areas
Initial	Heroes Sporadic process Black art Rewards individual creativity, does not promote engineering discipline	None
Repeatable	Software project management Project planning Repeatable processes Learning	Requirements management Project planning Project tracking Quality assurance Configuration management
Defined	Defined, documented, and used processes Integrated processes Active community participation and understanding	Process focus Process definition Training Peer reviews Software engineering Integration management
Managed	Measurement Statistical process control Variation analysis	Quantitative process management Software quality management
Optimizing	Focus on defects Continuous improvement Rapid technology transfer and adoption	Process change management Defect prevention Technology change management

shared within your architectural community. EAB, which is presented in Chapter 3, is a candidate for such a methodology. In evaluating EAB or an alternative, remember that methodological simplicity and intuitiveness are highly desirable but less so than the need for substantive content. Formal notational systems in all engineering disciplines first focus on the depth and selection of information to be communicated and then address the absolute simplest and intuitive way to present it. EAB, as would any meaningful alternative, requires education to learn, discipline to use, and professionalism to assure adherence. It is not the case that any formal notational system is too much work; it is the case that the necessary work must be done to express ideas in a predictable and understandable manner, a manner that is independent of any individual and that creates a persistent organizational memory. EAB, and its siblings, are not sketching systems. What is generally done now is unplanned and casual sketching. EAB is a communication system that serves as the mooring for most architectural work.

All engineering blueprinting systems are built on the same foundation logic:

1. The subject matter can be characterized in terms of a finite set of identifiable objects with well defined properties.
2. There exist general and persistent rules that apply to these objects, their properties, and the interrelationships of the objects.
3. The rules can be situationally and systemically applied to derive solution representations.
4. The establishment of the above (1–3) permits a diagramming and notational system to be created that enables preunderstanding across the stakeholder community. Since all members of the community, a-priori, know the representation system, they can read the diagrammatic with a specific expectation of what they will see and what each representation means. They preunderstand the notations and the symbols. The only thing that is novel is the problem-specific combinations and permutations of the symbols and notations.
5. The diagram creator (architect, engineer, etc.) uses the diagramming system to communicate a specific intent. Because of preunderstanding, the creator can convey a *literal* statement of his or her design.
6. The meaning of the diagram is, and solely is, embodied in the diagram. Each stakeholder is not free to develop or apply a personal interpretation. The intent of the creator, with its idiosyncratic meaning, transcends time, context, and audience.
7. As a consequence of the above, there exists a tight correspondence between the real world objects, the creator's intent (the diagram), and the interpretation of the diagram by the stakeholders.
8. If any of the above (1–7) is not accomplished, breakdown occurs. Breakdown means that correspondence does not occur and the stakeholders do not understand the creator's intent. If a formal diagramming system is being used, breakdown is visible and self correcting. If a formal system is not being used, breakdown is stealthy and continuous.

This universal logic applies to IT architecture drawings just as it does all other engineering disciplines and EAB, or EAB-like drawing systems are mandatory to assure correspondence and avoid disastrous breakdowns.

Knowledge and Architecture

Architecture work is very sophisticated knowledge work, and knowledge is the information resident in people's minds that is used for making decisions in unknown contexts. Knowledge management entails the practices and technologies that facilitate the creation and exchange of knowledge.

There are two types of knowledge: explicit, which is easily codified and communicated, and tacit, which is unique. Tacit knowledge has important characteristics:

- It can have a deep and far-reaching impact.
- It is often the basis of advantage.
- It is normally difficult to document and communicate.

Knowledge strategy is about expanding tacit knowledge throughout an organization.

Economic theory provides a way to think about how to grow and communicate architecture knowledge. It teaches that all production is, fundamentally, a function of three variables: factors of production (technology employed), methods of production (processes employed), and worker effort (worker morale, enthusiasm, commitment, etc.). To dramatically improve IT architecture blueprinting, it is necessary to design a set of actions that alter the factors of production (technology employed); alter the methods of production (processes employed); and alter the worker effort (morale, enthusiasm, commitment, zeal, dedication, ownership, etc.).

It is therefore our approach with EAB to eradicate the problems with IT architecture by:

> **Altering the factors of production (technology employed).** Architects utilize a formal blueprinting system.

> **Altering the methods of production (processes employed).** Architects do their work within the context of a structured configuration management process.

> **Altering the worker effort.** Architects are trained in EAB and structured configuration management, and the rewards and recognition system promote new professional behaviors.

In this way, your architects are transformed from individuals doing incomplete sketches to powerful architects of maneuver.

CONCLUSION

Figure 2.15 is a strategic analysis framework called a *consumption chain.*[4] A consumption chain analysis consists of looking at a product or service and asking the questions shown in Figure 2.15. From this critical self-analysis comes a plethora of ideas on how to improve the value proposition of the product or service—ideas that the business wants implemented yesterday.

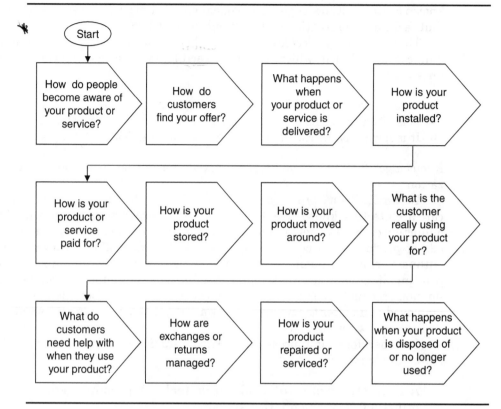

FIGURE 2.15   A consumption chain is a model of how consumers experience a product or service.

The implementation of these value-creation opportunities is centered in information technology, and requires you to change your IT architecture. Changing your IT architecture is a race against time because your hypercompetitors are doing the same thing. Companies are no longer content with slow or modest changes to the consumption chain. The faster a change can be made, the sooner a disruption can occur, and the sooner market exploitation can be achieved.

There is only one problem: To be fast and agile in revising your architecture to deliver the new value propositions, you need to understand precisely your as-is-built architecture and then you need to create the most flexible to-be-built architecture. Unfortunately, you do not have a blueprinting system. How will you cope as the trickle of architecture changes, common to moderate-level competition, turns into an inevitable flood of urgent change requests, which is common to a period of hypercompetition? What will you do?

ENDNOTES

1. In one of my previous books, *Practical Steps to Aligning Information Technology with Business Strategies*, (John Wiley & Sons, 1994), I introduced an architecture blueprinting system called Mulciber. Enterprise architecture blueprinting is a complete replacement for that system. To my knowledge, there are no other publicly offered blueprinting systems for IT architecture.
2. See Inmon, W. H., *Data Architecture: The Information Paradigm* (QED, 1992), or Martin, James, *Strategic Information Planning Methodologies* (Prentice Hall, 1989), for representative methodologies and modeling techniques of data architecture.
3. For information on functional business modeling, see Steven H. Spewak, Steven C. Hill, *Enterprise Architecture Planning: Developing a Blueprint for Data, Applications, and Technology.* (John Wiley & Sons, 1993).
4. Ian. C. MacMillan and Rita Gunther McGrath. "Discovering New Points of Differentiation," *Harvard Business Review*, May/June 1996.

CHAPTER 3

Enterprise IT Architecture Blueprinting

The purpose of this chapter is to teach the Enterprise IT Architecture Blueprinting (EAB) methodology. In reading and applying this chapter, keep in mind the imagery of a blueprint (an engineering drawing), a document that, by means of pictorial graphics, textual presentations, and rules of notation, depicts the physical and functional end-product requirements of an item. When you apply this definition specifically to IT architecture, any description of an architecture blueprint must, at minimum, answer the following questions:

Purpose. What is the problem to be solved?

Functions. What are the functional components and how have they been allocated or partitioned across the architecture?

Information technologies. What are the technical components and how have they been allocated or partitioned across the architecture?

Relationships. How do the components relate in space and time? How are functions allocated to technologies?

Dynamic interplay. How is control passed between and among components?

Flow. How does the data flow in space and time?

Resources. Which resources are consumed and where?

You must meet these requirements through the blueprinting building blocks of front matter, a bill of materials (a parts list), functional specifications, and diagrams. These four elements are collectively referred to as the *blueprint components*. The bill of materials, front matter, and functional specifications are collectively referred to as *support diagrams*.

EAB OVERVIEW: NOTIONS

The unit of instruction for EAB is a *notion*. A notion is an idea or set of ideas that you must understand to draw and interpret the blueprints. Notions are serially additive; the notions must be read in sequential order. At the end of the chapter, a table of notions is provided to serve as a reference index into all of those presented in this chapter.

Notion 1. Overview

An EAB is a rigorously structured document that is divided into sections and subsections (Figure 3.1). A given section exclusively hosts a front matter, parts list, functional specifications, or 1–n different types of diagrams. A diagram subsection will host only one type of diagram.

EAB embodies specific rules that define:

- How to draw each type of diagram—vocabulary, rules, graphics (a.k.a. icons, objects, and notations).
- How the diagrams and icons relate to each other.
- How to structure and specify the nondiagram blueprint components.
- In which (sub)section to place each blueprint component.
- How to package the finished EAB.

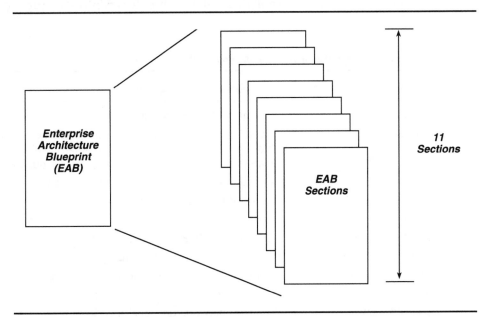

FIGURE 3.1   EAB definition. An EAB is a rigorously structured document that is divided into sections and subsections.

An EAB is rigorous, predictable, unambiguous, and easily drawn and read by anybody who understands the EAB rules and notations. The basic 11 sections and associated blueprint components that compose an EAB are shown in Table 3.1.

A method for creating user-defined sections (functional specifications) is also available (see Notion 57 ahead). Appendix B provides page templates for all the basic EAB sections.

The focal point of an EAB is the *core section*. All the other blueprint components elaborate the core diagrams. When you read an EAB, you read the front section and the core section. The core diagrams, as needed, point to components in the other sections to elaborate them. As routinely completed, an EAB would be structured as illustrated in Figure 3.2.

The domains of applicability for EABs are infrastructure and applications architectures. These are the Infrastructure Models and Application Models cells in Figure 2.3. As itemized in Table 3.2, an EAB can be used to document eight different types of blueprints that originate in those cells:

1. **Logical infrastructure architecture.** An EAB that shows the logical architecture components and their relationships for an infrastructure problem but does not specify a specific solution for each logical architecture element.
2. **Physical infrastructure architecture.** An EAB that shows the physical, architectural elements and their relationships for an infrastructure problem.

TABLE 3.1   EAB Basic Sections and Blueprint Components

Section Name	Associated Blueprint Component
Front Section	Contains introductory matter.
Core Section	Contains a drawing-dependent combination of system block diagrams, platform diagrams, interoperability diagrams, function block diagrams, and cut-out diagrams.
Annotation Section	Contains annotation functional specifications.
Dictionary Section	Contains the EAB dictionary that is a parts list.
Detail Section	Contains platform-detail functional specifications.
Database Section	Contains database functional specifications.
Transaction Section	Contains transaction functional specifications.
Portability Section	Contains portability functional specifications.
Scalability Section	Contains scalability functional specifications.
Network Section	Contains network functional specifications.
User Group Section	Contains user-group functional specifications.

Cover Page
Front Section
     Table of Contents Pages
     Overview Pages
     Design Definition
     Legend Pages
     Change Control Pages
Core Section
  SB Subsection
     System Block Diagram
  PL Subsection
     Platform Diagram
  Interop Subsection
     Interoperability Diagram
  FN Subsection
     Function Block Diagram
  Cut-Out Subsection
     Cut-Out Diagram
Annotation Section
  Annotation Functional Specification
Database Section
  Database Functional Specification
Detail Section
  Detail Function Specification
Dictionary Section
  Dictionary Bill of Materials
Network Section
  Network Functional Specification
Portability Section
  Portability Functional Specification
Scalability Section
  Scalabity Functional Specification
Transaction Section
  Transaction Functional Specification
User Group Section
  User Group Functional Specification

FIGURE 3.2   EAB structure. The structure of an EAB consists of a cover page, front matter, sections divided into subsections, and diagrams.

TABLE 3.2   EAB Applicability

Architecture Type	Architecture Perspective			
	Logical	Physical	Functional	Sketch (Conceptual Logical, Physical, Functional or Mixed)
Infrastructure Architecture (Infrastructure Models cell: Figure 2.3)	X	X	X	X
Application Architecture (Application Models cell: Figure 2.3)	X	X	X	X

3. **Functional infrastructure architecture.** An EAB that shows infrastructure functions and their relationships for an infrastructure problem.
4. **Infrastructure architecture sketch or infrastructure conceptual architecture.** The use of EAB icons in a casual manner to communicate key ideas about a physical, logical, or functional infrastructure architecture.
5. **Logical application architecture.** An EAB that shows the logical architecture elements and their relationships for an application-specific problem but does not specify a specific solution for each logical architecture element.
6. **Physical application architecture.** An EAB that shows the physical architectural elements and their relationships for a specific application problem.
7. **Functional application architecture.** An EAB that shows business functions and their relationships for a specific application problem.
8. **Application architecture sketch or application conceptual architecture.** The use of EAB icons in a casual manner to communicate key ideas about a physical, logical, or functional application architecture.

Infrastructure architectures illustrate how IT elements relate to each other independent of specific business application. Application architectures are the assignment of specific business systems and functions to subviews of the infrastructure architecture.

To elaborate the key points about an EAB, note that a core diagram provides a specific view of an architecture, and a given EAB may contain multiple types of core diagrams. It takes multiple architectural views to understand an architecture in its entirety.

There are three special instances of application architectures: *development,* an application architecture for the business application of application development; *operations,* an application architecture for the business application of production operations, administration, and maintenance (OA&M), used by production systems operations personnel to manage business applications; and *deployment,* an application physical architecture for the domain of all applications that execute on a given set of physical machines.

As shown in Table 3.3, the different types and perspectives of architectures are utilized to meet variant blueprint requirements using different EAB diagrams in alignment with varying time horizons. The contents of each intersection cell in Table 3.3 is called a *core diagram set.* The diagrams that compose a core diagram set have a structural relationship to each other and illustrate an architecture at increasing levels of detail.

TABLE 3.3   Core Diagram Utilization

Architecture Type and Perspective	*Architecture Time Horizon*		*Vision (Strategic Intent Conceptual Architecture)*
	As-Is-Built Today	*To-Be-Built Planned*	
Logical Infrastructure	Platform and Interoperability Diagrams	Platform and Interoperability Diagrams	Platform and Interoperability Diagrams
Physical Infrastructure	Platform and Interoperability Diagrams	Platform and Interoperability Diagrams	N/A
Functional Infrastructure	Function Block Diagrams	Function Block Diagrams	Function Block Diagrams
Infrastructure Sketch	Use of EAB icons	Use of EAB icons informally	Use of EAB icons informally
Logical Application	System Block, Platform, and Interoperability Diagrams	System Block, Platform, and Interoperability Diagrams	System Block, Platform, and Interoperability Diagrams
Physical Application	System Block, Platform, and Inteoperability Diagrams	System Block, Platform, and Interoperability Diagrams	N/A
Functional Application	Function Block Diagrams	Function Block Diagrams	Function Block Diagrams
Application Sketch	Use of EAB icons informally	Use of EAB icons informally	Use of EAB icons informally

Key EAB Diagrams

There are four core EAB diagrams:[1]

System Block Diagram   A diagram that illustrates an architecture where "systems" is the central element of granularity and presentation. The key icon is a *system block icon* that represents a system (Figure 3.3A). The system block icon, coupled with other icons such as network, information-exchange, database, and so on, illustrates the architectural structure—IT elements and their relationships—within an EAB domain from a system-level view.

Platform Diagram   A diagram that illustrates an architecture where "platforms" is the central element of granularity and presentation. The key icon is a *platform icon* that portrays an instance of an information technology device (Figure 3.3B). The platform icon, coupled with other icons such as network, information-exchange, database, and so on, illustrates the architectural structure—IT elements and their relationships—within the EAB domain from a platform-level view.

Interoperability Diagram   A diagram that illustrates an architecture where both "configured platforms" and "services" are the central elements of granularity and presentation. The key icons are a *configured platform icon* and a *service icon* that depict an instance of an information technology device with its associated interoperability (Figure 3.3C). These icons, coupled with other icons such as network, file, database, and so on illustrate the architectural struc-

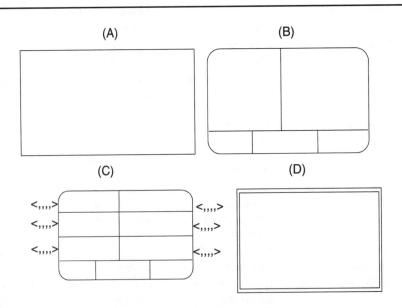

FIGURE 3.3   Key Icons. Each core diagram has a different central icon.

ture—IT elements and their relationships—within an EAB domain from an interoperability-level view.

Function Block Diagram A diagram that illustrates an architecture from a functional perspective where "function blocks" is the central element of granularity and presentation. The key icon is a *function block icon* that symbolizes a business function (Figure 3.3D). Function blocks provide a mechanism that enables the display of the functional relationships and decomposition of business functions. These icons, coupled with other icons such as file, database, and so on, illustrate the architectural structure within an EAB domain from a functional-level view.

Table 3.4, reading from top down, itemizes the relationships of these core diagrams with the other EAB icons. Note that the hierarchical view icon is used only by cut-out diagrams and is explained later.

TABLE 3.4 Icon Relationships

	System Block Diagram	Platform Diagram	Interoperatibility Diagram	Function Block Diagram
System Block Icon	x			
Platform Icon		x		
Configured Platform Icon			x	
Function Block Icon				x
Database Icon	x	x	x	x
File Icon	x	x	x	x
Annotation Icon	x	x	x	x
Any System Resource Icon	x	x	x	
Information Exchange Icon	x	x		x
Interoperability Icon			x	
Service Icon			x	
Connector Icon	x	x	x	x
User Group Icon	x	x	x	x
Information Appliance Icon	x			x
Grouping Icon	x	x	x	x
Decision Icon	x	x	x	x
Hierarchical View Icon				
Network Icon	x	x	x	
Scalability/Portability Icon			x	
Titling Notation	x	x	x	x
Footnotes/Endnotes	x	x	x	x

Each core diagram illustrates an architecture type by combining its key icon(s) with other icons. Table 3.4, reading top down, shows the sets of icons used by each type of diagram. Wherever possible, common IT industry symbols for the icons are utilized. This chapter explains all of the icons and their usage rules, and describes how to package the resulting diagrams into a finished EAB document. Appendix A contains a reference set of icon templates.

EAB changes are business- and technology-driven and are managed by using engineering change control and structured configuration management. As illustrated in Figure 3.4, blueprints are changed in response to three primary change drivers: new required business functionality cannot be met within the constraints of the existing architecture; existing business functionality can be done better with a change to the existing architecture; and a change to the existing architecture positions the architecture to do the preceding better (cheaper, faster, etc.) in the future. The change gives the business improved future option value. Chapter 4 suggests how to manage these changes by applying configuration management to EAB.

The remainder of this chapter is devoted to the presentation of the EAB. Keep in mind the following ideas:

- Architecture is about seeing structural relationships. EAB emphasizes visualization of an architecture at increasing levels of relational detail. Understanding EAB as a blueprint of relationships as opposed to a motionless graphic portrayal of parts is critical to appreciating the drawing's communication intent.
- In most conventional IT architecture packages, you read the architecture documentation, and it refers, as directed, to the included sketches. With

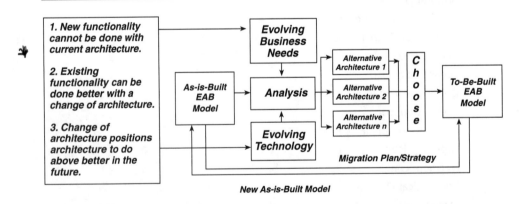

FIGURE 3.4 Configuration management. EABs are managed through their evolution using engineering-based configuration management.

EAB, you read the diagrams, and they refer, as required, to textual functional specifications.

- EAB defines the outcome of architecture work, the EAB drawing, but states nothing about the architecture design process. The architect remains completely free to envision or design whatever architecture he or she wishes. EAB only constrains the rules of expression of that design to ensure community communication and consistent representation. We do, however, propose a configuration management process (see Chapter 4) to keep drawings in synchronization as they change over time and suggest a way to do architecture design that maximizes the maneuverability of both infrastructure and application architectures (see Chapter 5).
- EAB is equally concerned about the blueprinting model and the packaging for that model. It is prescriptive in both the rules of notation and the structure (packaging) of the finished product.
- There is a fine line between doing architecture work and doing design work. In applying EAB, you may wish to move the line to align with your private view.
- There is an intractable problem between balancing simplicity and specificity. Ideally, any diagramming technique would be simple and intuitive; however, it must first convey required information in a concise and unambiguous form. As with the previous point, in adopting EAB, you may wish to refine the given balance point to be in closer harmony with your organization's traditions.
- EAB integrates with, but does not replicate, data models and business function models. It assumes that the other cells of the architecture framework (Figure 2.3) have been completed, and it references, uses, or points to them but does not duplicate them.

Figure 3.5 summarizes the key ideas that are introduced in this notion.
The most important take-away ideas are:

- The EAB, in its entirety, is the blueprint.
- The EAB is divided into sections that are, in turn, divided into subsections.
- Each core subsection hosts one, and only one, type of diagram.
- The complete expression of a diagram consumes 1–n pages.
- A diagram page is drawn using specific icons and variable text whose usage is dictated by EAB rules.
- There are structured relationships between EABs, diagrams, pages, and icons that are governed by EAB rules.

As a result of these ideas, EAB demonstrates the attributes of a rigorous blueprinting system.

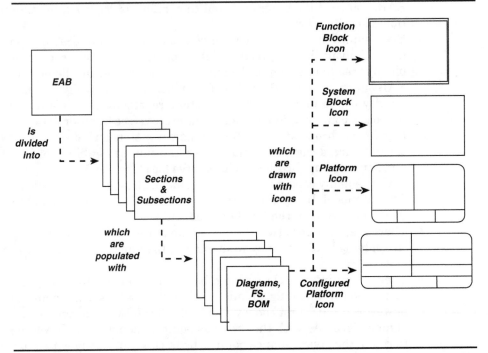

FIGURE 3.5   EAB summary. An EAB is composed of sections and subsections in which diagrams are drawn using specific sets of icons.

Notion 2: More Basic Ideas

A given EAB uses the appropriate subset of EAB components to solve the problem at hand. It is the responsibility of the architect to match the diagramming tools to the specific problem. A specific EAB diagram may occur multiple times within an EAB or no times within an EAB.

The diagrams within a given EAB have hierarchical, many-to-many, and horizontal relationships to each other. You can start an EAB at the system block level and decompose through subsystems to the platform level, or start at the platform level or configured platform level. The architect chooses the set of core diagrams appropriate to solve the specific problem.

As shown in Figure 3.6, the three core diagrams (system block, platform, and interoperability) have a very structured relationship. They participate in core diagram sets, as illustrated in Table 3.2. A given core diagram set portrays an increasingly detailed view of a specific architecture type (application or infrastructure), architecture perspective (logical, physical, or functional), and architecture time horizon. Core diagram sets have the following rules:

- In a given EAB, a core diagram set can be incomplete. You only draw the diagrams that you need to solve the problem at hand. If you draw multiple members of a set, you draw them with the structural relationships shown in Figure 3.6.
- An EAB may have multiple core sections where each core section hosts one, and only one, *core diagram set*. Though in practice, the problem at hand is normally addressed by one core diagram set per EAB, you can have multiple sets within an EAB (such as a complete row from Figure 3.2); and, if doing scenarios, you may have multiple instances of a given set. All the core diagram sets may share the same support components, or support diagrams may be identified to relate to a specific set. In practice, sharing the support diagrams permits reuse and enhances EAB productivity.

An EAB may have vertical and horizontal relationships to multiple other EABs. There may be numerous connections across blueprints. This permits large problems to be partitioned into dispersed but integrated drawings. When multiple distinct EABs have inter-EAB connections and are managed as a collection, the set of EABs is referred to as a *distributed EAB* or a *virtual EAB*.

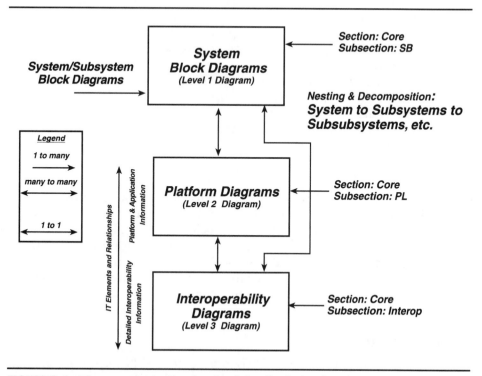

FIGURE 3.6   There are increasing levels of detail relationships between system block, platform, and interoperability diagrams.

Every EAB has a domain of interest. IT objects within the domain are called *in-scope;* those objects outside of the domain of interest are called *out-of-scope*. Most EAB drawings require the inclusion of out-of-scope objects to illustrate connections at the domain edge. However, you can declare a drawing to be *in-scope only*. This means that only in-scope objects may be drawn, and objects beyond the domain edge are related to by interdrawing connections. This method forces integration across multiple drawings, because a representation cannot be self-contained, and explicit references must be made to other drawings to complete the representation of the domain. Likewise, changes must be coordinated or the drawings will become out of sync.

To be successful, EAB, as is true for all shared diagramming techniques, requires standardization and adherence. As presented, EAB is a unified blueprinting system that should be customized to your specific needs. Color, size, or orientation of icons have no meaning in the EAB notation.

EAB is designed to manage large and complex architecture domains. By virtue of the following, it creates a robust blueprinting environment that can handle a wide range of problems:

- The (sub)section structure of EAB
- Its numbering conventions
- Its ability to engage in both page and icon decomposition
- Its ability to perform horizontal connections both within and between blueprints
- Its ability to manage distributed blueprints
- Its ability to perform architecture scenarios
- Its ability to create logical pages
- Its ability to model complex interoperability relationships
- Its modularization
- Its fundamental rigor

At the same time, simple problems can be addressed by using only basic EAB functionality. You employ EAB functionality with sensitivity and in proportion to the requirements of the problem. Initially, learning EAB, might seem complex and overwhelming because you are being presented with something new and highly functional in its entirety; in practice, architects start out using basic features and gradually integrate the more sophisticated options as both their skills mature and the problem demands.

Notion 3. Audience

The intended audience for EAB is the extended IT technical community. This embraces all those whose roles and responsibilities require them to understand or implement the architecture: architects, developers, project managers, capacity planners, system engineers, data center operations, vendors, business partner technical staff, performance engineers, reliability engineers, and others. The common denominator of this user community is the need to have a precise definition of the architecture to perform their work efficiently and effectively. EABs are primarily drawn and maintained by architects. The other stakeholders generally read, critique, and act based upon EABs.

When EAB icons are used in a casual manner to draw sketches (conceptual architectures), the intended audiences are business community executives, nontechnical management, and users. While the intent of an EAB blueprint is to be precise and directive, the intent of a sketch is to facilitate high-level idea and knowledge transfer by conveying conceptual meaning in a mode that is customized and highly sensitive to the viewpoint of the immediate audience. It is not EAB's purpose to deliver standardized sketches. The decision to use EAB icons for sketching must be evaluated against the use of other icons that may be more familiar and friendlier to each specific audience.

EAB is intended to be used to draw architectures of business information technology systems. This includes systems with cachets such as operational support systems, online transaction systems, management information systems, information exchange systems, data warehouse systems, decision support systems, datamart systems, workgroup systems, and personal systems. EAB, as currently designed, is not suitable for drawing network communications architectures, real-time systems, or embedded systems.

Notion 4. Notational Rules

The following are the basic notational rules used within EAB:

- A $lowercase_text_string denotes a text variable. Substitute the indicated text for the variable.
- A /$lowercase_text_string/ means a list of one to n entries. Remove the slash (/ /) delimiters upon text substitution.
- Text strings that are not preceded by a $ sign represent a literal.
- The forward slash (\) means a variable or text separator and is drawn.
- Left and right parentheses are used as start and end delimiters for an ordered list of comma-separated variables, such as ($lowercase_text_string, $lowercase_text_string, $lowercase_text_string, $lowercase_text_string). The parentheses are maintained after substitution. The relative position of a variable indicates its meaning. This format is used when the identity of the variable list may be ambiguous. Parentheses-delimited ordered lists may start and stop with more than one parenthesis. When the end variables of the list are not specified, the list may end with the last specified variable; the remaining variables are understood to be null-valued. When an interim variable is not specified, the comma must still be drawn to indicate a null value for the absent positional variable.

- When the substitution for a variable is made with more than one word, as and when required to avoid ambiguity, use quotation marks around the words to group them. For example, for the notation (/$role_list/), substitute ("database server" "process server") rather than the more ambiguous (database sever process server).
- When not required, variables are substituted with null values. Unless otherwise specified, null should be interpreted as meaning "blank."
- The n means an integer number. The n.n means an integer number followed by a user-determined sequence of .n. The n.n is referred to as a dotted number such as 4.1.3.

Notion 5. Cover Page

Figure 3.7 illustrates an EAB cover page. The purpose of the cover page is distinct EAB identification. The cover page is the only EAB page with a unique page layout. Each EAB is distinctly identified by its $arch_acronym and $version_nbr. The variables[2] on the cover page are as follows:

$architecture_name. The name of the architecture that this drawing represents, such as Marketing Warehousing Systems Architecture.

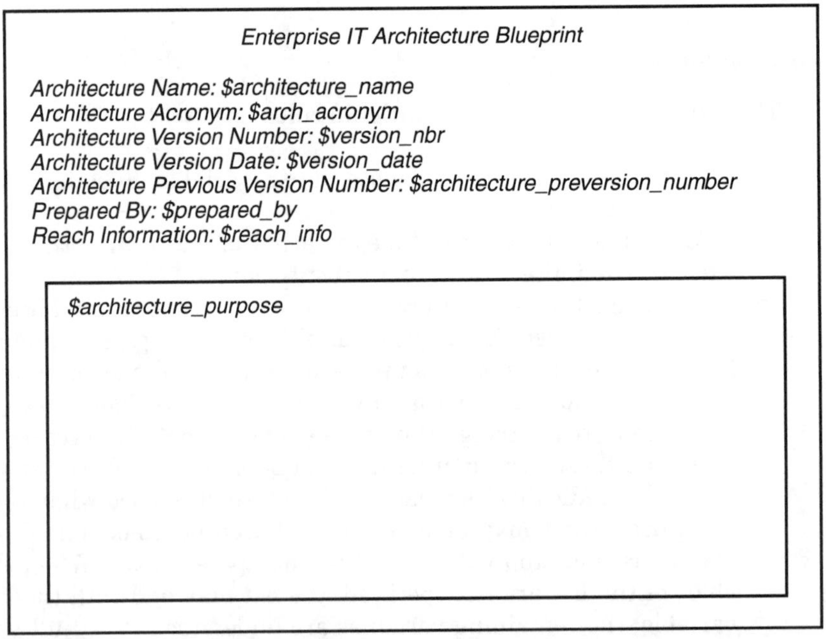

FIGURE 3.7   Cover page. The EAB cover page hosts basic identification information.

$arch_acronym. The acronym for the $architecture_name, such as MWS.

$version_nbr. The version number of this release of the blueprint. Version numbers have the format n.n., such as version 3.0.

$version_date. The publication date of the associated $version_nbr.

$architecture_preversion_number. The version number of the prior re-lease of the blueprint. Version numbers have the format n.n. such as ver-sion 2.0. This variable provides a backward chain to the previous release of the EAB. Assuming that an artifact library is maintained, you can trace the complete documentation history of the EAB. The initial release of an EAB is always version 1.0. An artifact library can prove invaluable as a resource for formal and informal training, doing research into best practices, as-sessing architecture quality, and evaluating the state of competence of your architecture community.

$status. The status of this drawing, such as draft, final, and so on.

$parent_architecture_name. The name of the parent EAB for this draw-ing when the drawing participates in a distributed EAB (see Notion 56).

$parent_arch_acronym. The acronym for the $parent_architecture_name (see Notion 56).

$prepared_by. The name of the person(s) or group responsible for the drawing.

$reach_info. The phone number, e-mail address, fax number, Web ad-dress, or other reach information of the $prepared_by.

$architecture_purpose. A short description of the purpose of the EAB. You would typically include statements as to the business problem solved, the domain of the EAB, the time horizon, and the core diagram sets pre-sented (Table 3.4).

Notion 6. Page Layout

Every page of an EAB (except the cover page) has a standard layout that uniquely distinguishes the page across all EABs (Figure 3.8).The following variables compose the standard page layout:

$architecture_name. As previously defined on cover page.

$arch_acronym. As previously defined on cover page.

$version_nbr. As previously defined on cover page.

$version_date. As previously defined on cover page.

$diagram_title. The title of the page.

$diagram_sub_title. The subtitle of the page.

$prepared_by. As previously defined on cover page.

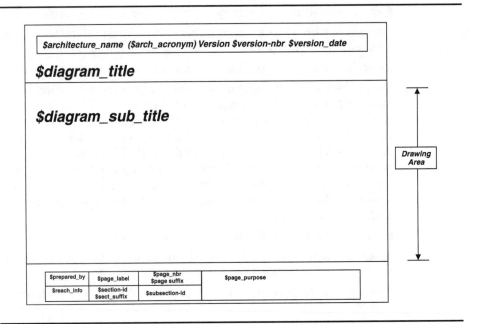

FIGURE 3.8 Standard page layout. Every page of an EAB (except the cover page) has a standard layout to uniquely identify the page.

$reach_info. As previously defined on the cover page.

$page_label. A unique name for the page. Labels must be unique within an EAB. Only pages that you want to refer to by name need a page label.

$section_id. The drawing section identifier.

$sect_suffix. A suffix to identify a specific core diagram set.

$subsection_id. The drawing subsection identifier.

$page_nbr. The page number. Page numbers are unique within a subsection of a section and have the format n.n.

$page_suffix. A page suffix (normally null). Page suffixes are used to distinguish *logical pages* (explained in Notion 7) or to identify *alternative pages* (explained in Notion 59).

$page_purpose. A short explanation of the objective (communication intent) of the page.

As illustrated in Figure 3.7, the actual drawing takes place within the boundaries of the *drawing area*.

The following rules refer to page identification:

- The concatenation of $arch_acronym\$version_nbr uniquely identifies a drawing.
- The concatenation of $arch_acronym\$version_nbr\$section_id$sect_suffix\ $subsection_id\$page_nbr uniquely identifies every page across all EAB drawings.
- $page_label is the symbolic equivalent to $section_id$sect_suffix\ $subsection_id\$page_nbr. The fully qualified identifier of a page is also $arch_acronym\version_nbr\$page_label.
- Within an EAB, if you wish to refer to another page, you must either:
  State the fully qualified page identifier.
  State the page label.
- Working backward from current page number, state the part of the fully qualified name of the target page that is different from the page you are on. The remainder of the fully qualified name is inherited from the page you are on.
- Refer to pages by their label; this is easiest and recommended.
- $page_address refers to any valid way to address a page.
- $page_header refers to $arch_acronym\$version_nbr.
- $page_trailer refers to either $page_label or $section_id$sect_suffix\ $subsection_id\$page_nbr, which are address equivalents.

Notion 7. Logical Pages

Sometimes, all the icons that you want to show on a page cannot fit and you do not want to use page and icon decomposition (see Notion 24). In such a case, you can define a logical page composed of up to x physical pages. Each physical page component has identical page identification, except that the page number is appended with a logical page suffix, in drawn parentheses, that denotes how the physical pages should be assembled to be read as one logical page. You can, therefore, create a single logical page composed of x physical pages.

The actual diagram should be drawn across the physical pages as though it were one continuous logical page. To read the logical page, you assemble it as directed by the page suffix. Figure 3.9 illustrates a logical page composed of two physical pages. The notation of (L), left, and (R), right, is used to denote how the physical component pages should be assembled to create this logical page. Since all the physical pages share the same $page_label, when you refer to a logical page by its page label, you are referring to all the physical page components that share the same label.

Each physical page component can still be functionally distinguished by the specification of $diagram_title, $sub_diagram_title, and $page_purpose. Each logical page should be positioned in the EAB based on its fully qualified page identifier of $arch_acronym\ $version_nbr\$section_id$sect_suffix\ $subsection_id\$page_nbr\$page_suffix. A user-determined rule should be established to further order the physical page components, relative to each other,

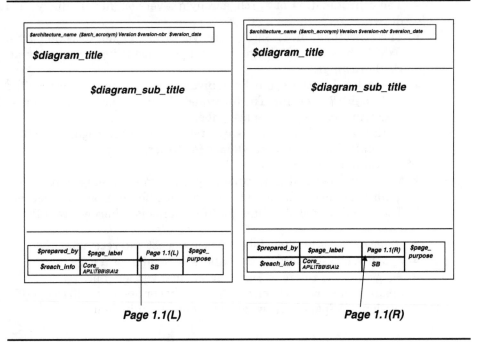

FIGURE 3.9   Logical pages. A logical page can be composed of any number of physical pages.

based on the code set of $page_suffix. This rule should be defined in the design definition part of the front matter (see Notions 10 and 11).

Notion 8. Sections

An EAB is divided into sections, which permits blueprint elements to be predictably located and modularizes the drawing. Standard section identifiers, $section_id, are:

Core. Contains system block, platform, interoperability, function block, and cut-out diagrams. Core diagrams illustrate the body of the blueprint; the support diagrams elaborate these diagrams.

Annotation. Contains annotation functional specifications.

Dictionary. Contains a dictionary parts list.

Detail. Contains detailed functional specifications.

Database. Contains database functional specifications.

Transaction. Contains transaction functional specifications.

Portability. Contains portability functional specifications.

Scalability. Contains scalability functional specifications.

Front. Contains the front matter.

Network. Contains network functional specifications.

User Group. Contains user-group functional specifications.

Appendix B provides page templates for all the EAB sections.

The focal point of an EAB is the core section; that is, all the support diagrams elaborate core diagrams. When you read an EAB, you read the front section and the core section. The core diagrams, as needed, point to support diagrams in the other sections to elaborate them. The other sections and their specifications, as a group, are referred to as *support diagrams*. Each support diagram is introduced and explained in the notions that follow, as an adjunct to the explanation of the core diagram(s) that it elaborates. Within an EAB, support diagrams are ordered in ascending page number sequence within alphabetical subsection identifiers within alphabetical section identifiers.

As routinely completed, an EAB would be structured as illustrated in Figure 3.2, with a front section, a core section, and, as required, the other sections. But note, it is possible to create an EAB that does not have a core section. This is an EAB that serves as a shared and common repository (e.g., dictionary for multiple EABs) and is referenced by multiple other EABs. Such an EAB is called a *reference EAB* and is explained in Notion 55.

A $section_id may be qualified by $sect_suffix (see Figure 3.8) to identify the specific core diagram set defined in the section.

For support diagrams, the default value for $sect_suffix is null. It is assumed that the support diagrams provide a common reference for all core diagram sets. If, however, you wish to strictly align support diagrams with core diagram sets, you may specify $sect_suffix to match the corresponding $sect_suffix for the core section. The $sect_suffix consists of an ordered set of variables and is defined as:

```
_$arch_type\$arch_form\$arch_time\/$arch_diagram/\$scenario_name\
$scenario_phase_nbr
```

where:

$arch_type identifies the drawings in this core section as being either an application (AP) or an infrastructure (IN) model. The default null value is AP.

$arch_form identifies the drawings in this section as being one of the following forms. The default null value is P:

- Logical (L)
- Physical (P)
- Functional (F)

- Mixed (M): Indicates that the drawing is a hybrid that crosses forms.
- Other (O): None of the above; the architecture team must explicitly specify what *other* means.

$arch_time identifies the drawing in this section from a time horizon perspective as follows. The default null value is AIB.

- As-Was-Built (AWB): A drawing of the architecture from a prior time period.
- As-Is-Built (AIB): The current architecture.
- To-Be-Built (TBB): A target architecture that is to be the result of an architecture initiative.
- Vision (V): Indicates a future vision drawing.
- Mixed (M): Indicates a drawing that crosses time period. May be used only by cut-out diagrams.
- Other (O): None of the above; the architecture team must specify what O means.

/$arch_diagram/ identifies the *core diagram set* that composes this core section. The diagram type codes are as follows:

- System block diagram: S
- Function block diagram: F
- Platform diagram: P
- Interoperability diagram: I
- Cut-out diagram: C

The /$arch_diagram/ is a nonspace-separated list of these codes, which specify the order of diagrams that compose this section. For example, if you were defining a core section composed of a core diagram set of a platform diagram and an interoperability diagram, /$arch_diagram/ would be PI. It is necessary to specify $arch_diagram because the actual diagrams drawn in a given core section may be different from the defining core set, and the reader needs to know what to expect. The null default value for /$arch_diagram/ is SPI.

$scenario_name. The name of a scenario. This is used primarily with TBB core diagram sets to distinguish multiple scenarios. It can also be used when multiple independent as-is-built diagrams need to be placed within one EAB.

$scenario_phase_nbr. A number that depicts the nth phase of a staged scenario implementation. This permits scenarios to be divided into time-phased implementation drawings.

If you leave the $sect_suffix set to null values, it is understood to mean _AP\P\AIB\SPI. Figure 3.9 provides an example of a specified $sect_suffix on a logical page. Table 3.5 provides some examples of how $sect_suffix could be specified. When the end variables of the list are not specified, the list may end with the last specified variable, and the remaining variables are understood to

TABLE 3.5   The $sect_suffix Specification

Architecture Type and Perspective	Architecture Time Horizon		
	As-Is-Built Today	To-Be-Built Planned	Vision (Strategic Intent)
Infrastructure Logical	IN\L\AIB\P	IN\L\TBB\I\A\2	IN\L\V\I
Infrastructure Physical	IN\P\AIB\PI	IN\P\TBB\PI\Scenario A	N/A
Infrastructure Functional	IN\F\AIB\F	IN\F\TBB\F\B\1	IN\F\V\F\Global\2
Application Logical	AP\L\AIB\S	AP\L\TBB\\Galaxy\3	AP\L\V\S
Application Physical	AP\P\AIB	AP\P\TBB\SI\Scen_a\ 3	N/A
Application Functional	AP\F\AIB\F	AP\F\TBB\F\21th Century\3	AP\F\V\F

be null-valued. When an interim variable is not specified, the \ must still be drawn to indicate a null value for the absent positional variable.

Notion 9. Subsections

Sections are divisible into subsections. Subsectioning makes it possible to easily identify and support core and supporting diagrams. The default value for all noncore subsections, $subsection_id on the bottom of each EAB page (Figure 3.8), is null value. The division of support sections into subsections is entirely up to the blueprinting team. Only subsections are prescribed in the core section. Each core subsection hosts a specific kind of drawing, as itemized in Table 3.6.

Notion 10. Design Definition

Based on what has been introduced in Notions 1 through 9, it should be clear that the first step in developing an EAB is to do some planning with regard to the structure of the blueprint. You need to ask and answer these basic questions:

What is the exact domain of the drawing?

Will your drawing be in-scope only?

Which EABs exist to define objects at the edge of the domain?

Do artifact EABs exist that can expedite your efforts?

TABLE 3.6 Core Subsections

Subsection	Drawing Content	Comments
SB	System Block Diagrams	A drawing of the architecture domain, with *systems* as the focal point.
PL	Platform Diagrams	A drawing of the architecture domain, with *platforms* as the focal point.
Interop	Interoperability Diagrams	A drawing of the architecture domain, with *interoperability* as the focal point.
FN	Function Block Diagrams	A drawing of the architecture domain, with *functions* as the focal point.
Cut-Out	Cut-and-paste mixture of the above diagrams	A drawing of the architecture domain that provides selected views from each of the other core diagrams and across the other types of core diagrams.

What will be your cover page variable definitions?

Which core diagram set(s) will be presented in the drawing?

What is the definition of the $sect_suffix that will define each core diagram set?

Which support diagrams do you need?

Do you use (and if so how) subsections within the support diagrams?

Are your support diagrams shared across all core diagram sets; are they mirror core diagram sets, or is there a mixture?

If you specify an $arch_form or $arch_time of *other*, exactly what does *other* mean?

If you specify an $arch_form or $arch_time of *mixed*, exactly why are you creating a hybrid drawing?

What will be the definition of $arch_diagram list?

Will you use (and if so how) logical pages? What are the notational rules for $page_suffix that instruct the reader on how to assemble the logical page from the physical component pages?

Resolving these questions as the first agenda item will eliminate project fog, eradicate uncertainty as to the objectives of the effort, and bound a well-defined sandbox for the EAB team effort. The answers to these questions are, in practice, much simpler than might initially appear. A typical EAB package doesn't need to avail itself of all the exotic choices and functionality that has been described to handle atypical and complex diagramming situations. The more typical EAB has one core diagram set (a $sect_suffix of _AP/P/AIB); logical pages are not used; $arch_diagrams is set to the default null value of SPI; and support diagrams neither use mirroring nor subsections.

In the front section is a specific page called *design definition* (see Notion 11). It serves as the repository for your design selections. A reader can, therefore, quickly ascertain the design choices that were made for this EAB. As we continue through the notions, additional design points will need to be specified in the *EAB design definition*.

FRONT SECTION

Notion 11. Front Matter

The front of an Enterprise Architecture Blueprint ($section_id = Front, $subsection_id=null) consists of the five different types of pages: Table of Contents, Overview, Design Definition, Change Control, and Legends (Figure 3.10). These pages provide the customary context setting and introductory material that is mandatory for any documentation.

Table of Contents

Figure 3.11 illustrates an EAB table of contents. The table of contents itemizes every page in the package. Tables of contents pages are numbered sequentially, starting with 1.0. For additional pages, 1 remains constant and the dot number is incremented.

Overview

Figure 3.12 illustrates an overview page. It contains the normal explanatory subjects that would accompany any technical documentation. The variables shown

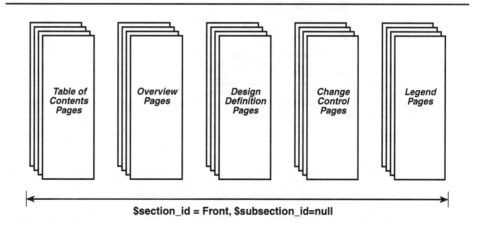

FIGURE 3.10 Front section. The front section is composed of five different types of pages.

$architecture_name ($arch_acronym) Version $version-nbr $version_date

TOC for $architecture_name

Section	Subsection	Page	Label	Diagram Title (& Diagram Subtitle)

$prepared_by	$page_label	Page 1.n	This page illustrates a TOC.
$reach_info	Front		

FIGURE 3.11   Table of contents. The table of contents provides an index into every EAB page in the blueprint.

$architecture_name ($arch_acronym) Version $version-nbr $version_date

Overview for $architecture_name

1. Introduction/Purpose: $introduction
2. Overview: $overview
3. Scope: $scope
4. Problem Statement: $problem
5. Objectives: $objectives
6. Audience: $audience
7. Assumptions: &assumptions
8. Team and Contact List : &teamlist
9. Highlights: $highlights
10. Executive Summary: $esummary
11. Change Summary: $change_summary
12. Related EABs: $related_eabs
13. Other: $your_choice

$prepared_by	$page_label	Page 2.n	This page illustrates an Overview page.
$reach_info	Front		

FIGURE 3.12   Overview. The overview provides the context setting information for the EAB.

on Figure 3.12 are self-explanatory and exemplary. You must choose what to include, the order of presentation, and the form of expression (text, graphics, tables, etc.) as appropriate for each subject. Overview pages are numbered sequentially starting with 2.0; 2 remains constant and the dot number is incremented for additional pages.

Design Definition

Figure 3.13 illustrates an EAB Design Definition. The Design Definition provides a repository to explain all the EAB design options that were selected for this drawing. For example, all of the questions asked in Notion 10, design definition, would be answered here. Design Definition pages are numbered sequentially starting with 3.0; 3 remains constant and the dot number is incremented for additional pages.

Change Control

Figure 3.14 illustrates an EAB Change Control page, which provides a summary itemization of the changes made to this version release of the EAB. For the initial release of an EAB, just a single line needs to be entered with Section, Subsection, Page, and Label set to the value of *All* and Change Action set to the value of *Initial Release*. Change Control pages are numbered sequentially starting with 4.0; 4 remains constant and the dot number is incremented for additional pages.

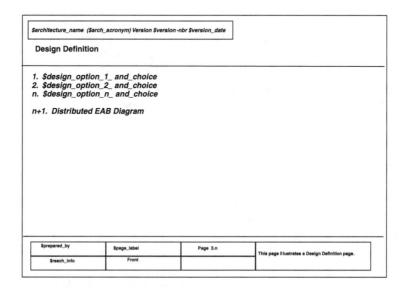

FIGURE 3.13   Design Definition. The Design Definition page documents the EAB optional design selections made by the architecture team.

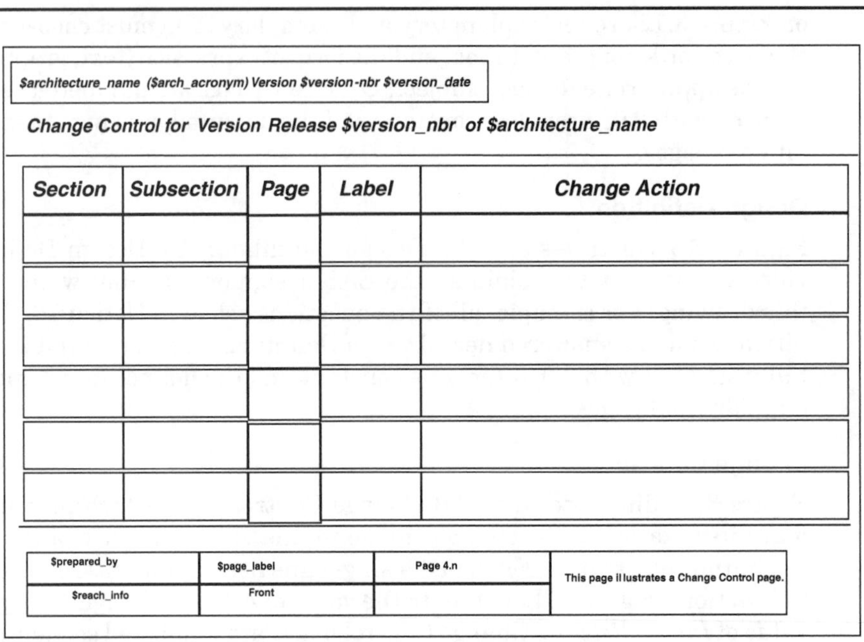

$architecture_name ($arch_acronym) Version $version-nbr $version_date			
Change Control for Version Release $version_nbr of $architecture_name			

Section	Subsection	Page	Label	Change Action

$prepared_by	$page_label	Page 4.n	This page illustrates a Change Control page.
$reach_info	Front		

FIGURE 3.14   Change Control. The Change Control pages itemize what has been changed in this release of the EAB.

Legends

Figure 3.15 illustrates an EAB Legends page. The Legends page illustrates and names all the icons used in this EAB. It is simply a reminder reference for readers. Legend definition is customary in all blueprinting methodologies. Legend pages are numbered sequentially starting with 5.0; 5 remains constant and the dot number is incremented for additional pages.

User Extensions

An architecture team may create any additional front matter pages they require. To create user extension pages, execute the following four steps:

1. Follow the standard EAB page layout.
2. Give the page a unique diagram title.
3. Number the pages sequentially starting with n.0 with n remaining constant, n being greater than 5, and n being sequentially unique within the Front Section.
4. Define the user extension pages in the Design Definition.

The complete front matter, therefore, consists of the five standard pages, plus any user-defined pages.

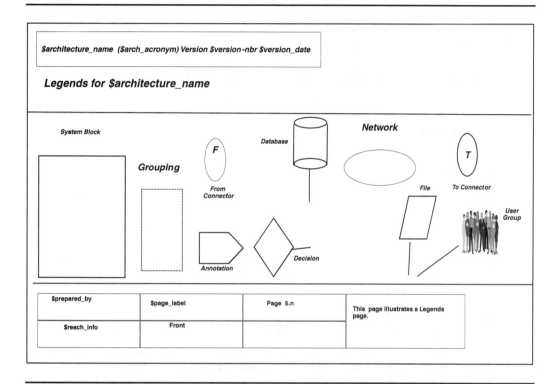

FIGURE 3.15   Legends. The Legends pages define all icons used in the blueprint.

Notion 12. Separator Pages

A separator page is placed in front of each section and subsection to partition the EAB; $intro_notes should be used to introduce the (sub)section (Figure 3.16). Separator pages are always numbered 0.0. The first separator page is inserted after the front section. For the core section, or any other section that is divided into subsections, a distinct separator page introduces the section and each subsection.

SYSTEM BLOCK DIAGRAMS

This section explains the icons and rules for drawing system block diagrams (section core: subsection SB). Support diagrams are introduced and explained at the point of instruction where the system block diagram relates to them.

Notion 13. System Block Icon

A system block diagram is a diagram that illustrates an architecture with *systems* as the central element of granularity and presentation. The key icon is a *system block icon* (a solid line rectangle, as shown in Figure 3.17) that represents a sys-

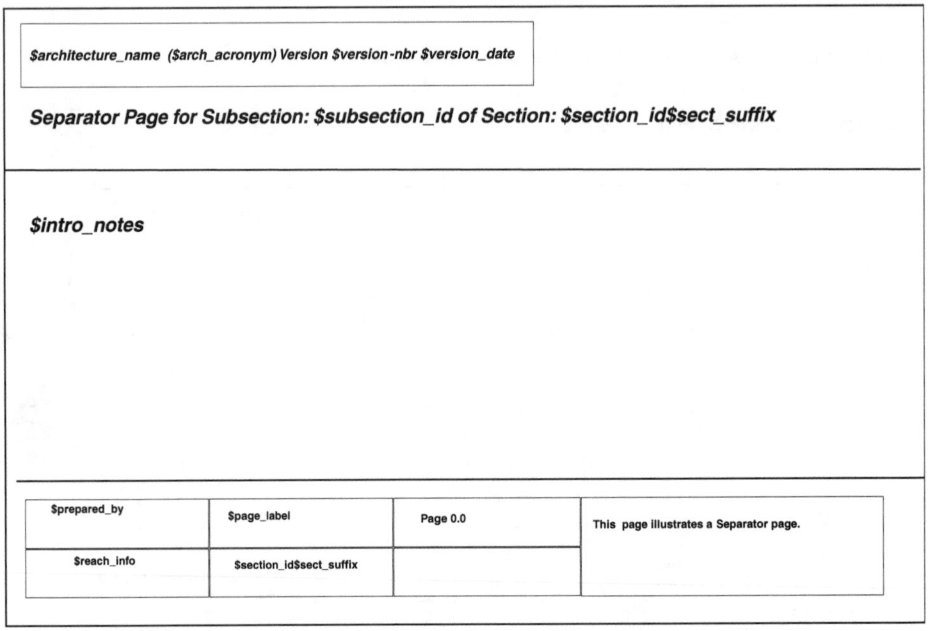

$architecture_name ($arch_acronym) Version $version-nbr $version_date			
Separator Page for Subsection: $subsection_id of Section: $section_id$sect_suffix			

$intro_notes

$prepared_by	$page_label	Page 0.0	This page illustrates a Separator page.
$reach_info	$section_id$sect_suffix		

FIGURE 3.16   Separator page. A separator page is used as a divider between sections and subsections.

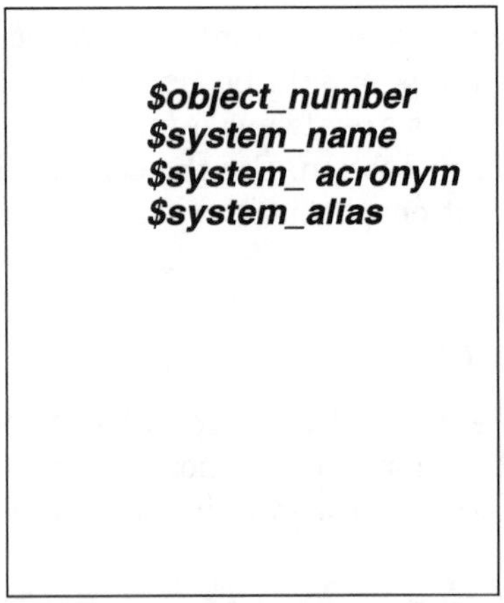

$object_number
$system_name
$system_ acronym
$system_alias

FIGURE 3.17   System block icon. A rectangle is used as the icon to represent a system.

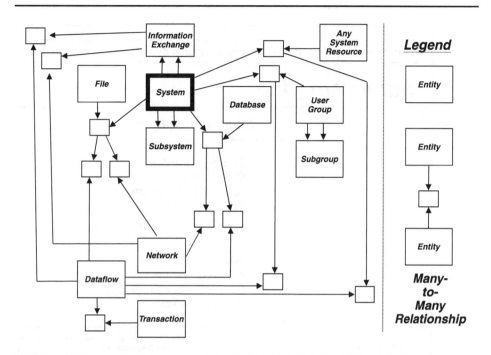

FIGURE 3.18   System block diagram entity relationship model. This high-level entity relationship model shows the relationships that system block diagrams model.

tem or subsystem. You draw a system block icon to represent each (sub)system in the domain of interest. The system block icon, coupled with other icons such as network, information-exchange, or database, illustrates the architectural structure (IT elements and their relationships) within the EAB domain at a system-level view. Figure 3.18 is a sketched entity relationship data model that shows all the relationships that need to be modeled by system block diagrams. System block diagrams are drawn in subsection SB within section Core$sect_suffix of the EAB.

The system block icon (a solid line rectangle) is used to identify a system and/or a subsystem. If you wish to distinguish a (sub)system as being out-of-scope, the rectangle is drawn with a broken line. Figure 3.19 illustrates both in-scope and out-of-scope system block icons.

The variables[3] on a system block icon are defined as follows:

$object_number. A unique number that identifies the (sub)system of the form Sn.n. Notion 24 explains the rules for system block object numbering.

$system_name. A unique name that identifies the (sub)system.

$system_acronym. A unique acronym that identifies the (sub)system.

$system_alias. An alias name for the (sub)system.

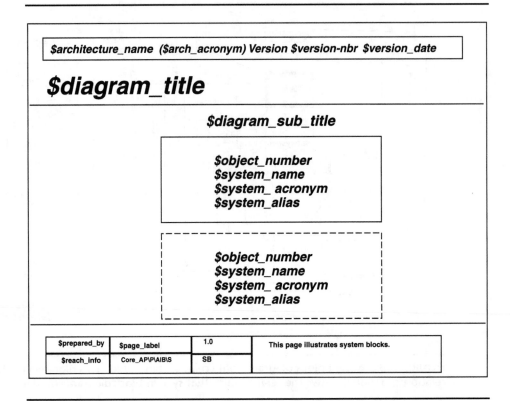

FIGURE 3.19 In-scope and out-of-scope system block icons. A solid rectangle is used to represent an in-scope (sub)system and a broken line rectangle is used to represent an out-of-scope (sub)system.

Figure 3.20 provides an example of completed system blocks.

Definitions

The construction of system block diagrams begs the question of what is a system and what are system derivative concepts. A system is a coherent and ordered collection of IT objects arranged in a purposeful manner to deliver function to the business. A subsystem, a recursive concept, is a partition of a system (or subsystem) that delivers a meaningful component of the functionality of the overall system. Subsystems eventually reach a point of decomposition at which further partitioning is no longer meaningful, when they are apportioned into function-centric applications that are dispersed across IT elements to deliver the business functionality. EAB system block diagrams, platform diagrams, and interoperability diagrams, collectively, illustrate these definitions.

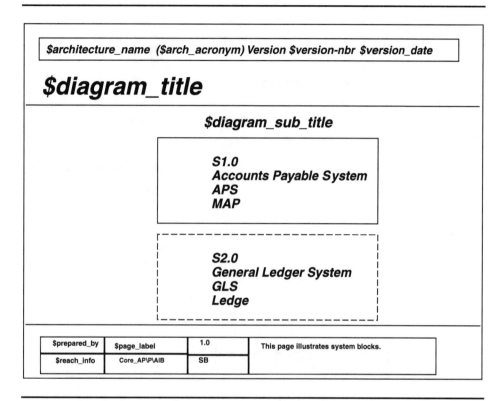

> $architecture_name ($arch_acronym) Version $version-nbr $version_date
>
> # $diagram_title
>
> ### $diagram_sub_title
>
> **S1.0**
> **Accounts Payable System**
> **APS**
> **MAP**
>
> **S2.0**
> **General Ledger System**
> **GLS**
> **Ledge**

$prepared_by	$page_label	1.0	This page illustrates system blocks.
$reach_info	Core_AP\P\AIB	SB	

FIGURE 3.20   System block icon example. This figure illustrates both in-scope and out-of-scope system blocks.

Notion 14. Source and Sink System Blocks

A *source* system block is used to represent a system that is unknown but provides information to other system blocks. The $system_name is set to *Source*. A *sink* system block is used to represent a system that is unknown but receives information from other system blocks; $system_name is set to *Sink*. See Figure 3.21. When an unknown system both receives and sends information, it can be referred to as a Source_Sink, and $system_name is set to Source_Sink. If multiple sources and/or sinks exist in a diagram, qualify $system_name to make it unique.

Notion 15. System Block Nesting

System blocks can be nested within system blocks. In this way, you may illustrate subsystem structures. Subsystem structures may also be illustrated through decomposition, which will be explained in Notion 24. In drawing

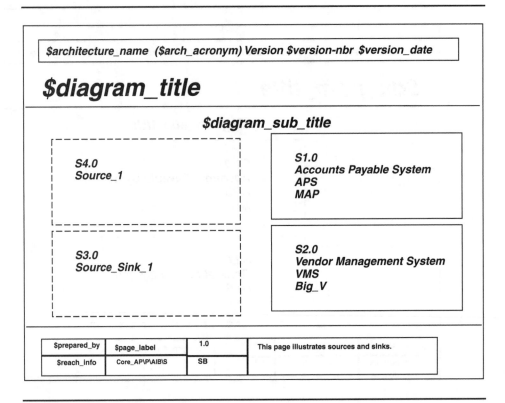

FIGURE 3.21   Source and sink system blocks. Source and sink system blocks are used to represent systems that engage in information exchange with domain systems but are unknown.

nested structures, the child system block icon is drawn as a rectangle or broken rectangle, consistent with its parent. Nested system blocks are numbered in a hierarchical relationship to their parent, which also will be explained in Notion 24. Figure 3.22 shows a system block diagram page containing nonnesting, two-level nesting, and three-level nesting.

Notion 16. File Icon

A file icon (a parallelogram with a connection line) is used to identify a file. The connection line links the file to the relevant system block(s) icon. A system block can have *n* files connected to it. The connection line may be an arrowhead to show information flow direction. A nonarrowheaded connection line indicates that information flow direction is unstated. The connection line may link to the system block at any point on its edge; the point of connection has no meaning. The variables related to the file icon (Figure 3.23) are as follows:

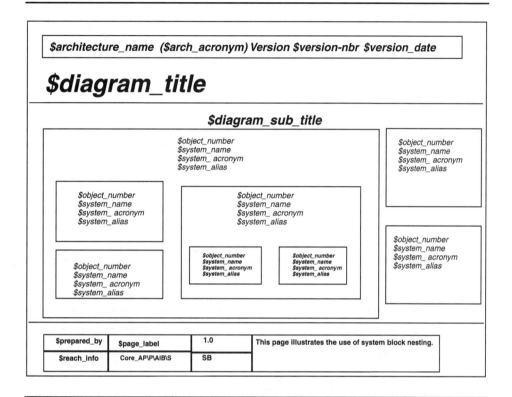

FIGURE 3.22 Nested system blocks. System blocks may be nested to illustrate subsystem relationships.

$file_name. The name of a file.

$data_flow. The name of the data item(s) exchanged.

As indicated by the notation, you may list multiple files and/or multiple data flows per file icon. Generally, you only draw persistent files such as those that are both durable and important to the architecture. Figure 3.24 shows an example of using the file icon.

The use of lists, for files as well as other EAB icons, provides for *economy of notation*, so that you can express yourself using the fewest number of icons. While this is highly desirable, be very careful not to create an incorrect or ambiguous representation. The nonuse of lists is called *normalized notation*.

If you use a file list within the file icon, and all the files use the same data flows with the same information flow direction, a single (non)arrowheaded connection line can be interpreted as applying to all (an economy of notation situation). If data flows and/or flow directions are different, individual connector

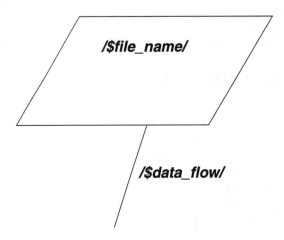

FIGURE 3.23   File icon. A parallelogram with a connection line is used to represent a file.

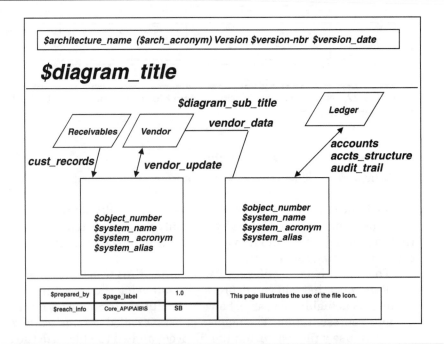

FIGURE 3.24   File icon example illustrating stated direction flows, unstated direction flows, concurrent usage of multiple file icons, and multiple data flows per connection.

lines must be drawn with the nth connection line, left to right applying to the nth file, top to bottom (normalized notation situation). Figure 3.25 illustrates these rules. In a normalized situation, an inconsistency between the number of items in the list and the number of connectors is a drawing error.

Notion 17. Database Icon

A database icon (a cylinder with a connection line) is used to identify a database. The connection line links the database to the relevant system block(s) icon. A system block can have n databases connected to it. The connection line may be arrowheaded to show information flow direction. A nonarrowheaded connection line indicates that information flow direction is unstated. The connection line may link to the system block at any point on its edge, and the point of connection has no meaning. The variables[4] related to the database icon (Figure 3.26) are as follows:

$database_name. The unique name of a database.

$data_flow. The name of the data item(s) exchanged.

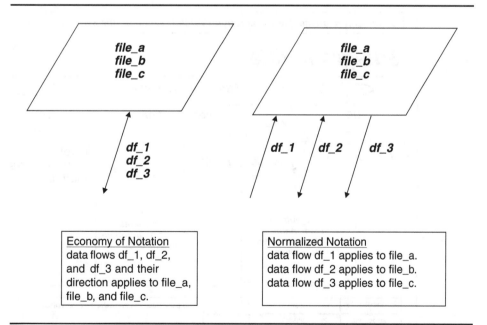

FIGURE 3.25 File icon and economy of notation. If all the files in the file list use the same data flows with the same flow direction, a single connection line can define the relationship for all the listed files.

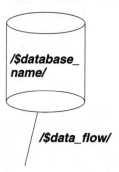

FIGURE 3.26 Database icon. A cylinder with a connection line is used to represent a database.

As indicated by the notation, you may list multiple databases and/or multiple data flows per database icon. Figure 3.27 shows an example of using the database icon.

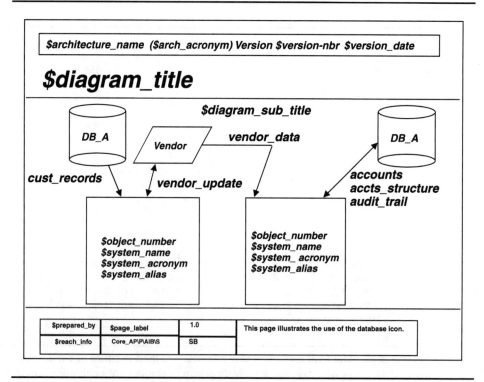

FIGURE 3.27 Database icon example illustrating the use of the database icon.

The same economy of notation and normalized notation rules that apply to the file icon apply to the database icon. If you use a database list within the database icon and all the databases use the same data flows with the same information flow direction, a single (non)arrowheaded connection line can be interpreted as applying to all (economy of notation situation). If data flows and/or flow directions are different, individual connector lines must be drawn with the nth connection line, left to right applying to the nth database, top to bottom (normalized notation situation).

Notion 18. Database Functional Specification

A Database Functional Specification is a support diagram that provides the detailed specifications for a database (Figure 3.28). It has a $section_id of Database, a $diagram_title of Database Functional Specification for $database_name, and a $page_label of the $database_name on the defining database. The $database_name on the database icon serves as a direct pointer to its own Database Functional Specification. Figure 3.29 illustrates this relationship between the database icon and the Database Functional Specification.

$architecture_name ($arch_acronym) Version $version-nbr $version_date

Database Functional Specification for $database_name

The Database Functional Specification may contain any of the following (or other) to define the database:
- **References to other documentation that defines the database**
- **The database documentation; i.e., database entity diagrams, multidimensional database diagrams, physical database designs, etc.**
- **Sizing information**
- **Integrity information**
- **Other**

$prepared_by	$database_name	1.0	This page illustrates a Database Functional Specification
$reach_info	Database		

FIGURE 3.28   Database Functional Specification. A Database Functional Specification is used to provide detailed information about each database in the EAB.

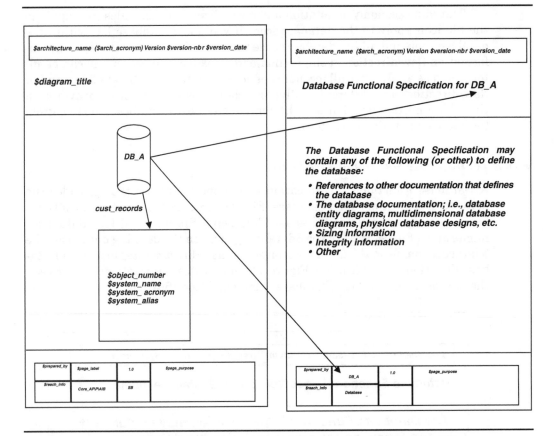

FIGURE 3.29   Database Icon-Database Functional Specification relationship. The $database_name in the database icon points to its own Database Functional Specification.

Each Database Functional Specification starts with an integer page number of the format n.0. If the Database Functional Specification is longer than one page, n remains the same, the dot number is incremented, but the page label remains constant. Database Functional Specifications should be sequenced by page number within $page_label. Though inclusion of Database Functional Specifications is architect-determined, databases are such an important architectural object that it is good practice to include one for every database.

Normally, the Database Functional Specification serves only as a reference pointer to the detailed, database documentation that is defined as part of the data architecture. As shown on Figure 3.30, an EAB defines infrastructure or application models but not the data architecture model. It is therefore the superior IT architecture practice to decouple data architecture and database documentation from an EAB; the Database Functional Specifications should point to that documentation. EAB, therefore, does not normally define database documentation because that is the responsibility of the data model cell in Figure 3.30.

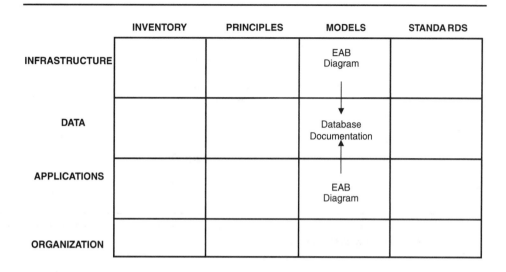

	INVENTORY	PRINCIPLES	MODELS	STANDA RDS
INFRASTRUCTURE			EAB Diagram	
DATA			Database Documentation	
APPLICATIONS			EAB Diagram	
ORGANIZATION				

FIGURE 3.30   Database documentation. A Database Functional Specification should point to the appropriate data and database models that are defined as part of the data architecture.

Notion 19. Any System Resource Icon

A system resource icon (a trapezoid with a connection line) is used to identify any system resource (peripheral, scanner, etc.) that the architect would like to include in the drawing. The connection line links the system resource to the relevant system block(s) icon. A system block can have n system resources connected to it. Whether a system resource can connect to more than one system block depends on the character of the system resource. The connection line may be arrowheaded to show information flow direction. A nonarrowheaded connection line indicates that information flow direction is unstated. The connection line may link to the system block at any point on its edge; the point of connection has no meaning. The variables related to any system resource icon (Figure 3.31) are as follows:

$resource_type. The type of resource, such as printer, scanner, and so on.

$resource_name. A unique name for the resource.

$data_flow. The name of the data items exchanged.

Figure 3.32 shows an example of using any system resource icon. Note that files and databases are special instances of a system resource. You can use the system resource icon, as well as the file or database icon, to represent them. Also realize that files, databases, and other system resources exist within the relevant system block(s). They are extracted from inside the system block(s) to be highlighted.

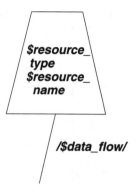

FIGURE 3.31 Any system resource icon. A trapezoid with a connection line is used to represent any system resource.

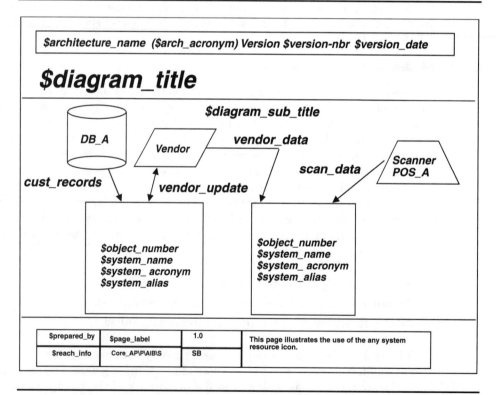

FIGURE 3.32 Any system resource icon example illustrating the use of the any system resource icon.

Notion 20. User Group and Information Appliance Icons

An icon depicting a cluster of people, together with a connection line, is used to represent the user groups of a (sub)system. The connection line links the user group to the relevant system block(s) icon. A system block can have n user groups connected to it. A user group can connect to more than one system block. The connection line may link to a system block at any point on its edge; the point of connection has no meaning. The connection line should be arrowheaded to show information flow direction. If the connection line is nonarrowheaded, it means that information flow is unstated.

If a list of user groups is specified and they share the same data flows and the same number of concurrent users, then only one connection line is drawn; it is understood to represent the data flows for the entire list of user groups. If you list the user groups and they have different data flows and/or number of concurrent users, then the nth connection line refers to the nth user group. Unless a single connection line is being used, if the number of user groups is different from the number of connection lines, your diagram is structurally in error.

The variables related to the user group icon (Figure 3.33A) are:

$user_group_name. The functional title of the user group.

$total_users. Total number of users.

$concurrent_users. Normal concurrent users.

$geo. The geographical location of the user group.

$data_flow. The name of the data items being exchanged.

Figure 3.34 shows an example of using the user group icon.

Only use icons with human forms to represent user groups; do not use PCs, laptops, workstations, or any type of intelligent, programmable, or dumb information technology appliance. Such symbols are used to represent information appliances (see following section).

An alternative to a single user group icon is to include various user group icons to represent different classes of users, for example, to uniquely represent internal users, customers, and suppliers. If the actual user community for a (sub)system is a mixture of these groups, you can either depict each user group individually with the associated definitions and connection to the (sub)system block or create a concatenated icon to depict the set of user groups.

Distinct user group icons, while adding some complexity, make the drawing easier to comprehend, because the reader can immediately distinguish the classes of users. Distinct user group icons should be defined in the Design Definition (Notion 11).

In addition to relating user groups to system block icons, a user group icon may also connect a user group to an any system resource icon or engage in an in-

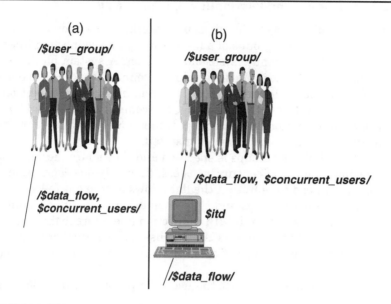

FIGURE 3.33 User group icon. A cluster of people with a connection line is used to represent a group of users.

formation exchange with another user group. Whether a user group icon can connect to an any system resource icon depends on the type of the system resource. When two user group icons engage in an information exchange (see Notion 23), you are using the information exchange icon to represent a noninformation technology-based exchange of information (i.e., phone call, postal mail, overnight mail, etc.). In such a case, it is good practice to use an annotation (see Notion 22) to explain the process or logic of the information exchange.

Information Appliance Icon

To highlight the user interface device (information appliance) used to interface with the system and make it explicit in the drawing, the connection between the user group icon and the system block icon can be broken by an information appliance icon (Figure 3.33b). The information appliance icon represents the information technology device ($itd) that the user group uses to execute presentation services. Use an icon that graphically portrays the type of device. Set the $itd (Figure 3.33b) equal to a generic type of device (desktop PC) or a specific instance of a device (COMPAQ Presario PC). If the data flows emanating from the information appliance are the same as those associated with the user groups, the data flows need not be restated.

The connection line from the information appliance icon to the system block icon should be arrowheaded to illustrate data flow direction and be consistent

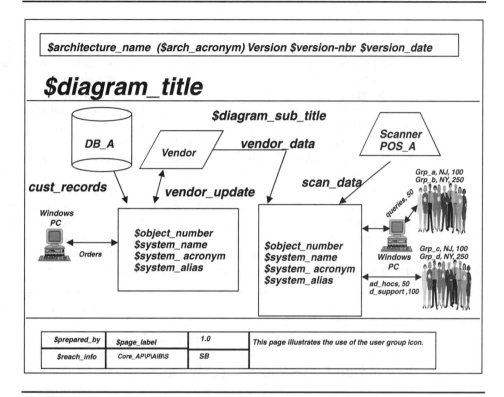

FIGURE 3.34   User group icon example illustrating the use of the user group icon.

with the data flow direction from the user group to the information technology appliance. An information technology appliance may be decorated with databases, files, and any system resources. Data flows to multiple system block icons may emanate from an information appliance icon, and a user group may connect to multiple information appliance icons.

By combining the user group icon with the information appliance icon, the architect has five representation alternatives:

1. Show neither information appliances nor user groups (not recommended).
2. Show only users group and connect them directly to the system block icon.
3. Show only information appliances and connect them directly to the system block icon (Figure 3.34).
4. Show both user groups with their associated information appliances (Figure 3.34).
5. Any combination of the above.

The optimum representation is situation determined by the architect.

Notion 21. *User Group Functional Specification*

A User Group Functional Specification ($section_id = User Group) should be drawn to show the network relationship of all the user groups (Figure 3.35). Every user group referred to in the core section should be represented. If you are using multiple user group icons, the top (root) level of the drawing should have at least one entry for each distinct type of user group icon. If subuser groups are mixtures of these classes of user groups, concatenate the icons in the lower-level depiction.

The User Group Functional Specification starts with page number 1.0, and is dot-incremented as required for additional pages. If necessary, use the connection icons (see Notion 26) to link user groups across pages. The User Group Functional Specification should be drawn top down and read bottom up, meaning that any specific user group is a subset of its vertical parents. To improve readability, you may choose to use arrowheaded connection lines between user groups to show the vertical relationships or label the connection lines with the selection criteria that defines the criteria used to place a subset of the parent user group into the child user group. In this way, it is clear to the EAB reader who the users are and what their interuser group relationships are.

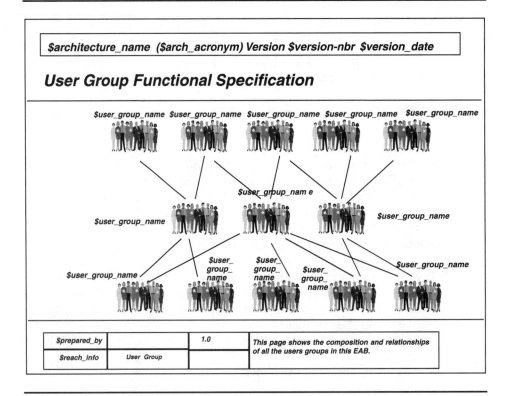

FIGURE 3.35 User Group Functional Specification.

Notion 22. Annotation Icon

An annotation icon (a pentagon with an optional arrowheaded pointer) is used to highlight any object for which the architect would like to provide commentary or extended explanation (Figure 3.36). The annotation icon points to the object that is the subject of the commentary. Use the arrowhead only when the pentagon point is too gross to clearly identify the subject of the annotation, or you want to annotate multiple objects with a singe commentary.

An object may be annotated multiple times, and an annotation may comment on multiple objects. You may annotate any EAB object or an entire page by pointing the annotation icon to the edge of the page. The annotation may contain an annotation note or a $page_label. In the former case, the entire annotation takes place within the annotation icon. In the later case, the $page_label points to an Annotation Functional Specification where the actual annotation takes place. The annotation may be placed anywhere in the drawing area. A typical use of an annotation would be to note the service level agreements that are necessary to support each user group.

The variables related to the annotation icon (Figure 3.36) are as follows:

$story_nbr. The story sequence number of this annotation in the format n.n.

$annotation. Short notes or comments that will fit entirely within the annotation icon. This is called an annotation note and must be more than one word.

$annotation_label. The $page_label of an Annotation Functional Specification. The resulting annotation may be of any length.

Figure 3.37 shows an example of using the alternative formats of an annotation icon.

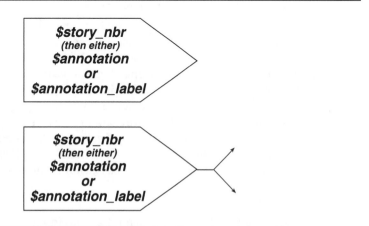

FIGURE 3.36 Annotation icon. A pentagon with an optional arrowheaded pointer is used to represent an annotation icon.

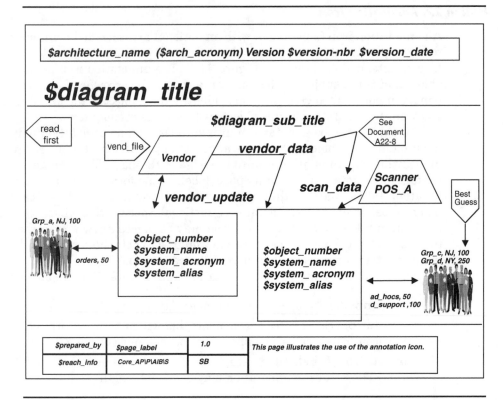

FIGURE 3.37 Annotation icon example illustrating the use of the annotation icon.

Annotation Functional Specification

An Annotation Functional Specification provides the page(s) for documenting the commentary about the selected object. It has a $section_id of Annotation and a $page_label of the $annotation_label on the pointing annotation icon. Each Annotation Functional Specification starts with an integer page number of the format n.0. If the specification is longer than one page, n remains the same, the dot number is incremented, but the $page_label remains the same. Annotation Functional Specifications are ordered within the Annotation Section by page number. Figure 3.38 illustrates this relationship between the annotation icon and the Annotation Functional Specification. The /$object_name/ on the Annotation Functional Specification is the name of the annotated object.

Object Naming

Although many EAB objects do not have an identifier (name or number), it may be desirable to refer to them explicitly elsewhere within the EAB. This is called *object naming*. An annotation icon is used to assign an identifier to any icon or

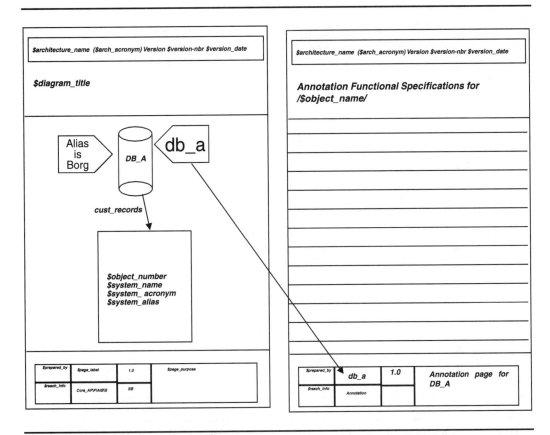

FIGURE 3.38 Annotation icon-Annotation Functional Specification Relationship. The $annotation_label in the annotation icon points to an Annotation Functional Specification.

part of an icon to which you would like to be able to explicitly refer. The tip of the annotation icon (or arrow tip from the pentagon) points to the identified object. Unless you want to assign a synonym, it is not necessary to assign an additional identifier to named objects. In the annotation note, simply write, "Name is /$xxx/" or "Synonym is /$xxx/" or "Alias is /$xxx/" where $xxx is the name you want to assign to the object or object part. Figure 3.38 illustrates object naming.

Ordered Annotations or Stories

It is often necessary to have annotations read in a specific order because the ordered annotations tell a sequential story (Figure 3.39). This may be accomplished in two ways, using annotation notes or annotation labels.

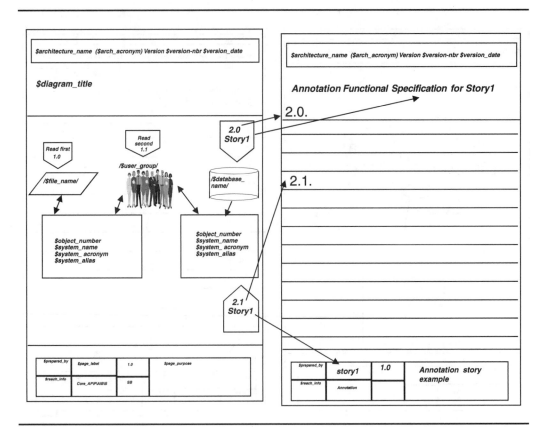

FIGURE 3.39 Annotation stories. This example illustrates the use of the annotation icon to present stories.

Annotation Notes A story is a set of annotation notes in which the first entry within a note is a $story_nbr in the format integer_number.n; all members of the same story have the same integer number, and the notes are read in order based on their .n number. The first note in the story has an .n number of .0. Multiple stories may be told concurrently on a page or across pages by varying the integer number. Story annotation notes may span pages.

Annotation Labels A story is a set of annotation labels in which the $annotation_label is preceded by a number, $story_nbr, in the format integer_number.n, where all members of the story share the same integer number and the story is read in order based on the .n number. Multiple stories may be told on a page by varying the integer number. The first label to be read has a .0 number. Story annotation labels may span multiple pages. The label that follows the story number points to an Annotation Functional Specification, where the .n number is a paragraph name on the Annotation Functional Specification.

Each story in an EAB must have a unique story number. Therefore, on the Annotation Functional Specification, instead of identifying the target $object_name, state the name of the story that is the annotation_label. Both forms of stories, notes and labels, may be intermixed for a given story. A story is often used to explain a sequence of data flows or explain where system controls/metrics need to be inserted.

General Architecture Elaboration

Blueprints are diagram-centric. As stated previously, in adopting EAB, you want the reader to read the diagrams; and the diagrams should point, as required, to functional specifications for elaboration. The broadest use of the annotation icon is, therefore, to clarify and elaborate the meaning of a drawing by supplementing the schematic with explanatory text. This can be accomplished concurrently at both the individual icon and page levels.

Notion 23. Information Exchange

A dashed line with a directional arrow illustrates an information exchange, within or between system blocks. When the information exchange connects an object to itself, it is highlighting a data movement within the system block. The points of contact on each system block have no meaning. There is no limit on the number of information exchanges a system block may participate in.

The variables related to the information-exchange icon (Figure 3.40) are as follows:

$information exchange. Defines the information flowing between system blocks. An information exchange is defined by an ordered set of the form /$data_flow, $frequency, $onoffline, $middleware_def/.

$data_flow. The name of the data items exchanged.

$frequency. The frequency of the exchange, such as real time, daily, on-demand, and so on.

$onoffline. Indicates whether the exchange is done online or batch.

$middleware_def. The name of the middleware that governs the exchange.

$information_exchange

– – – – – – – – – – – – – – – –

FIGURE 3.40 Information exchange icon. A dashed line is used to represent an information exchange icon.

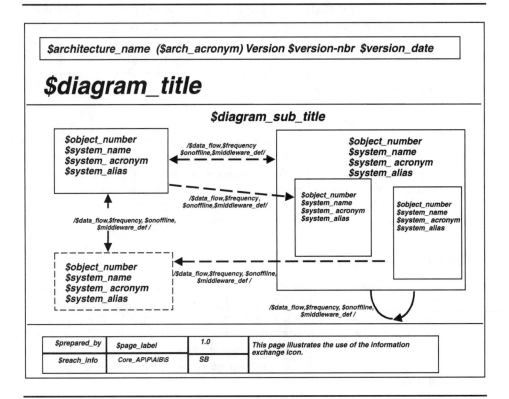

FIGURE 3.41   Information exchange icon example illustrating the use of the information exchange icon.

Figure 3.41 illustrates the use of the information exchange icon. Notice that with nested system blocks, the point of connection is very important to the meaning. A nested system block may not engage in an information flow with a parent system block. In other words, information exchanges may occur only across diagrams at the same balanced level (see Notion 25).

Notion 24. Hierarchical Decomposition of System Blocks and Pages

Page Decomposition and Numbering

As presented so far, a system block diagram is literally restricted to a page. System block diagrams are hierarchically decomposable across pages into (sub)system block diagrams, meaning the system blocks are decomposed into subsystem blocks (the same system block icon is used). When doing decomposition, both the page numbers and subsystem block object number have to be managed to maintain hierarchical numeric relationships between pages and (sub)system blocks, respectively. You continue decomposing (sub)system blocks until termination conditions are realized:

1. It no longer makes sense to decompose the (sub)system into further subsystems. In this case, the next decomposition would be into the applications and actual information technology devices embodied within the subsystem block. (This will be explained later when we discuss applications and (configured) platforms.)
2. The (sub)system block is the only (sub)system block on a page. We call this an *atomic (sub)system block*[5] since this diagram provides an individual view of one, and only one, (sub)system block.

The hierarchical level 0 system diagrams are called the base, root, or anchor diagrams. They are integer-page numbered starting with 1.0 within each core diagram set. All anchor pages must have a core diagram set unique integer page number. Page decomposition proceeds using hierarchical numbering conventions. Hierarchically decomposed diagrams, levels 1-n, are sequentially page numbered within the parent page as (parent diagram page number).n. From any core diagram page number, you can deduce the parent diagram page number.

Decomposition is only hierarchical. You cannot have a decomposed page that has multiple parents. You connect horizontally across pages using connectors (Notion 26). Multiple anchor pages can exist within a core diagram set. You read system block diagrams in hierarchical sequential order; that is, top to bottom, left to right. Figure 3.42 illustrates the concepts related to page decomposition.

System Block Decomposition and Numbering

System blocks on the anchor page(s) are numbered uniquely across the entire EAB in the format Sn.o, where n is an EAB unique integer number for all anchor system blocks across all core diagrams sets with the same architectural perspective (i.e., logical, physical, or functional). Nested system blocks are numbered in the format parent-object-number.n. Only the most decomposed nested system blocks can be further decomposed. All anchor (sub)system blocks are therefore uniquely identified across the EAB. When you engage in (sub)system block nesting or decomposition, you are partitioning the (sub)system into further refined subsystems.

(Sub)system blocks on nonanchor pages are numbered in the format parent-object-number.n across hierarchically decomposed pages. From any (sub)system block, you can deduce its parent. There is no necessary relationship between hierarchical page numbers and hierarchical (sub)system block numbers because of (sub)system block nesting. Figure 3.43 illustrates the concepts of hierarchical (sub)system block numbering. Decomposed (sub)system blocks must be placed on a decomposed page from the parent page that its par-

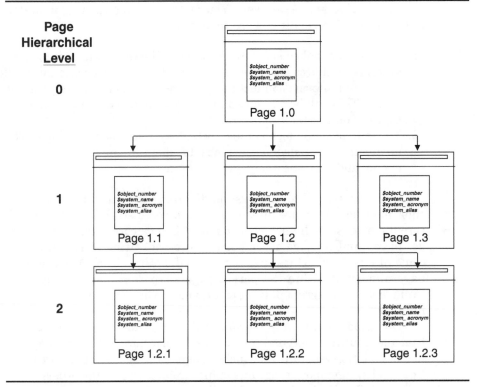

FIGURE 3.42 Hierarchical page decomposition numbering. This example illustrates how page decomposition is managed.

ent (sub)system block is on. A (sub)system block may do a null decomposition into itself.

Summary

Think about page and (sub)system block decomposition and numbering as follows:

1. The (sub)system blocks exist on a page.
2. The page is decomposed into n hierarchical child pages with page numbers assigned in the format parent_page-number.n.
3. The (sub)system blocks on the parent page are decomposed across the child pages. The children subsystem blocks may be dispersed or concentrated across the child pages and are numbered in the format parent_object_number.n.
4. This process continues recursively until termination conditions are realized.

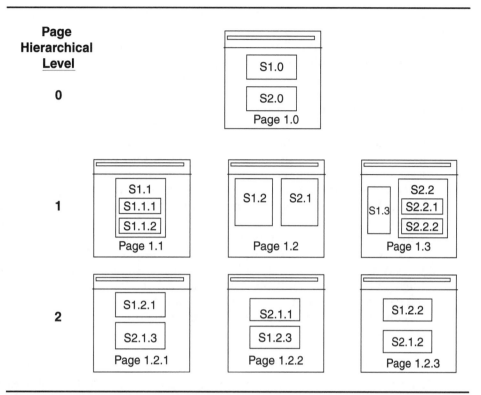

FIGURE 3.43   Hierarchical (sub)system block decomposition numbering. This example illustrates how (sub)system block decomposition is managed.

Notion 25. Decorating

Decorating means adding files, databases, or any system resources, and so on to a (sub)system block skeletal hierarchical structure, but only the root level and the lowest level of the hierarchical structure should be decorated. Interim decomposed levels are for structural information only and should not be decorated.

Horizontal connecting across pages (see Notion 26) should be done only across the root level or across the lowest vertical leaf of each tree branch, because a meaningful horizontal-level view across decomposed pages implies that all the system blocks are at same level of decomposition. When this is true, you have a balanced drawing. Even if you do not implement nesting and decompose all (sub)system blocks the same number of levels, it does not automatically mean that the same level of decomposition represents the same level of decomposed abstraction. Assuring balancing is extremely difficult at interim levels, so the simplest rule is to limit decorating to the root and lowest decomposed levels which, by definition, are balanced. If you want to decorate the decomposition trees at each interim level, it is your responsibility to assure that each level is balanced.

These rules imply how to approach drawing system block diagrams. Develop the hierarchical structure first. After iterating and stabilizing the hierarchical structure, decorate the root and lowest level leafs. The lowest levels leafs should be atomic (sub)system blocks. The reason for this will become clear later when we discuss cut-out diagrams in Notion 51.

A specific numbered (sub)system block, platform, or configured platform cannot appear more than once across a core diagram set. For decorating, the general rule is that a specific file, database, or user group icon should be specified only once per balanced level of decomposition across the PL, SB, and Interop subsection diagrams. They should be drawn next to the (sub)system block, platform, or configured platform icon that most "owns" it. Connectors are then used to connect the file, database, or user group (and information appliance) to other (sub)system block, platform, or configured platform icons.

If you follow this rule and you go to the database, file or user group icon, you get an object-centric view of the drawing. It is not wrong to draw the same file or database icon multiple times at a balanced level but, if you do, you cannot go to an instance of it and see all the connections.[6] Whether the any system resource icon should be drawn once or multiple times per balanced decomposition level depends on the nature of the resource.

Anomalous Situation

An anomalous situation can occur when a root system block is not decomposed and other system blocks are. The nondecomposed system block would, therefore, concurrently participate in two different leveled views: the root level and the lowest leaf view. Information exchanges for both views would originate or terminate in the same system block. In this case, groupings (see Notion 29) or footnotes (see Notion 32) should be used to associate the information exchanges with the appropriate view.

Notion 26. Horizontal Connectors

Connector icons serve as interpage connectors. They define a logical continuation of connection lines across pages. The connection is drawn consistent with the relationship of the involved objects. The connector icons may link icons across pages within a specific diagram perspective (logical, physical, or functional).[7] The connector icons have no directional meaning and should be interpreted simply as communicating where to reconnect the cross-page broken connection lines.

As shown in Figure 3.44, $connection_name is a unique identifier within architectural perspective (logical, physical, or functional) within an EAB. Connections contain the idea that you connect "from" a page (the F connector) "to" another page (the T connector), and therefore require a pair of connectors. Both connectors, the F and the T, must share the same $connector_name.

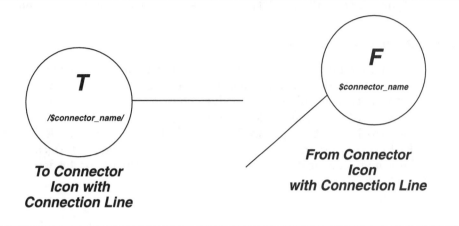

FIGURE 3.44   Connector icons. A circle with a T or an F is used to represent connector icons.

Connector Rules

1. Multiple *F* objects can connect to the same *to* object using the same connector identifier, as long as all the *F* objects are the same type of object.
2. The T connector has a list option. A T connector can therefore be the receiver for multiple F connectors, as long as they are all the same type of object.
3. It is good practice to annotate the F connector with a note annotation that concisely indicates what is being connected to, and to annotate the T connector with a note annotation that concisely indicates what is being connected from.
4. Connections must be made only at the same hierarchical level, thereby providing complete horizontal level views across the root level or across the lowest level of decomposition.
5. If on the connect from icon, you provide a list of connect to connectors, all the to objects should be the same type of object.
6. When database or file icons are involved in a connection situation, they are using the list option, and each database or file has distinct data flows, it is necessary to have a connection line for each file or database. In this case, the T connector should always be placed next to the database or file. The F connector should connect to the system block with as many connection lines as necessary to match the number of files or databases so that the individual data flows may be specified.
7. Connectors link broken data flow lines. The associated definitions of connection variables for the broken database, file, any system resource, and so on should be placed on whichever sides makes sense.
8. The directional arrow of the connection should appear on the side of the connection on which it would have appeared had a connector not been required.

Figures 3.45, 3.46, and 3.47 illustrate the use of the connector icons.

Notion 27. Decision Rule Icon

The decision rule icon, a diamond with connection lines, is used to broker conditional data flows (Figure 3.48). The connection lines are drawn consistent with the relationship of the involved objects. The three exit points are labeled A, B, and C; $decsion_rule is defined by standard "If then else logic," which uses the logical tools of "AND, x, OR, NOT, and ()." Stating Exit A, Exit B, or Exit C is used to indicate where to exit from the diamond. Decision icons may be sequentially nested. Figure 3.49 illustrates the use of the decision rule icon.

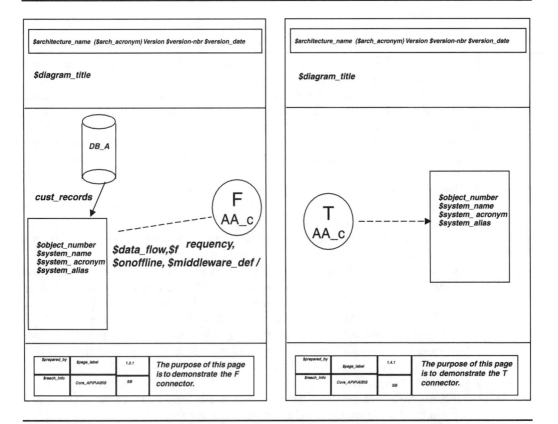

FIGURE 3.45   Connector example 1 illustrates a simple information exchange connection across page.

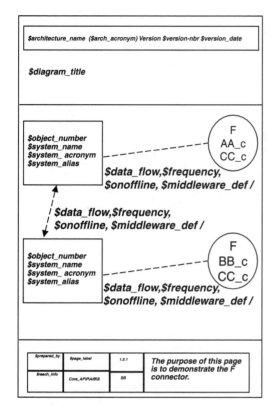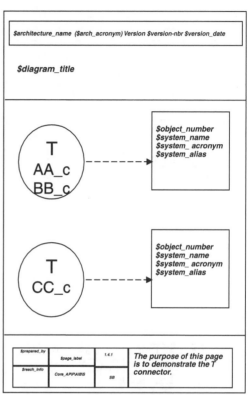

FIGURE 3.46 Connector example 2 illustrates connecting using the list options in both the F and the T connectors.

Notion 28. Dictionary Bill of Materials: Parts List

The dictionary provides bill of materials support for an EAB (Figure 3.50). It contains definition entries for all objects within the core section of the EAB. The selection of EAB parts should be a subset of the Standards column of the architecture framework (Figure 2.3). The architect must decide whether to create subdictionaries and to arrange entries alphabetically or alphabetically within object type. The dictionary design decisions should be recorded in the Front Matter on the Design Definition page (Notion 11). Dictionary pages are numbered sequentially within subsection, starting with number 1.0.

Notion 29. Object Grouping

Any selection of EAB objects may be grouped by drawing a perimeter line (in any shape) around them using dotted lines. The perimeter line need not be

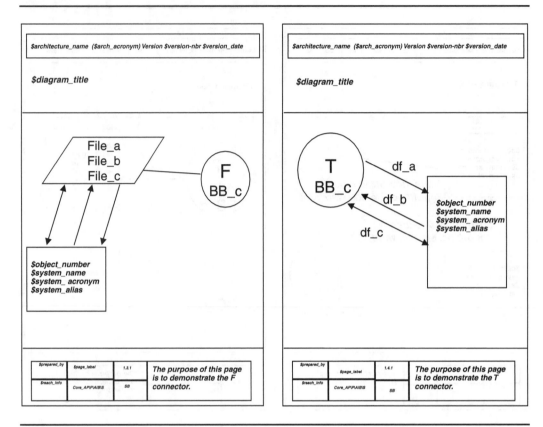

FIGURE 3.47 Connector example 3 illustrates connecting when the list option is used with the file icon.

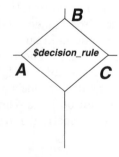

FIGURE 3.48 Decision rule icon. A diamond with connection lines is used to represent the decision rule icon.

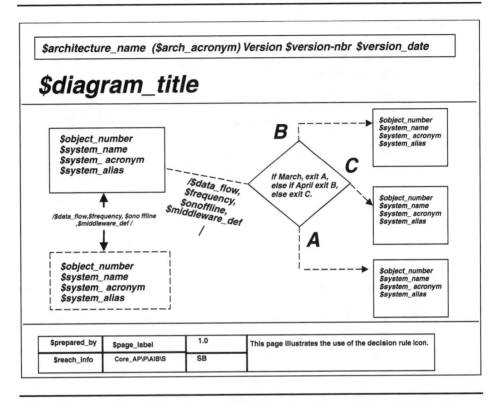

FIGURE 3.49 Decision rule icon example illustrating the use of the decision rule icon.

closed. The grouping only has informational meaning; it has no structural meaning, and connections should not be made to the grouping perimeter. Groupings may be annotated, may overlay each other, or be nested. Figure 3.51 illustrates a grouping.

Notion 30. Titled Lists

A titled list is a title (a set of words) sandwiched by dashes with a list of 0 – n entries under it. When the titled list has no list entries, it is called a null-titled list. Titled lists may be used anywhere within an EAB by dash-sandwiching a list of words (the title), and as required, by providing a list of entries under it. Typical uses of null-titled lists are to title objects arranged on a page in columns or to assign a name, a title, to an object grouping. The structure of a title list is $title_list_name in a dash-sandwiched title name, and $list_entry_n is a list entry.

Object Type	Object	Definition	Comments

$architecture_name ($arch_acronym) Version $version-nbr $version_date

Dictionary Bill of Materials

$prepared_by		1.0	Dictionary example page.
$reach_info	Dictionary		

FIGURE 3.50   Dictionary bill of materials.

$title_list_name
  1. $list_entry_1
  2. $list_entry_2
  3. $list_entry_n

Figure 3.52 illustrates the use of a null-titled list.

Titled Lists and Database Icons or File Icons

A titled list may be placed within a database icon or a file icon. This enables an alternative way to use annotations to highlight critical attributes of the database or file. To use titled lists within database or file icons, do the following:

1. Define the name of the titled list and the attribute represented by each line entry on the Design Definition page of the Front Matter (Notion 11). Each line entry is numbered.
2. Place the completed titled list within the database or file icon.

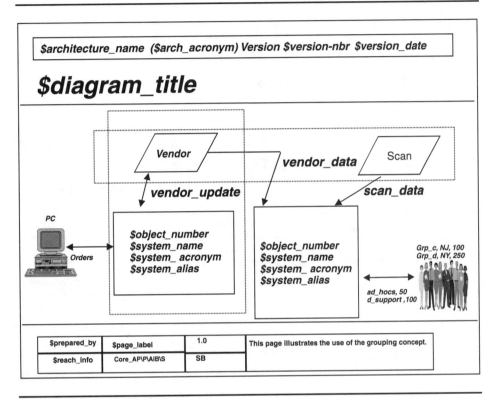

FIGURE 3.51   Grouping example illustrates performing a grouping of EAB icons.

3. When populating a list, each entry is identified with its entry number. Any given list on a drawing may present only a subset of the entire list entries.

Each titled list name must be unique within the EAB. There can be multiple different titled lists assigned to database icons or file icons. The titled list name given inside the icon identifies the meaning of the entries within a specific icon. Multiple titled lists can be stacked within an icon. If a titled list is used with a database or file icon, and the file or database list option is being used, it indicates that the titled list attributes apply to all listed databases or files.

Figure 3.53 illustrates the use of a titled list within both the database and file icons. The respective design definitions (Notion 11) in the Front Matter would have been as follows:

- Database Titled List Definition
  $title_list_name: –DB Attributes–

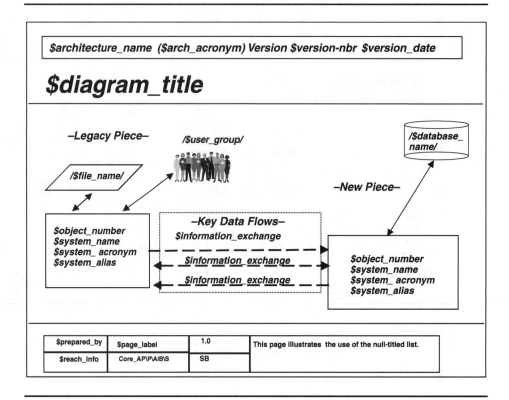

FIGURE 3.52   Null-titled list example illustrates the use of the null-titled list construct.

$list_entry_1: 1. database manager name

$list_entry_2: 2. size of database in gigabytes.

- File Titled List Definition
  $title_list_name: –File Attributes–

  $list_entry_1: 1. type of file system

  $list_entry_2: 2. size of file in megabytes.

Titled Lists and (Sub)System Block Icons

There are three standing titled lists associated with (sub)system block icons: –Function List–, a –Product List–, and a –Function_Product List–. These lists do not have to be defined on the Design Definition page in the Front Matter. The function list is a list of 1 – n business functions performed by this (sub)system. The functions listed on a –Function List– should correlate with a business function model (Figure 2.6) or with a corresponding function blueprint.

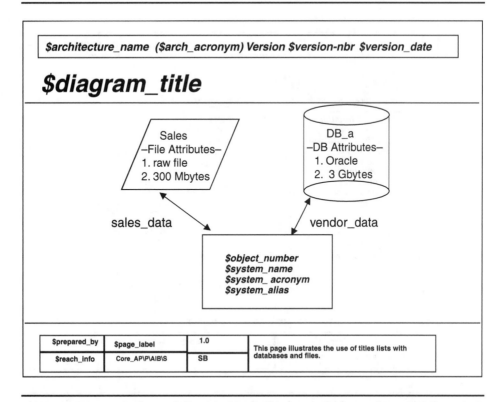

$architecture_name ($arch_acronym) Version $version-nbr $version_date

$diagram_title

Sales
—File Attributes—
1. raw file
2. 300 Mbytes

DB_a
—DB Attributes—
1. Oracle
2. 3 Gbytes

sales_data

vendor_data

$object_number
$system_name
$system_ acronym
$system_alias

| $prepared_by | $page_label | 1.0 | This page illustrates the use of titles lists with databases and files. |
| $reach_info | Core_AP\P\AIB\S | SB | |

FIGURE 3.53 Database- and file-titled lists. This example shows the use of the titled list with the database and file icon.

Functions on a –Function List– may or may not be decomposed across decomposed (sub)system blocks. If you choose to decompose them, you must do the following:

1. Give all functions listed on root system blocks integer identifier numbers.
2. To decompose the functions on the decomposed (sub)system blocks, dot number each subfunction with the function number of its parent.
3. Dot number the functions listed on the application layers (to be discussed).
4. Declare in the Design Definition (Notion 11) that you are doing a structured decomposition of functions across decomposed (sub)system blocks.

The default is not to do a structured function decomposition.

The –Product List– is a list of 1–n business products supported by this (sub)system. Figure 3.54 illustrates the utilization of these lists with the (sub)system block. The –Function List– and –Product List– are independent; if both are listed on a (sub)system block, they should be read together to mean that each listed function is performed for all listed products.

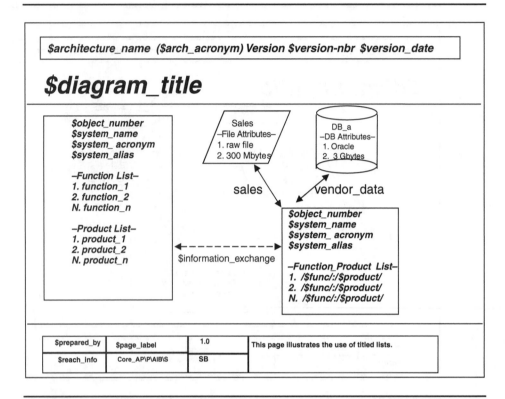

FIGURE 3.54 (Sub)System block title lists. This example shows the use of the standing function and product titled lists.

A –Function_Product List– shows the specific relationships that exist between functions and products. It explicitly itemizes which functions are done for which products. A–Function_Product List– should not be listed together with either a –Product List– or a –Function List–. The format of each entry in the –Function_Product List– is /$func/:/$product/, where $func is a business function (or the name of a group of business functions), and $product is a business product (or the name of a group of business products). Figure 3.54 illustrates using this list.

Applications Lists and (Sub)System Blocks

On the lowest, and only on the lowest, level of the decomposed (sub)system blocks (Notion 25), you should create an application list for each (sub)system block. The application list is a standing titled list that defines the business applications embodied within the (sub)system block. If you decompose the system blocks to an atomic level, such as the recommended one block per page, there will only be one application list per page. Otherwise, there will be an application list for each (sub)system block on the page. The applications on this list will later be mapped to application layers on platforms and configured platforms (Notion 38).

The title of the application list has the format Application List for $system_ acronym-. The list has 1– n entries that itemize the business applications embodied within this (sub)system block. Figure 3.55 illustrates application lists. If there is room within the (sub)system block, the application list may be placed within the (sub)system block rather than as a separate object grouping. In this case, it is not necessary to specify the $system_ acronym.

Nesting-Titled Lists

Titled lists may be nested. When nested, each should be indented to illustrate the level of nesting. The following illustrates nested-titled lists:

–Function List–
    Function1
    Function2

$architecture_name ($arch_acronym) Version $version-nbr $version_date

$diagram_title

$diagram_sub_title

S1.2.1.3 **Accounts Payable System** **APS**	**S2.2.2.3** **Vendor Management System** **VMS**
–Application List– 1. APS1 2. APS2	–Application List for VMS– 1. VMS1 2. VMS2

$prepared_by	$page_label	1.1.2.1	This page illustrates an application list.
$reach_info	Core_AP\P\AIB\S	SB	

FIGURE 3.55 Application list. This example shows the use of an application list.

            –Subfunction List–
            Subfunction1
            Subfunction2
            Subfunction3
        Function3

Unless it is a standing titled list, each list should be defined in the Design Definition (Notion 11).

Notion 31. Network Icon

A network icon (an oval) is used to represent a network (Figure 3.56). One or more network icons may be used to break any data flow connection line, except a data flow that originates from a user group; $network_name may be the name of an actual network, the name of a network type or ". . . " to represent an unknown network. Multiple networks may be represented by listing them in transversal order within a network icon or concatenating network icons. Figure 3.57 illustrates the use of the network icon.

OSI List

A standing titled list for the network icon is the OSI list that specifies the OSI reference model for the network. Figure 3.58 defines the OSI list. On the network icon, you can list each line entry or only the numbered entries that you want to itemize. Additionally, in the way described for file or database icons, you may create your own titled lists for network icons.

Network Functional Specification

The $network_name within the network icon points to a Network Functional Specification that provides documentation about the network or pointers to other documentation about the network. Each Network Functional Specification

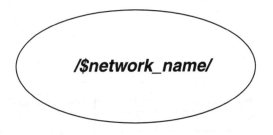

FIGURE 3.56 Network icon. An oval is used to represent a communications network.

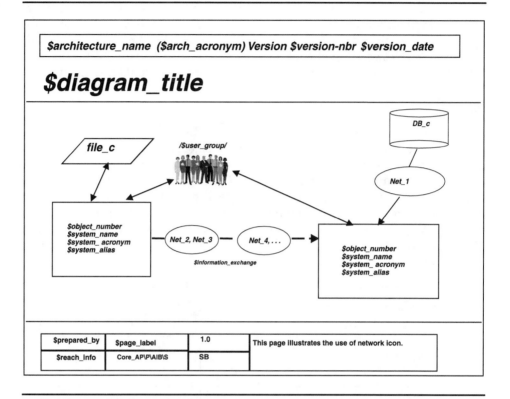

FIGURE 3.57   Network icon example illustrates the use of the network icon.

	Layer Number	Layer Name	Layer Definition
Application Interface	7	*Application*	*User-level formats and interfaces*
	6	*Presentation*	*Management of entry, exchange, display of data*
	5	*Session*	*Session administration*
Network Interface	4	*Transport*	*Transfer of data between sessions*
	3	*Network*	*Formatting and routing of packets*
	2	*Link*	*Dataflow initialization, control, and recovery*
	1	*Physical*	*Electrical and mechanical interfaces*

FIGURE 3.58   OSI list. This figure illustrates the definition of the OSI list for the network icon.

starts with an integer page number of the form n.0 and is dot incremented, as required, for additional pages. Network Functional Specifications are ordered sequentially within (sub)sections. The $network_name is the $page_label name for its Network Functional Specification. Figure 3.59 illustrates the relationship between the network icon and the Network Functional Specification.

Notion 32. Footnotes and Endnotes

Any text item or EAB object may be footnoted. To footnote, append a superscript footnote number after the text or object and create a titled footnote grouping with the footnotes. Footnotes are a less intrusive method than annotations for providing concise commentary on the drawing. Footnote numbers must be unique within a page, but multiple items may share the same footnote number. An item may be footnoted multiple times by separating the footnote numbers with commas. You may footnote the entire page (which means it should be read before reading the page) by footnoting the diagram title. Figure 3.60 illustrates the use of footnoting.

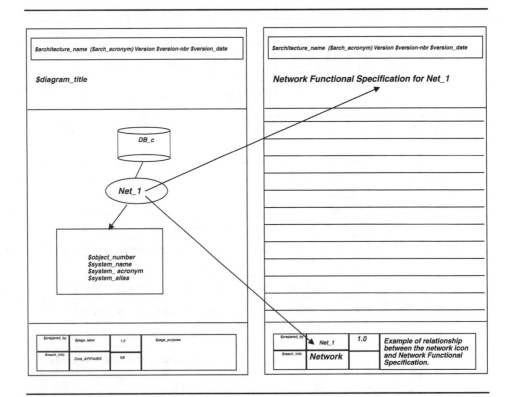

FIGURE 3.59 Network icon-Network Functional Specification relationship. The $network_name in the network icon points to its own Network Functional Specification.

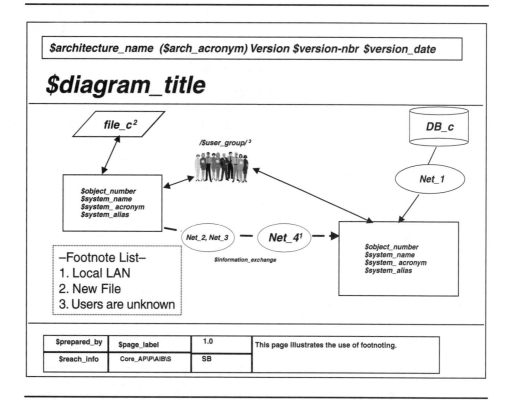

FIGURE 3.60   Footnote example illustrates the use of footnoting.

An alternative to footnotes are endnotes. Footnotes and endnotes are mutually exclusive. To substitute endnotes for footnotes do the following:

1. Make an entry in the Design Definition (Notion 11) in the Front Matter that this EAB is using endnotes. Footnotes are the default.
2. Create a user-defined section called Endnotes (see Notion 57 for the definition of user-defined sections).
3. List all notes in numerical order in this subsection.
4. Number the initial endnote page 1.0 and dot-number increment additional pages.

Endnotes offer a number of advantages over footnotes: The same endnote number can be used on multiple pages to note multiple objects that require the same commentary; footnotes are removed from each diagram page, so pages are less crowded and this frees page "real estate" for other purposes; endnotes are a shared repository for all diagrams within the EAB, thus enabling an endnote to be reused across all EAB core diagram sets within the EAB.

If you prefer to group endnotes by core section, create subsections within Section Endnote where the $subsection-id is set equal to $section_id$sect-suffix.

Notion 33. Transaction Functional Specification

Any $data_flow definition from a database, file, any system resource, user group, information appliance, information exchange, or interoperability definition (see Notion 46) may point to a Transaction Functional Specification, which explain the details of the data flow. Each Transaction Functional Specification starts with an integer page number of the form n.0 and is dot incremented, as required, for additional pages. Transaction Functional Specifications are ordered sequentially within (sub)sections. The $data_flow is the $page_label name for its transaction diagram. Figure 3.61 illustrates the relationship between the $data_flow and the Transaction Functional Specification. Each EAB architecture community should standardize the data required to document a transaction.

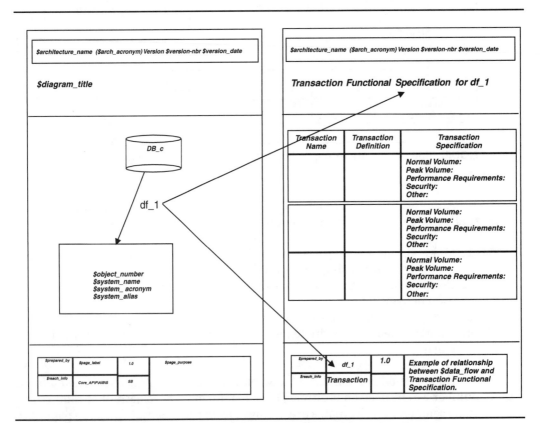

FIGURE 3.61   The $data_flow-transaction diagram relationship. A $data_flow points to its own transaction diagram.

PLATFORM DIAGRAMS

This section explains the icons and rules for drawing platform diagrams (Section Core: Subsection PL). Support diagrams will be introduced and explained at the point of instruction where the platform diagram relates to them.

Notion 34. Platform Icon

A platform diagram illustrates an architecture in which "platforms" are the central element of granularity and presentation. The key icon is a platform icon (a solid-line rounded rectangle, shown in Figure 3.62) that portrays an instance of an information technology device with its associated attributes; it presents platform and application information. The platform icon, coupled with other icons (network, information-exchange, database, etc.), illustrates the architectural structure (IT elements and their relationships) within the EAB domain at a platform-level view. Figure 3.63 is a sketched entity relationship data model that shows all the relationships that need to be modeled by the platform diagrams. Platform diagrams are drawn in subsection PL within section Core$sect_suffix of the EAB.

The platform icon is used to identify an in-scope platform. To distinguish a platform as being *out-of-scope*, the rounded rectangle is drawn with a broken line. Figure 3.64 illustrates both in-scope and out-of-scope platform icons.

Notion 35. Platform Diagram Page Numbering

Platform diagram pages are sequentially integer-numbered starting with page 1.0. There is neither page nor object decomposition within the Platform subsection. All the platform diagrams represent one continuous flat service view

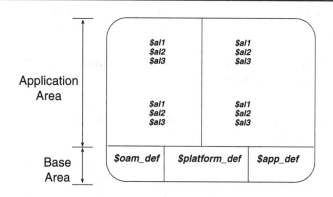

FIGURE 3.62   Platform icon. A rounded rectangle is used as the icon to represent a platform.

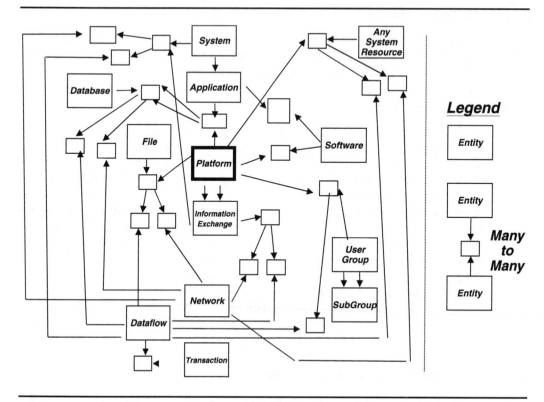

FIGURE 3.63   Platform diagram entity relationship model. This high-level entity relationship model shows the relationships that platform diagrams model.

of the architecture. Although you could alternatively draw an entire Platform subsection as one logical page, it is recommended that platform diagrams be drawn at an atomic[8] level with only one platform icon per page.

Notion 36. Platform Diagram Relationships to (Sub)System Block Diagrams and Interoperability Platforms

The relationships of platform diagrams to (sub)system block diagrams and interoperability diagrams depends on the core diagram set that the architect has chosen to illustrate. The following possibilities exist:

1. The core diagram set consists of only platform diagrams. In this case, the platform diagram is independent. It is self-contained and provides an independent representation of the architecture at the platform view level.
2. The core diagram set consists of a system block diagram and a platform diagram. In this case, each platform icon exists in a many-to-many relationship with the lowest level (sub)system block icons. Each application (from

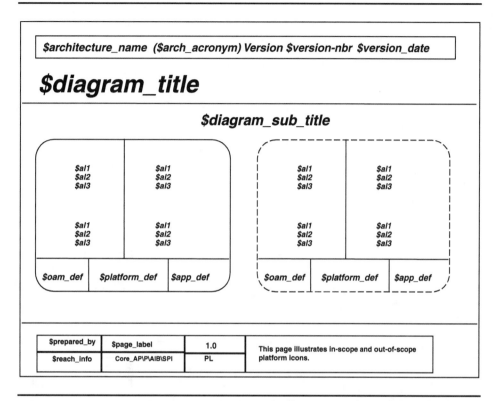

FIGURE 3.64   In-scope and out-of-scope platform icons. A solid rounded rectangle is used to represent an in-scope platform and a broken-line rounded rectangle is used to represent an out-of-scope platform.

the (sub)system block icon-associated application list; Notion 30) will reside on one or more platforms, and each platform may host 1–n applications from 1–n (sub)system blocks.

3. The core diagram set consists of a platform diagram and an interoperability diagram. There is an exact one-to-one relationship between platform icons and configured platform icons. A configured platform is a platform to which interoperability definitions have been added. If your intent is to create an interoperability diagram, it is not necessary to draw the platform diagram since everything illustrated on the platform diagram is included in the interoperability diagram.

4. The core diagram set consists of a platform diagram, a system block diagram, and an interoperability diagram. This is a combination of situations 2 and 3. It is important to note that each configured platform icon has the same relationships to the (sub)system block icons as its corresponding platform icon.

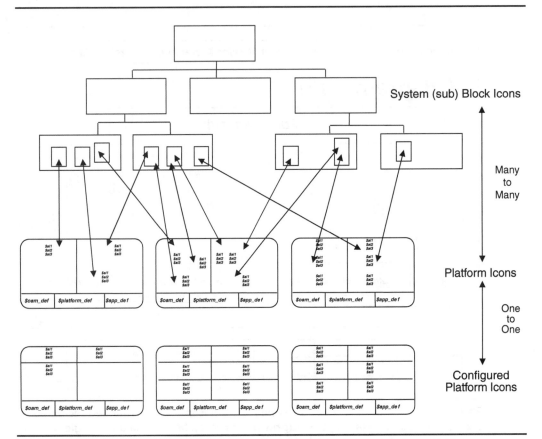

FIGURE 3.65   Platform relationships. Platform icons exist in a many-to-many relationship with (sub)system block icons, and in a one-to-one relationship with configured platform icons.

Figure 3.65 conceptually illustrates situation 4. To visualize the other situations, look at Figure 3.65 and block out the absent diagram types. Though not illustrated in Figure 3.65, remember that each configured platform icon has the same relationships to (sub)system block icons as does its corresponding platform icon.

Also understand that in situations where platform diagrams are coupled with (sub)system block diagrams, the platform icons inherit their in-scope or out-of-scope definition from the (sub)system blocks from which the mapped applications come, as follows:

- If all the applications originate in in-scope, (sub)system blocks, the platform icon is in-scope.
- If all the applications originate in out-of-scope, (sub)system blocks, the platform icon is out-of-scope.
- If the origin of the applications is mixed, the platform icon is in-scope.

Notion 37. Platform Base Area Variables

The platform icon is divided into two areas: the base area and the application area (Figure 3.62). The base area defines the information technology device at a global level. The application area defines the attributes of each application that runs on the platform. The base area variables are as follows:

$platform_def. Defines global attributes for the platform.

$app_def. Defines global application attributes for the platform.

$oam_def. Defines global OA&M attributes for the platform.

OA&M is the acronym for operations, administration, and maintenance, and indicates production operations support and monitoring functions. Operations architectures can be drawn together with the business systems they support or on separate drawings. In either case, they use the same notation system for representation. Table 3.7 summarizes the high-level OA&M functions that must exist within an architecture to manage and monitor business applications. The EAB team must decide how they will document the OA&M component of the application architecture.

Definition of $platform_def

The $platform_def is a comma-separated ordered list of the variables $object_nbr, $platform_name, $itd, /$role/, $os, $spec, $geo, and $machine-id. Variable definitions are as follows:

$object_nbr. Defines a core diagram set unique number for this object, of the format Pn where n is an integer.

TABLE 3.7   OA&M Functions

Application Level OA&M	System Level OA&M
Software Release Management	Software Release Management
Monitoring	Monitoring
Performance Management	Performance Management
Change Management	Change Management
Backup/Restore	Backup/Restore
Database Administration	Help Desk
Security Administration	Fault Management
Controls and Metrics	Controls and Metrics
Help Desk	Accounting
Job Management	Configuration Management

$platform_name. Assigns a name to the platform.

$itd. Defines either the generic type of information technology device or the specific type of information technology device that this icon represents, such as Intel PC, COMPAQ Presario, PBX, or other.

$role. Defines the architectural role(s) that the platform plays, such as Web server, enterprise server, desktop client, and so on.

$os. Defines the operating system that runs on this platform. For dumb devices such as terminals, this variable is set to null.

$spec. Defines a $page_label that points to a Detail Specification diagram.

$geo. Defines the physical location of the $itd.

$machine-id. Defines the real-world physical identifier of the platform.

Figure 3.66 illustrates a completed $platform_def.

Information Appliance Icon

Each information appliance icon that appears on a system block diagram becomes exactly one platform icon on a platform diagram. Instead of the user

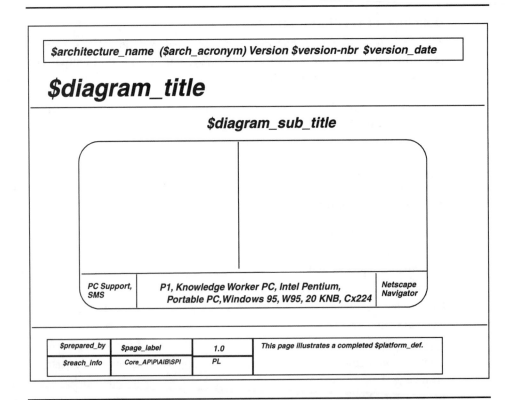

FIGURE 3.66   Platform base area example of a completed platform base area.

group icon connecting to the information appliance icon, it now connects to the platform icon, which provides a more detailed representation of the information appliance. Information appliance icons should not appear on platform or interoperability diagrams.

Detail Functional Specification

A Detail Functional Specification provides a detailed definition of the platform. It has a $section_id of Detail, a $diagram_title of Detail Functional Specification for /$platform_name/, and a $page_label equal to $spec on the pointing platform icon. The first page of each Detail Functional Specification is a (sub)section unique integer number of the format n.0. If it is longer than one page, the label remains the same but the page number is dot incremented. The detail data shown on Figure 3.67 is for illustration purposes only; each architect community should define its own specification.

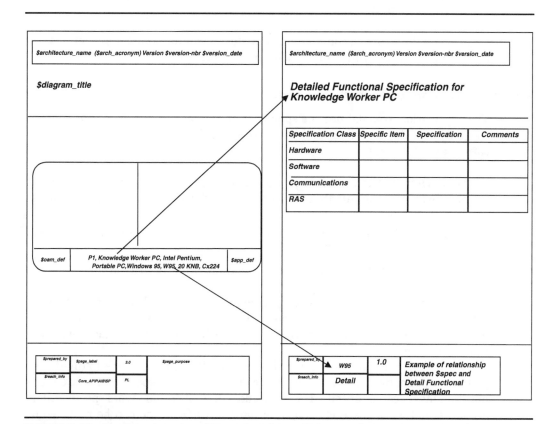

FIGURE 3.67   Platform icon-Detail Functional Specification relationship. The $spec in the platform icon points to its own Detail Functional Specification.

Definition of $app_def

The $app_def is a list of the variable /$appenv/. The $appenv is the name of an application environment (Lotus, Netscape, Explorer, etc.) under which all business applications on this platform run. If even one application does not run under this environment, do not specify $appenv. The list form of $appenv permits application environments to be vertically stacked. Figure 3.66 illustrates a completed $appenv. The $os plus /$appenv/ defines the environment under which all business applications run.

Definition of $oam_def

The $oam_def is a comma-separated ordered list of the variables $support_domain and /$oam_env/. Variable definitions are as follows:

> **$oam_env.** Defines the name of an OA&M environment under which all OA&M applications on this platform run.
>
> **$support_domain.** Defines the organizational unit responsible for supporting this platform.

Figure 3.66 illustrates a completed $oam_def. $os; plus, /$oam_env/ defines the environment under which all OA&M applications run.

Notion 38. *Platform Application Area Variables*

The application area defines the specification for each application that runs on the platform. Each application is defined by a set of three multivariable application layer (al) lists:

> **$al1.** Defines the application, its classification, the business products it supports, and the functions it performs, and relates it back to a (sub)system block icon.
>
> **$al2.** Provides an opportunity to define application-specific operating system or environment definitions.
>
> **$al3.** Defines the language(s) that the application is written in.

As shown in Figure 3.62, you specify one application layer for each application that runs on the platform. The application layer may be placed anywhere within the application area. Each application list should be space-separated from adjoining lists.

The vertical line down the middle of the platform icon serves to divide the platform application area into two halves to enlarge the specification area (application layers can be specified on both sides). If application layers specifications are large and more space is needed, either the vertical line can be removed or shifted to one side as required; the vertical line is not material to the drawing.

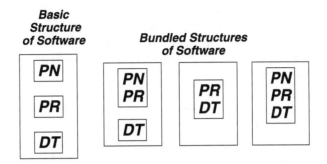

FIGURE 3.68   Software layers.

Software Layers

All software applications should be understood as consisting of three basic types of software layers that interact with each other (Figure 3.68): presentation (PN), processing (PR a.k.a. function layer), and data layer (DT). As illustrated in Figure 3.68, software is best designed when it is decoupled into the three primitive layers. When software is designed using the bundled structures, it reduces portability, scalability, interoperability, and reconfigurability because you cannot distribute the layers individually across your platforms.

Definition of $al1

The $al1 is a parentheses-enclosed (parentheses are single and are drawn), comma-separated ordered list of the form ($app_id, $app_name, $app_layer, $app_type, $system_block_object_nbr, //$func/:/$product//).

Variable definitions are as follows:

$app_id. A core diagram set unique identifier number assigned to identify the application, in the format An where n is an integer.

$app_layer. The type of application layer, such as PN, PR, DT, and so on.

$app_type. Identifies whether the application is an OA&M application or business APP (the default).

$app_name. The name of the application. If this platform diagram is part of a core diagram set that includes a system block diagram, then the application name should be selected from the application list that corresponds to the (sub)system block icon in which this application originates (see Notion 36).

$system_block_object_nbr. If this platform diagram is part of a core diagram set that includes a system block diagram, then this is the $object_nbr of the (sub)system block icon in which this application originates (see Notion 36); otherwise, it is null.

$func. A business function (or the name of a group of business functions) performed by this application. If this platform diagram is part of a core diagram set that includes a system block diagram, then these functions should be a subset of the –Function List– or –Function_Product List– (Notion 30) on the (sub)system block icon from which this application originates (see Notion 36).

$product. Defines a business product (or the name of a group of business products) supported by this application. The $product is explicitly associated with each $func that is performed for it. If this platform diagram is part of a core diagram set that includes a system block diagram, then these products should be a subset of the –Product List– or –Function_Product List– (Notion 30) on the (sub)system block icon from which this application originates (see Notion 36).

Figure 3.69 illustrates the $all definition and its relationship to a (sub)system block diagram.

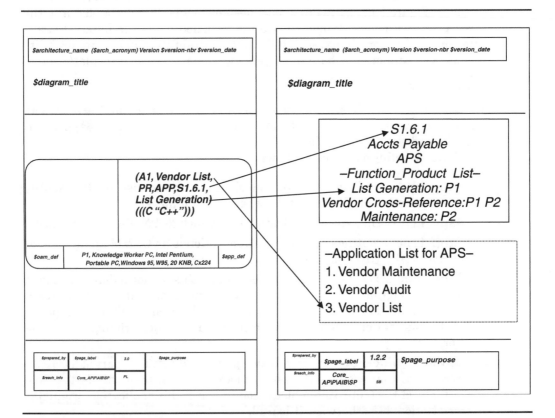

FIGURE 3.69 Application layer example of the specification of an application layer.

Definition of $al2

The $al2 is a double-parentheses enclosed (parenthesis are drawn), comma-separated ordered list of the form ((/$os/, /$env/)). Variable definitions are as follows:

$os. Defines an application-specific operating system that runs on top of the previously defined operating system for the platform.

$env. If the $app_type from $al1 is OA&M, it defines an application-specific OA&M environment that runs on top of the previously defined oam_def (Notion 37); otherwise, $app_type is APP and it defines an application-specific business application environment that runs on top the previously defined $app_def (Notion 37).

The $al2 permits you to create an application-specific operating system and environment per application. The list options permit you to stack operating systems and/or environments. The $al2 only needs to be used when the definition of the operating system or the environments in the platform base area variables (Notion 37) is insufficient to deal with the operating system and environment uniqueness for each application. This will often be the case when specialized development tools require run-time execution environments.

Definition of $al3

The $al3 is a triple-parentheses enclosed (parentheses are drawn) list of the form ((((/$language/))). Variable definitions are as follows:

$language. A language that the application is written in.

Figure 3.69 illustrates a specification of $al3.

Notion 39. Database Icon Revisited

Generally, a specific application on a platform manages a database accessed by applications on the platform (Figure 3.70). An additional variable, $app_id, is specified in the database icon to identify the specific $app_id in an $al1 definition that manages the database. The associated $app_layer in the $al1 must include a layer of type DT. In all other ways, the relationship definition of database icons to platform icons is identical to that of system block icons to database icons. Figure 3.71 illustrates the association of the revised database icon with a platform icon.

Notion 40. Platform Diagram Usage of Other EAB Icons and Notational Rules

Table 3.8 summarizes the rules for using other EAB icons with the platform icon. In general, the use is analogous except, of course, that the platform icon replaces the system block icon in the relationships and definitions.

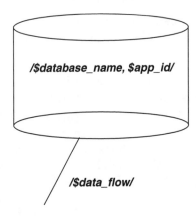

FIGURE 3.70 Database icon revisited. The definition of the variables on the database icon is extended to include the $app_id that manages the database.

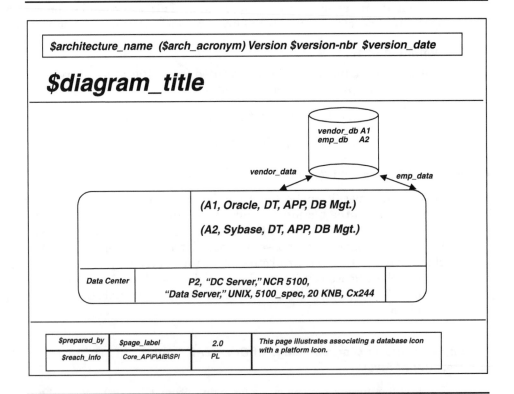

FIGURE 3.71 Database icon-platform icon example of drawing a database icon with the associated platform icon.

TABLE 3.8 Platform Diagram Use of Other EAB Icons and Notations

EAB Icon or Notation Rule	Reference Notion Number	Platform Icon Usage or Relationships within Platform Diagrams
System Block Icon	Notion 13	System block icons are not utilized within platform diagrams. The $system_block_object_nbr within the $al1 application layer definition (Notion 38) points to the (sub)system block in which applications that run on the platform originate.
Sources and Sinks	Notion 14	Platforms may be defined as sources or sinks. In this case, the $itd is set to source, sink, or source-sink, and the operating system and environment base variables are set to null values.
Nesting	Notion 15	Platform icons may not be nested.
File Icon	Notion 16	Same rules as for system block diagram.
Database Icon and Database Functional Specification	Notion 17 Notion 18	Same rules as for system block diagram, as amended by Notion 39.
Any System Resource	Notion 19	Same rules as for system block diagram.
User Group Icon, Information Appliance Icon, and User Group Functional Specification	Notion 20 Notion 21	Same rules as for system block diagram, except that a platform icon replaces the information appliance icon. Note that the point at which the user group icon connects to the platform icon does not indicate the applications the user groups use. This information is communicated in interoperability diagrams via service paths.
Annotation Icon and Annotation Functional Specification	Notion 22	Same rules as for system block diagrams. A story may transcend all members of a core diagram set.
Information Exchange Icon	Notion 23	Same rules as for system block diagrams. A platform icon may only engage in an information exchange with another platform icon. Note that the point at which the information exchange touches the platform icon does not indicate which applications are involved in the exchange. This information is communicated in interoperability diagrams via service paths.
Decomposition	Notion 24	Platform diagrams and platform icons do not undergo decomposition. It is recommended that each diagram page be drawn at an atomic level with only one platform icon per page.
Decorating	Notion 25	A platform diagram is balanced and should be decorated across all pages.

continues

TABLE 3.8   *(continued)*

EAB Icon or Notation Rule	Reference Notion Number	Platform Icon Usage or Relationships within Platform Diagrams
Horizontal Connectors	Notion 26	Same rules as for system block diagrams.
Decision Rules	Notion 27	Same rules as for system block diagrams.
Dictionary Bill of Materials	Notion 28	Same rules as for system block diagrams.
Object Grouping	Notion 29	Same rules as for system block diagrams.
Titled Lists	Notion 30	Same rules as for system block diagrams.
Network Icon and Network Functional Specification	Notion 31	Same rules as for system block diagrams.
Footnotes and Endnotes	Notion 32	Same rules as for system block diagrams.
Transaction Functional Specification	Notion 33	Same rules as for system block diagrams.

INTEROPERABILITY DIAGRAMS

This section explains the icons and rules for drawing interoperability diagrams (Section Core: Subsection Interop). Support diagrams will be introduced and explained at the point of instruction where the interoperability diagram relates to them.

Notion 41. Configured Platform Icon and Service Icon

An interoperability diagram illustrates an architecture with "configured platforms" and "services" as the central elements of granularity and presentation. The key icons are a configured platform icon and a service icon, which define an instance of an information technology device, a platform, with its associated interoperability (Figure 3.72). These icons coupled with other icons (network, file, database, etc.) illustrate the architectural structure (IT elements and their relationships) within an EAB domain from an interoperability level view. The configured platform icon is identical in structure to the platform icon, except that horizontal lines are drawn to partition the application layers from one another. Figure 3.73 is a sketched entity relationship data model that shows all the relationships that need to be modeled by interoperability diagrams. Interoperability diagrams are drawn in subsection Interop within section Core$sect_ suffix of the EAB.

The configured platform icon (a solid-line rounded rectangle with application layer separators) is used to identify an in-scope configured platform. To dis-

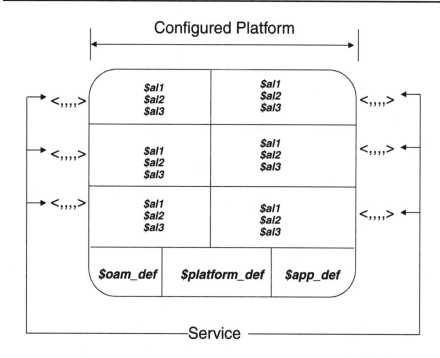

FIGURE 3.72   Configured platform icon and service icon. A rounded rectangle with application layer separators is used to represent a configured platform; a comma-separated list delimited by greater than and less than signs is used to represent a service.

tinguish a configured platform as being out-of-scope, the rounded rectangle is drawn with a broken line. This is analogous to the platform icon (Figure 3.64).

Notion 42. *Configured Platform Icon*

A configured platform icon is identical to a platform icon except that:

- Separator lines are drawn between application layers to clearly partition them. This is necessary because interoperability definitions must relate explicitly to specific application layers.
- The $object_nbr in $platform_def is assigned a number in the format In instead of Pn. If a platform diagram is part of the core diagram set, then the value of n for the configured platform should be identical to its corresponding platform icon. Otherwise, it should be assigned a unique diagram set In number.

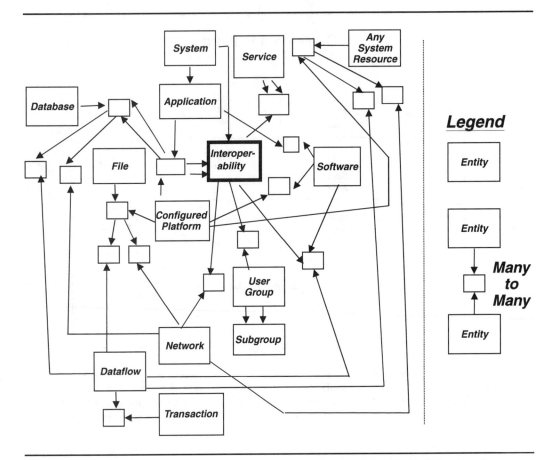

FIGURE 3.73 Interoperability diagram entity relationship model. This high-level entity relationship model shows the relationships modeled by interoperability diagrams.

In all other cases, the definition of the configured platform is identical to the description for the configured platform given in Notions 35 through 39. Simply reread those notions and substitute configured platform for platform. As stated, since a configured platform icon includes the information defined in a platform icon, if it is your intent to draw an interoperability diagram, it is not necessary to draw a platform diagram.

Notion 43. Service Icon

Configured platforms exchange information with other configured platforms through services and service paths. The basic concept of a service is as follows:

- Applications confine their domain of interest to business presentation, processing, or data logic on the resident configured platform.
- When an application needs to engage in interoperability, it invokes it through standardized service requests. An application may invoke 0–n services.
- A service is invoked through either an application program interface (API) or protocol format.
- Typical services are transaction management, data access, messaging, file transfer, or mail.
- The service interface hides the complexity and means of service delivery.
- When an entire set of services are bundled together to deliver interoperability between two application layers, it is called middleware.
- Service paths are the sequence of services through which application layers interoperate. Each application layer that participates in the interoperability invokes a service path composed of 1 to n ordered services. The dual service paths are referred to as an end-to-end service path.

A comma-separated list delimited by a greater than or less than sign is used to represent a service (Figure 3.74). An application initiates interoperability by invoking a service. The service definition is placed next to the application layer that invokes it (Figure 3.75).

A service icon is a comma-separated ordered list of the form <$service_type, /$api/, $sproduct, //$func/:/$product//, $svc_role, /$language/>. Variable definitions are as follows:

$service_type. Defines a unique type of service.

$api. Defines the API or protocol that is invoked to interface with the service.

$sproduct. Defines the software product that delivers the service.

//$func/:/$product//. Defines a subset list of the //$func/:/$product// list in the associated and invoking $al1. Itemizes the subset of associated functions and products within the application that this service innovation is supporting. If it is set to null, blank, it should be interpreted as meaning *all*.

$svc_role. Defines the interoperability role of the application layer.

$language. A language in the associated $al3 that invokes the associated API(s).

<$service_type, /$api/, $sproduct, //$func/:/$product//, $svc_role, /$language/>

FIGURE 3.74 Service icon. A comma-separated list delimited by a greater than and less than sign is used to represent a service.

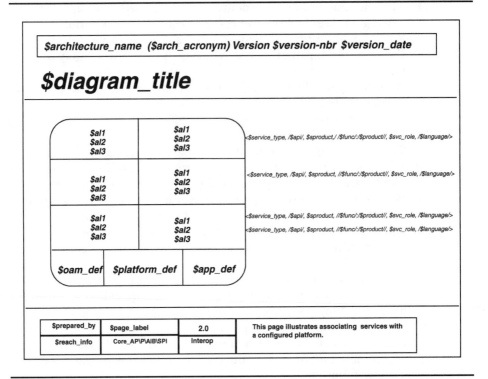

FIGURE 3.75   Service placement. Service icons are placed next to the application layer that invokes them.

An application layer may invoke 0–n services. An application layer may invoke the same service 1–n times; 0–n application layers per configured platform may invoke a service.

Definition of $service_type

The $service_type is a code that defines each unique type of service that may be invoked by any application layer. Sample $service_types are as follows:

Service Type	Service
DTM	Distributed transaction management
RPC	Remote procedure call
DA	Data access
OS	Operating system service
FT	File transfer

The architecture team should establish a finite standard set of $service_types for their environment.

Definition of the $api

The $api defines the API or protocol invoked by the application layer to invoke the service. The $api is invoked by the service-associated $language. Sample APIs are ANSI SQL, Oracle API, CGI, TAPI, and Teradata CLI. The list structure of $api permits the architect to specify multiple alternatives. The architecture team should establish a finite standard set of $api for their environment.

Definition of $svc_role

The $svc_role defines the interoperability role of the application layer. Permitted roles are:

CL: Client
SR: Server
CLSR: Client and server
PR: Peer
SD: Sender in file transfer sense
RR: Receiver in file transfer sense
SUB: Subscriber
PUB: Publisher

The most comprehensive role executed by the application layer should be denoted. The architecture team should extend this code set as required for their environment. Figure 3.76 shows an example of using the service icon.

Notion 44. Service Path

A service may, in turn, invoke from 0–n additional services. The service directly invoked by the application layer is called the *header service*. Only a header service should have a //$func/:$product//, $svc_role, and /$language/ defined. The header services on each side of the end-to-end service path must have a valid pair of service roles. Table 3.9 shows the valid pairs.

A concatenated string of services is called a *service path*; it has the form /$service/. The last service in a service path is called the *trailer service*. In the most common single-service path, a service path of one service, the header and trailer service are the same. There are four types of service paths:

1. **Single-service path.** The service path is one service long.
2. **Simple service path.** Any service in the service path invokes, at most, one additional service.
3. **Complex "or" service path.** Any service in the service path may invoke more than one additional service in an "or" relationship. When the service path reaches the "or" point, it may invoke one service or the other, then continues. An "or" situation is denoted by a thin vertical bar line.

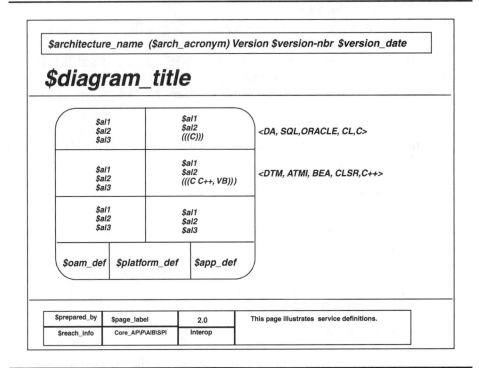

FIGURE 3.76   Example of specifying a service.

4. **Complex "and" service path.** Any service in the service path may invoke more than one additional service in an "and" relationship. Having invoked a service, the service path continues but eventually back-tracks to the "and" point and transverses the other service alternative as well. An "and" situation is denoted by a thick vertical bar line.

The last three cases handle complex situations. In practice, most service paths are only one service long. Service paths usually terminate with layer 7 of the OSI reference model (Notion 31; Figure 3.58). Figure 3.77 illustrates the alternative structures for service paths. Figure 3.78 revises Figure 3.75 with the more general structure of service paths replacing a single service as the object invoked by an application layer.

Notion 45. *Global Application Layers*

Some service paths on a configured platform may be used by all other application layers of the same type. To economize notation, you can define global application layers. A global layer, $al1 (Notion 38) is defined as follows:

TABLE 3.9   Valid Pairs of Service Roles

	Client	Server	Client/Server	Peer	Receiver	Sender	Publisher	Subscriber
Client		x	x					
Server	x		x					
Client/ Server		x	x	x				
Peer				x				
Receiver						x		
Sender					x			
Publisher								x
Subscriber							x	

$app_id. A core diagram set unique identifier number is assigned to identify the global layer in the format Gn where n is an integer.

$app_layer. The type of application layer, for example, PN, PR, DT, and so on, to which this global definition applies.

$app_type. Identifies the type of application, OA&M or business APP (default), to which this global definition applies.

$app_name. Null value.

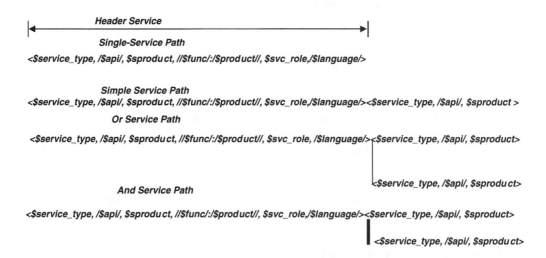

FIGURE 3.77   Service path structure. This is an example of the alternative structures of service paths.

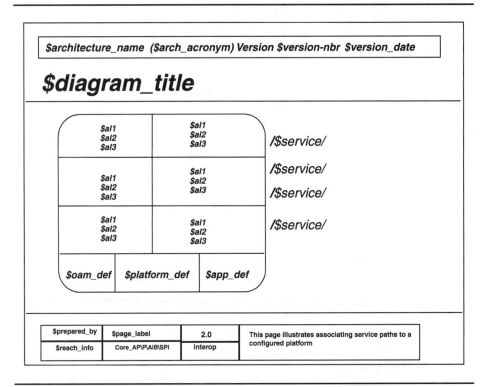

FIGURE 3.78 Service path placement. Service paths are placed next to the application layer that invokes them.

$system_block_object_nbr. Null value.

//$func/:/product//. Null value.

The service path is placed next to the global application layer and defines an end-to-end service path. All other application layers that have the same $app_layer and $app_type inherit the end-to-end service paths associated with the global layer and must have in their $al3 definition the $language defined in the header service. The //$func/:/product// in all the service paths associated with a global layer must be set to null. There can be multiple global application areas per configured platform, and each global layer area may have 1–n service paths connected to it.

Notion 46. Interoperability Definition

Interoperability is defined by a nonarrowheaded dashed connection line between service paths with an associated interoperability definition (Figure 3.79). The

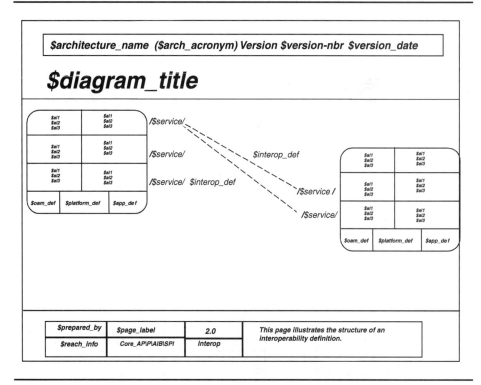

FIGURE 3.79 Interoperability definition. A dashed line connecting two service paths defines interoperability.

$role on the header service on each side defines the direction(s) of information movement. Interoperability can occur between applications on different or the same platforms. Interoperability, $interop_def, is defined by a comma-separated, ordered list of the form $middleware_def, $trans_def, /$data_flow $frequency/.

Variable definitions are as follows:

$middleware_def. Defines the middleware framework that governs the interoperability.

$trans_def. Defines whether the interoperability supports transactions. Codes are Y (yes) or N (no). The default is no.

$data_flow. Defines the name of the data items being exchanged.

$frequency. Defines the frequency of the exchange, such as interactive, daily, on-demand, and so on.

Multiple interoperability connections can originate from one service path. Figure 3.80 illustrates an interoperability definition.

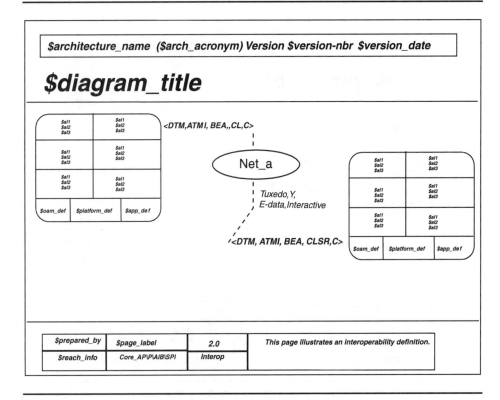

FIGURE 3.80 Interoperability definition example.

For interoperability diagrams, interoperability definitions with the associated end-to-end service paths replace information exchanges as the way to depict information flow between the key objects. While developing the interoperability diagram, you may use information exchanges as a placeholder; it is the excruciatingly detailed depiction of the service paths and associated interoperability definition that is the essence of interoperability diagrams.

Notion 47. User Group Icon Revisited

User interface definitions are the same as presented in Notion 20, except that a service with a $service_type = UI replaces the connection line. User interface services may be issued only by PN applications layers and are often defined in a global application area for a configured platform. The service definition explicitly connects a user group(s) to the application layer that the user group(s) uses. Figure 3.81 illustrates the structure of a user interface definition on an interoperability diagram.

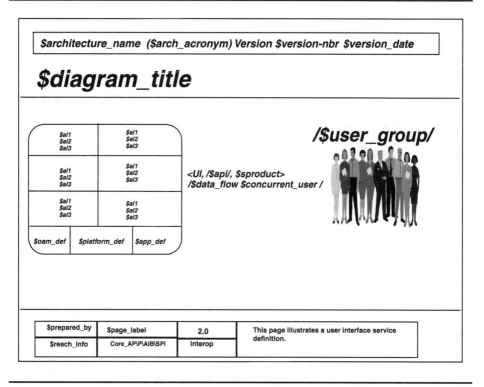

FIGURE 3.81   User interface definition. On interoperability diagrams, a service definition is created to explicitly relate each user group to the application layers that they use.

Notion 48. Scalability and Portability Icon

Scalability is defined as the ability to move all application layers at the execution level to another configured platform and maintain all end-to-end service paths. Portability is defined as the ability to move the source code for all applications layers to another configured platform, rebuild them, and maintain all end-to-end service paths. A scalability/portability icon, a hexagon with a pointing arrow, is used to specify the $page_label of the Scalability Functional Specification and/or Portability Functional Specification for a configured platform. Figure 3.82 illustrates the use of the scalability/portability icon.

Variable definitions are as follows:

S: $scale_def: Defines the $page_label of a Scalability Functional Specification.

P: port_def: Defines the $page_label of a Portability Functional Specification.

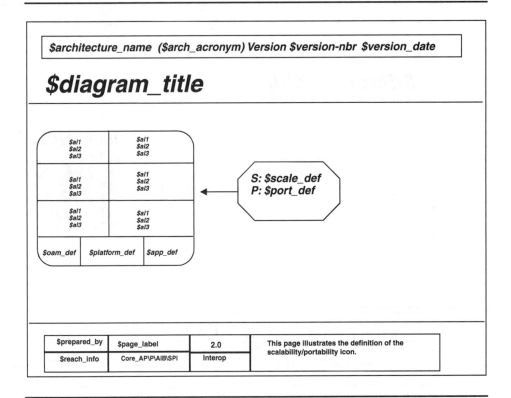

FIGURE 3.82 Scalability/portability icon. The scalability/portability icon defines the $page_label of Scalability and/or Portability Functional Specifications for the configured platform.

Figure 3.83 illustrates the pointing relationship between the scalability/portability icon and the Scalability Functional Specification. The Scalability Functional Specification defines a set of configured platforms across which all application layers are scaleable. This means that all application layers at the execution code level can be moved between the set of configured platforms, and all end-to-end service paths are maintained. Figure 3.84 illustrates the pointing relationship between the scalability/portability icon and the Portability Functional Specification.

The Portability Functional Specification defines a set of configured platforms across which all application layers are portable. This means that for each language on an application layer on a configured platform, there exists a minimum set of build software (compilers, linkers, etc.) with which to remake the application layer on another configured platform; all end-to-end service paths are maintained.

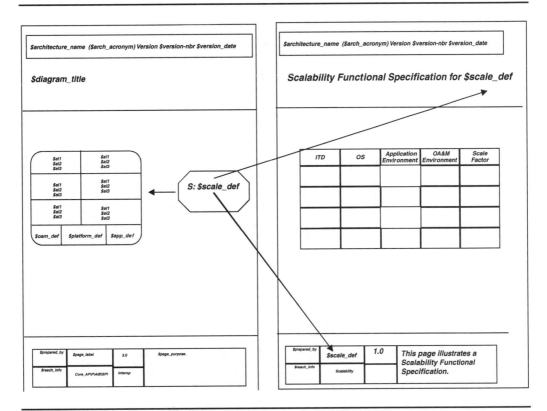

FIGURE 3.83   Scalability/portability icon relationship to Scalability Functional Specification. The scalability/portability icons point to the Scalability Functional Specification.

The actual requirements for portability or scalability may exceed the minimum definitions provided on the sample Scalability Functional Specification and the Portability Functional Specification. For example, it may be necessary to provide emulation software on a target platform; or there may be hardware-dependent issues that need to be addressed. It is the responsibility of the architecture team to provide adequate specifications to assure scalability or portability. For both functional specifications, pages are numbered sequentially within subsections. If a definition is longer than one page, the successive pages are dot-numbered.

Notion 49. Interoperability Diagram Use of Other EAB Icons and Notational Rules

Table 3.8 (Notion 40) summarized the rules for using other EAB icons with the platform icon. In general, the use of a configured platform icon is analogous, ex-

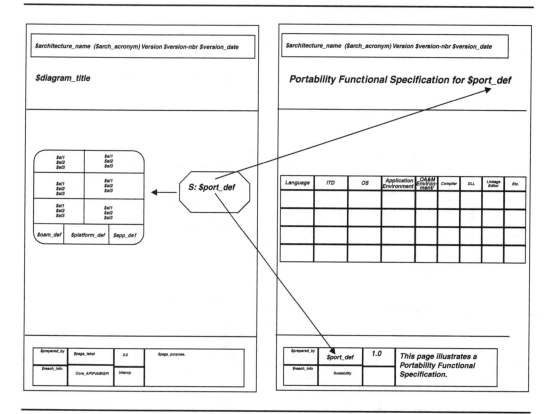

FIGURE 3.84   Scalability/portability icon relationship to Portability Functional Specification. The scalability/portability icons point to the Portability Functional Specification.

cept of course, that the configured platform icon replaces the platform icon in the relationships and definitions. Two specific points of difference are:

- A service definition replaces the connection line on the user group icon definition (Notion 47) to connect a user group to the configured platform. The configured platform is the detailed representation of an information appliance. The original user group icon notation is still applied to relate user groups to an any system resource icon or to engage the user group in an information exchange with another user group.
- The information exchange icon is replaced in its entirety by the interoperability definition (Notion 46) and end-to-end service paths (Notion 45).

Remember, on platform diagrams, the relationships between user groups and information exchanges to applications layers are not explicit. They are made explicit on interoperability diagrams by the service paths and the delimiter lines on the configured platform that partition application layers. If a platform diagram would meet your needs, but you require the explicit relationship of user groups and information exchanges to applications, draw the interoperability diagram with the information exchange icon explicitly connecting application layers, and connect the user groups to the specific application layer.

FUNCTION BLOCK DIAGRAMS

This section explains the icons and rules for drawing Function diagrams (Section Core: Subsection FN). Support diagrams will be introduced and explained at the point of instruction where the function diagram relates to them.

Notion 50. Function Icon

A function block diagram illustrates an architecture from a functional perspective, in which function blocks are the central element of granularity and presentation (Figure 3.85). The key icon is a function block icon that defines business function. The function block icon, coupled with other icons (information exchange, file, database, etc.) illustrates the architectural structure within an EAB domain from a function level view. Figure 3.86 is a sketched entity relationship data model that shows all the relationships that need to be modeled by function block diagrams. Function block diagrams are drawn in subsection FN within section Core$sect_suffix of the EAB.

Often, an architect, especially when doing vision architectures, wants to draw a functional architecture that depicts the packaging and location of major

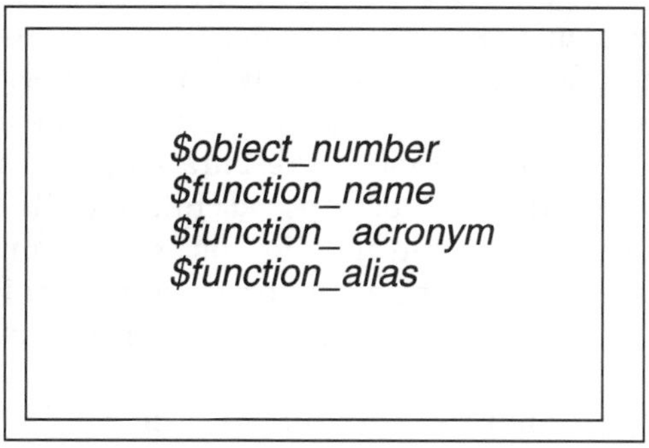

$object_number
$function_name
$function_ acronym
$function_alias

FIGURE 3.85   Function block icon. A double-edged rectangle is used to represent a function.

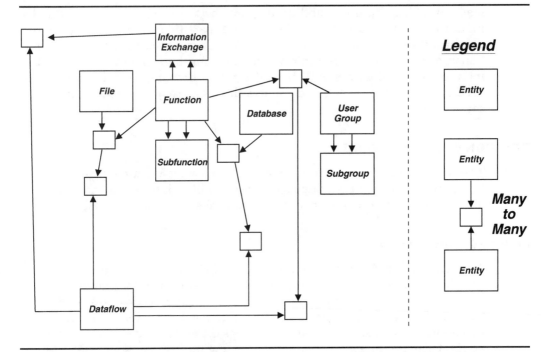

FIGURE 3.86   Function block diagram entity relationship model. This high-level entity relationship model shows the relationships modeled by function block diagrams.

business functions without specifying systems or technologies. To do this, you use the same icons/rules/notations as for system blocks (modifications to be explained shortly) but replace the notion of a system block with the notion of a function block with an Fn.n number.

As illustrated in Figure 3.87, the idea of a function block diagram is to allocate and package relevant functions from the business models[9] (application inventory cell, Figure 2.3) and show the architectural relationship of these functions. A typical way to do this is to create the anchor function block page with the three basic functions—presentation, processing, and data—then map the business functions as decomposed children of these basic IT functions. Figure 3.88 illustrates a child function block diagram of a presentation anchor function. The use of nesting structures is prevalent in function block diagrams.

Variable definitions on the function icon (Figure 3.85) are as follows:

$object_number. An EAB unique number identifying the function or subfunction of the format Fn.n.

$function_name. A unique name identifying the function or subfunction.

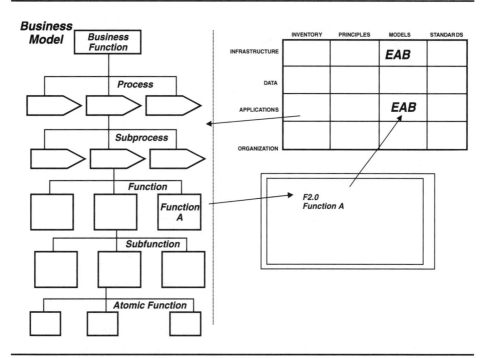

FIGURE 3.87 Function block relationship to business model. The functions placed on function block icons originate in the business model.

$function_acronym. A unique acronym identifying the function or sub-function.

$function_alias. An alias name for the function/subfunction.

Function block diagrams generally use the same rules as system block diagrams, except that the unit of focus is a function rather than a system. Table 3.10 explains the use of other icons and notational rules with function block icons and diagrams.

When drawing function block architectures, at the out-of-scope perimeter, it is desirable to show the existing systems with which the functions will eventually have to interface. Do this by creating a function block icon and populating it with a –Systems List– (another standing titled list; Notion 30) that contains a list of 1–n systems. Generally, this function block will be a dashed perimeter because it is out of scope. An information exchange between a function block defining a function and a function block containing a system list means that the indicated data flows move between the indicated systems and the designated function.

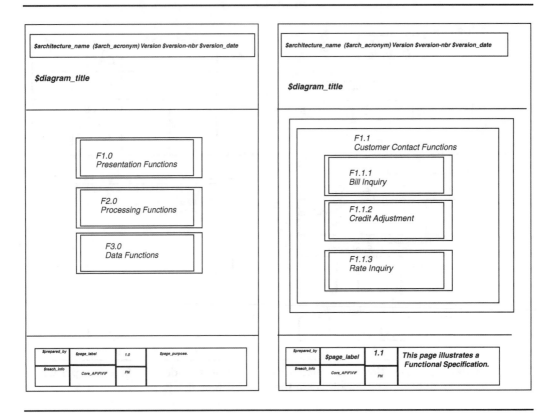

FIGURE 3.88 Function block diagram example.

CUT-OUT DIAGRAMS

This section explains the icons and rules for drawing cut-out diagrams (Section Core: Subsection Cut-Out).

Notion 51. Cut-Out Diagrams

A cut-out is a selective regrouping of any desired set of icons from across all pages within a core diagram set or across core diagram sets. It permits you to show a selected composite view of objects that are dispersed across multiple pages on one page. It is the only time that a numbered object may reappear on another core diagram page. The redrawing only has to show those parts of the original drawings that are relevant to what you are trying to express. No new objects (except *joined platforms* or *joined configured platforms,* discussed later) may be added; however, connection icons may be replaced with actual connec-

TABLE 3.10 Function Block Diagram Use of Other EAB Icons and Notations

EAB Icon or Notation Rule	Reference Notion Number	Function Block Icon Usage or Relationships within Function Block Diagrams
System Block Icon	Notion 13	System block icons are not utilized within function block diagrams.
Sources and Sinks	Notion 14	Sources and sinks are not utilized within function block diagrams.
Nesting	Notion 15	Function block icons may be nested.
File Icon	Notion 16	Same rules as for system block diagram, except that file icons should be thought of as datastores.
Database Icon and Database Functional Specification	Notion 17 Noton 18	Same rules as for system block diagram, except that database icons should be thought of as datastores.
Any System Resource	Notion 19	Same rules as for system block diagrams, but rarely used.
User Group Icon and User Group Functional Specification	Notion 20 Notion 21	Same rules as for system block diagrams.
Annotation Icon and Annotation Functional Specification	Notion 22	Same rules as for system block diagrams.
Information Exchange Icon	Notion 23	Same rules as for system block diagrams. A function block icon may only engage in an information exchange with another function block icon.
Decomposition	Notion 24	Same rules as for system block diagrams.
Decorating	Notion 25	Same rules as for system block diagrams.
Horizontal Connectors	Notion 26	Same rules as for system block diagrams.
Decision Rules	Notion 27	Same rules as for system block diagrams.
Dictionary Bill of Materials	Notion 28	Same rules as for system block diagrams.
Object Grouping	Notion 29	Same rules as for system block diagrams
Titled Lists	Notion 30	Same rules as for system block diagrams, except that function lists and application lists are not applicable.
Network Icon and Network Functional Functional Specification	Notion 31	Network icons are not utilized within function block diagrams.
Footnotes and Endnotes	Notion 32	Same rules as for system block diagrams.
Transaction Functional Specification	Notion 33	Same rules as for system block diagrams.

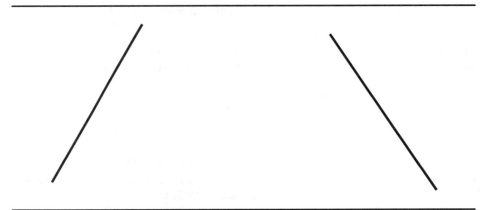

FIGURE 3.89   Hierarchical view icon. The hierarchical view icon is used only on cut-out diagrams to show hierarchical relationships of decomposable icons.

tions and explanatory features, such as annotations, footnotes/endnotes, object groupings, and null-titled lists. Cut-outs normally have a page annotation associated with them to explain why the cut-out was made. If you include objects from multiple hierarchical levels of a decomposition path (decomposition levels may be skipped), you must use a hierarchical view icon to illustrate and maintain the hierarchical relationship (Figure 3.89).

You use cut-outs to create any and all desired views or perspectives of the architecture by combining selected objects from the other core sections. This is why we recommended creating atomic drawings in the other core sections. In the cut-out section, you regroup the atomic diagrams from the system, platform, interoperability, or function block diagrams into any and all views that are necessary to express your architecture. Atomic drawings preposition their elements as Lego blocks, to be recombined in the cut-out section. Figure 3.90 illustrates a cut-out diagram. Pages are numbered sequentially starting at 1.0 within subsections. A cut-out may be only one page.

Cross-Core Diagram Sets Cut-Outs

If you have an EAB that has multiple core diagram sets, you may create an additional core diagram set that includes only a cut-out, which may include objects from across core diagram sets. This is highly desirable when you are drawing scenarios and have an as-is-built core diagram set and multiple to-be-built core diagram sets and would like to show pieces of each core diagram set together. The $sect_suffix for such a cut-out diagram could look like _AP\P\M\C\ (Notion 8). If you mix objects on a cut-out diagram page from different types of diagrams and/or different time periods of diagrams, it is wise to use object groupings with a null-titled list to separate and identify each distinct collection.

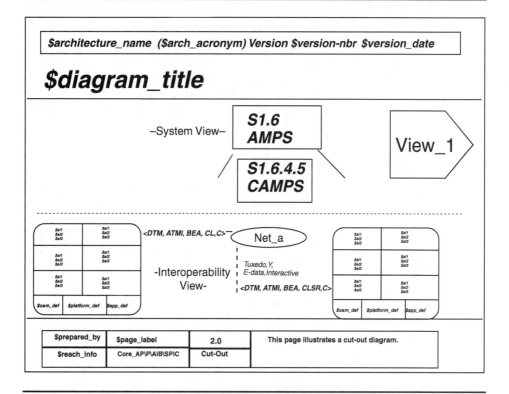

FIGURE 3.90   Cut-out diagram example.

Temporal Views

A particularly valuable utilization of cut-outs is to show comparative architectural changes over time on a single page. Each of the other core diagrams can only show an architecture at a given point in time. The different time views of the architecture can be colocated on a single cut-out to illustrate the time impacts of the changes being proposed.

Joined Platforms or Joined Configured Platforms

If you have created atomic platforms or atomic configured platforms in the PL or Interop subsections respectively, you may want to create consolidated user group cut-outs that show the (configured) platforms from a user group perspective. In this case, you can join platforms or configured platforms with others that share the same base data (Figure 62) to create a single (configured) platform that has the consolidated application layers for all *joinable* (configured) platforms. In this case, it may also be advantageous to create global application layers (Notion 45) to simplify the joined (configured) platform.

DISTRIBUTED EABS

EABs may hierarchically and horizontally interconnect with each other. This permits the partitioning of architecture efforts into manageable units and makes it possible for new drawings to include other drawings by connecting to them rather than redrawing the reference/shared entities. When a set of EABs is managed and evolved as a single virtual EAB, it is referred to as a *distributed EAB*. An EAB may also connect to support diagrams, dictionaries, or functional specifications in another EAB.

Notion 52. *Horizontal Connecting of Objects across EABs*

Horizontal connecting between distinct EABs is done by prefacing the $connector_name on the From connector with the $page_header ($arch_acronym\ $version_nbr\) of the target EAB. All other connection rules, as previously defined in Notion 26, must be followed. If $version_nbr is set to null, it is read as meaning the most current version. Figure 3.91 illustrates the revised definition of the connector icons. Variable definitions are as follows:

$connector_id: $page_header\$connector_name

$connector_name: A connector identifier

$page_header: $arch_acronym\$version_nbr

Figure 3.92 illustrates a horizontal connection across EABs. A connector may only connect objects on balanced drawings of the same architectural perspective. As shown in this figure, it is good practice to annotate the To connector with the $page_header of the From connector.

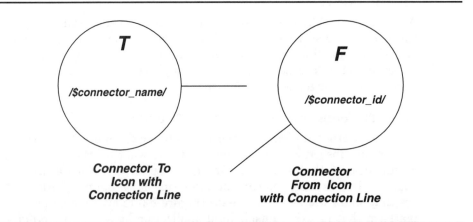

FIGURE 3.91   Connector icons revisited. The definition of the From connector is revised to indicate the EAB and version number that hosts the To connector.

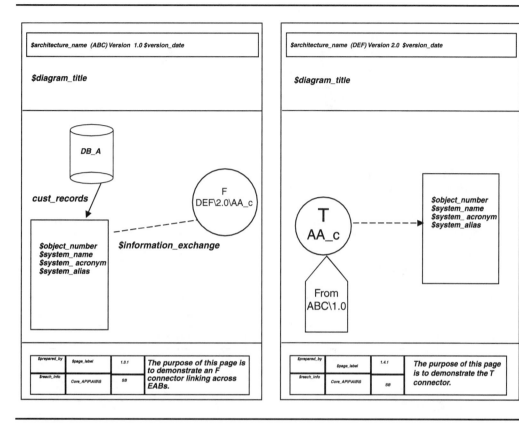

FIGURE 3.92   Cross EAB horizontal connection. This is an example of horizontally connecting two blueprints.

Notion 53. Vertical Connecting of System Block Icons or Function Block Icons across EABs

The vertical connection of system blocks to system blocks (or function blocks to function blocks) treats one system block (function block) as the parent and the other as the child. Vertical connecting is done by populating the child system block (function block) with the $parent_id of the system block (function block) on the parent EAB, and populating the parent system block (function block) with the $child_id of the system block (function block) on the child EAB. The parent block must be the lowest leaf on its decomposition tree; the child block must be a root block.

Figure 3.93 shows the revised definitions of the system block icon and the function block icon. The $parent_id is defined on the child block as $page_header\$object_number, where $page_header equals $arch_acronym\ $version_nbr of the parent block. The $child_id is defined on the parent block as

$object_number
$system_name
$system_ acronym
$system_alias
$parent_id
/$child_id/

$object_number
$function_name
$function_ acronym
$function_alias
$parent_id
/$child_id/

FIGURE 3.93   System block icon and function block icon revisited. Both icons are revised to permit vertical connections.

$page_header\$object_number, where $page_header equals $arch_acronym\ $version_nbr of the child block. If $version_nbr is set to null, it is read as meaning the most current version. Figure 3.94 illustrates a hierarchical connection of system blocks across EABs.

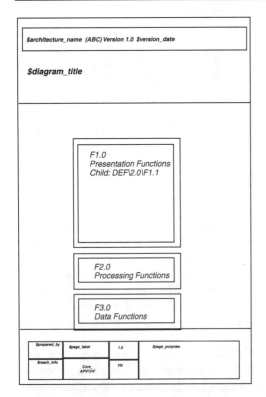
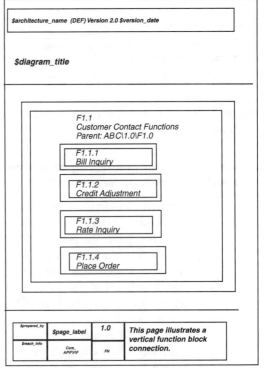

FIGURE 3.94   This is an example of a vertical connection between function block icons.

Notion 54. Vertical Connecting of Application Layers to System Block Icons across EABs

Vertical connecting of a (configured) platform to the system block that owns its applications is done by prefacing the $system_block_object_nbr on $all with $page_header. The parent must be the lowest-level system block on the parent EAB. The definition of $all is revised to ($app_id, $app_name, $app_type, $app_env, $page_header\$system_block_object_nbr, //$func/:/$product//), where $page_header equals the $arch_acronym\$version_nbr of the parent system block. If $version_nbr is set to null, it is read as meaning the most current version. Figure 3.95 illustrates a hierarchical connection of a platform icon to a system block icon across EABs.

Notion 55. Core Diagram Referencing of Support Diagrams in Other EABs

It is efficient to create EABs that contain dictionaries and functional specifications that can be reused by other EABs. These EABs do not have a core section

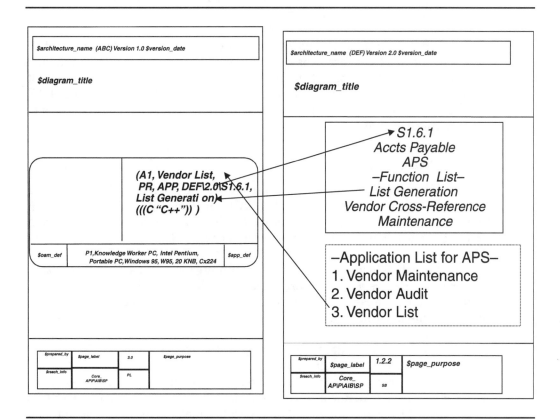

FIGURE 3.95 This is an example of a platform icon connecting back to a system block icon in a different EAB.

but contain one or more other sections shared by EABs with core sections. We call such EABs *reference EABs*. There are two ways for an EAB to point to reference EABs:

1. *Create the EAB that has a core section with a full complement of support diagrams; on each support diagram, provide a concatenated list of reference EABs to search.* In this case, you create a chained list from the EAB's own functional specification to a concatenated list of reference EABs to search. When you specify the concatenated list of reference EABs, you may include the current EAB either first or last. The format of the pointer to the reference EAB is $arch_acronym\$version_nbr. If $version_nbr is set to null, it is read as meaning the most current version.

2. *In the Design Definition (Notion 11) of the EAB with a core section, for all support diagrams or by specific support diagram, declare concatenated lists of reference EABs to be used to resolve dictionary and functional specification requirements.* The format of the pointer to the reference EAB is $arch_acronym\$version_nbr. If $version_nbr is set to null, it is read as meaning the most current version.

Though you can mix and match these two methods, it can become confusing very quickly. Therefore, it is recommended that you choose a simple and consistent approach across all reference EABs. When developing to-be-built EABs, it is common to use the most current as-is-built EAB as a reference EAB to reduce the need to create dictionary entries and functional specifications to only additions and changes.

Notion 56. Distributed EABs

When EABs use any of the interconnection techniques explained in Notions 52 to 55, but evolve independently, the EABs are said to be *loosely coupled*. Though the owners of each interconnected EAB have to be sure to maintain proper linkages, in a loosely coupled design, each EAB maintains its independence.

An alternative to loosely coupled interconnected EABs is a *distributed EAB*. A distributed EAB is a set of interconnected EABs managed as a single virtual EAB. The EABs are carefully designed, managed as a unit, and go through configuration management in a structured and coordinated manner (see Chapter 4).

Each EAB that participates in a distributed EAB includes in its Design Definition (Notion 11) an identical drawing of the structure of the distributed EAB. Figure 3.96 illustrates the two icons that are used.

A thick-line rectangle is used to represent an EAB, and a line with arrows at the ends is used to define interconnections. A linkage line between two EABs means that at least one horizontal or vertical connection exists between them. Only reference EABs (no core section) have an R in their definition. EAB icons

$architecture_name
$arch_acronym
R

FIGURE 3.96   Distributed EAB icons. An EAB icon and a linkage icon are used to show the structure of distributed EABs.

are nested to show the unity of the blueprints. Figure 3.97 illustrates a distributed EAB drawing within a Design Definition; as shown there, a distributed EAB is normally organized in a tree structure with the top EAB referred to as the root EAB.

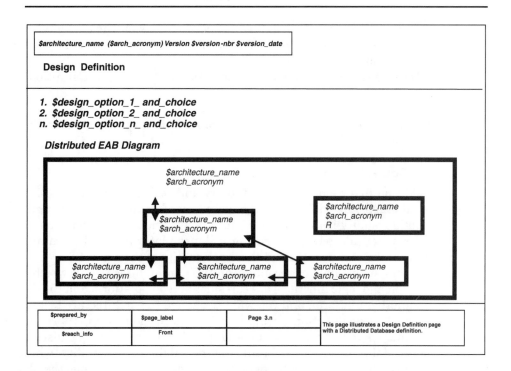

FIGURE 3.97   This is an example of a Distributed EAB drawing within a Design Definition.

Open Connections

In the discussion of loosely coupled EABs and distributed EABs, it is necessary to emphasize that horizontal connections will not necessarily resolve themselves within a given EAB. A From connector in one EAB may resolve itself with a To connector in another EAB. This is called an *open connection* and is a perfectly valid construct.

LOOSE ENDS

Notion 57. User-Defined Functional Specifications

Each EAB user community can extend the types of functional specification sections in an EAB. In the basic EAB that has been presented, its sections could have, but were not, defined for entities such as applications, systems, APIs, files, middleware, or languages. To extend an EAB with these or other functional specifications do the following:

1. Create a section with the $section_id of the entity, such as API.
2. Create a $page_label within the $section_id with the name of the entity, such as ANSI_SQL.
3. Populate the page with agreed-to specifications for the entity type.
4. Integer-number the pages. If a specification extends beyond one page, dot-increment the page number.
5. Declare the new functional specification in the Design Definition (Notion 11).

The entity that you have chosen now points from its place in a core diagram to a functional specification page.

Reconfigurability Functional Specification

In addition to demonstrating portability and scalability (Notion 48), more advanced blueprints will include the definition of architecture reconfigurability. Reconfigurability is the ability to migrate application function across existing platforms (or add new platforms or collapse platforms) and maintain the integrity of the architecture and the functionality of the system.

A simple example of reconfigurabity is an architecture in which the presentation and logic functions are coresident on one platform and the data layer is on another platform, and you want to change the architecture to a three-tier model. The logic functions would be migrated to their own platform, but their relationships to the presentation and data layers would not be disrupted. Reconfigurability is clearly different from portability or scalability, whereby the configuration of IT elements remains the same; you just change the platforms. In reconfigurability, you change the relationships and packaging of the IT elements.

To demonstrate reconfigurability in your blueprint, do the following:

1. Establish a $section_id of reconfigurability.
2. Revise the portability and scalability icon (the hexagon) to include the notation R: $reconf, where $reconf is a page label within the Reconfigurability section. Point the icons with the R: $reconf definitions to each platform involved in the reconfigurability.
3. In the Reconfigurability section, draw both a cut-out of the configured platforms and end-to-end service paths for which you want to demonstrate reconfigurability and the revised reconfigured architecture.
4. Use object groupings to distinguish them, and include a page annotation to explain the differences.

Documenting reconfigurability is a powerful action but rarely done because of effort and time constraints. It very vividly demonstrates the capability of portions of your architecture to change their shape without disruption; and that is what architecture design for extreme maneuverability is all about.

Notion 58. Sketching

EAB icons can also be used to draw sketches (a.k.a. conceptual architecture drawings). When you use EAB icons for sketching, the purpose shifts from rigor to communicating important ideas to an audience primarily interested in the big picture. EAB icons may then be used casually or informally. Casual usage means:

- Ignore packaging.
- Use minimum data attributes with icons.
- Ignore page-numbering rules.
- Draw only core diagrams.
- Add non-EAB objects or notations of your choice to the core diagrams.
- Mix logical, functional, and physical notations.
- Use color or other highlighting features to illustrate changes over time.

The advantage of using EAB icons for sketches is continuity of the representation system. Nevertheless, EAB may not be your best choice of tools for doing sketching, and you should carefully match sketching tools to your audience's needs.

Notion 59. Scenarios

The most prevalent use of EABs is to document as-is-built architectures. The next most common use is to document to-be-built (TBB) architectures. When developing to-be-built drawings, it is often necessary to develop a set of scenario proposals for consideration. To create multiple scenario architectures, you may:

1. Create multiple EABs each with a distinct status to differentiate them.
2. Create an EAB with multiple TBB core diagram sets.
3. Footnote questionable variables with a list of choices.
4. Create a TBB EAB with alternative pages (described next).

Alternative Pages

When drawing TBB EABs, you may want to illustrate multiple ways to implement the architecture on a given page. In this case, you can define an alternative page (Figure 3.98). On the Design Definition page (Notion 11), define an alternative page and an identifier for the alternative page to be placed in the $page_suffix. Each alternative page will have identical page identification to the base page, except that the page number is appended with an alternative page suffix, *in brackets*, to denote the type of alternative page. By declaring multiple types of alternative pages in the Design Definition, you can illustrate multiple alternatives per page.

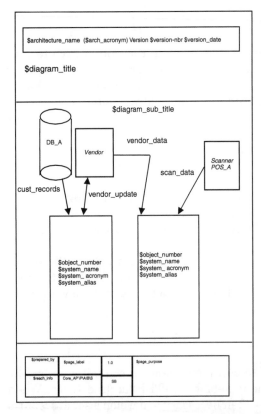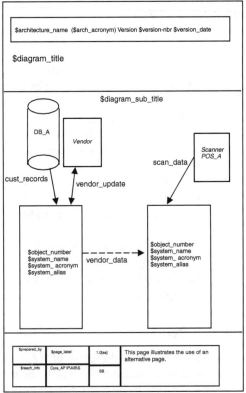

FIGURE 3.98 This is an example of defining an alternative page to support a scenario.

A TBB with alternative pages is read as follows:

1. The base pages are a TBB scenario.
2. For the first alternative page identifier, replace the base pages with the alternative pages and read the resulting mix of base pages and alternative pages as a TBB scenario.
3. Repeat steps 1 and 2 for each alternative page identifier.

Since an alternative page is a substitute for the base page, it will normally have the same off-page connectors as the base page.

Although alternative pages enable you to create multiple complete sets of alternative architectures within one drawing, such as for every page for which there is a substitute, this is not the intent. The intent of alternative pages is to avoid creating additional drawings when only a few items on a few pages are in doubt and you want to present scenarios with economy of effort.

Using alternative pages inappropriately can create confusion with regard to cut-out diagrams, especially if you want to show portions of a base page with its alternatives on the same cut-out diagram. To eliminate ambiguity, when using alternative page objects on a cut-out, the alternative page objects should be grouped with a null-titled list that identifies the alternative page identifier.

The base page and all alternative pages can still be functionally distinguished by the specification of $diagram_title, $sub_diagram_title, and $page_purpose. Each alternative page should be positioned in the EAB based on its fully qualified page identifier of $arch\_acronym\$version\_nbr\$section\_id$sect_suffix\ $subsection\_id \$page\_nbr$page_suffix. By concatenating the alternative page brackets with logical page parentheses, you can create alternative logical pages. In this case, only the components of the logical page that are different need an alternative page defined.

Highlighting Changes

On TBB drawings, it is highly desirable to distinguish (highlight) the changes that have been made relative to the AIB EAB. Table 3.11 summarizes how to communicate changes in different situations. If the TBB is a baseline (initial) drawing, the change notation rules need not be followed because the entire

TABLE 3.11 Communicating Changes

Core Diagram Change Situation	Method to Highlight Changes
Addition or change of data variable	Underline the data variable.
Deletion of data variable	X the data variable.
Addition of a new object	Footnote, endnote, or annotate the object as new.
Deletion of any object	X the object.

blueprint is an *add*. Once the TBB is promoted to AIB status, change notations should not be included on the AIB drawing.

Notion 60. Roles and Responsibilities

EAB team members must be assigned the roles and responsibilities listed in Table 3.12. One team member may assume multiple roles or take on multiple responsibilities; conversely, a role or responsibility may be assigned to multiple team members. Managers of distributed EABs must hierarchically coordinate these roles across EABs.

Notion 61. Architecture or Design?

As stated in Notion 1, there is a fine but ill-defined line as to where architecture ends and design begins. EAB, as presented in the prior 60 notions, has made explicit choices to clearly draw that line. Nevertheless, there are three special situations for which you may choose to move that line:

1. **Transaction Layout Definition.** As presented, the functional specification for the transactions that compose data flows (Notion 33: Transaction Functional Specifications) does not include the definition of the message layouts. Is this an architectural issue or a design issue? If the architecture team doesn't do it, who will?
2. **Internal API Definition.** Who is responsible for the rigorous definition of internally defined API sets? If your architecture will include an internally defined API to enable information movement between your own applications, is the definition of that API set an architecture problem or a design

TABLE 3.12   EAB Roles and Responsibilities

EAB Role	EAB Responsibility
Team Leader	Senior architect with overall responsibility and accountability for the delivery of the EAB.
Architect	Member of the team with responsibility for developing one or more components of the blueprint.
Librarian	Member of the team responsible for coordinating and managing the EAB as an integrated object being worked on by multiple team members.
Dictionarian	Member of the team responsible for coordination and management of the dictionary.
Functional Specification Manager	Member of the team responsible for coordination and management of the functional specifications.

problem? If it is an architecture issue, you need to create a User Defined Functional Specification (Notion 57) to house it.

3. **Application Structure Definition.** Who is responsible for the megalevel design of each application? To meet architectural requirements, do applications need to be designed in a specific way, or does architecture end with the definition of the IT components that touch the application at its boundaries? As presented, the application architecture ends with the allocation of application layers to configured platforms, full definition of each application layer ($al1, $al2, and $al3), the definition of the application's relationships to the configured platform, and interoperability definition through service paths. Is this sufficient, or in a given case is an Application Functional Specification (Notion 57) necessary to provide the detail needed to assure alignment between the architecture and the application design?

Notion 62. Reconciling EAB

Table 3.13 reconciles EAB with the definition of an engineering blueprint. EAB finally brings the integrity of engineering blueprints to IT architecture work. Figure 3.99 reconciles EAB with the other cells of the Index Architecture Framework (Figure 2.3). It shows how the EAB cells integrate with the other cells. Figure 3.100 provides a one-page EAB cheatsheet with all the EAB icons. Table 3.14 provides an index into all of the notions used in this chapter to teach EAB.

TABLE 3.13   EAB Reconciliation

Engineering Blueprint Requirement	EAB Equivalent
Front Matter	Front Matter
Diagrams	Core Section
	System Block Diagrams
	Platform Diagrams
	Interoperability Diagrams
	Function Diagrams
	Cut-Out Diagrams
Bill of Materials	Dictionary Bill of Materials
Functional Specifications	Annotation Functional Specification
	Database Functional Specification
	Detail Functional Specification
	Network Functional Specification
	Portability Functional Specification
	Scalability Functional Specification
	Transaction Functional Specification
	User Group Functional Specification
	User-Defined Functional Specification

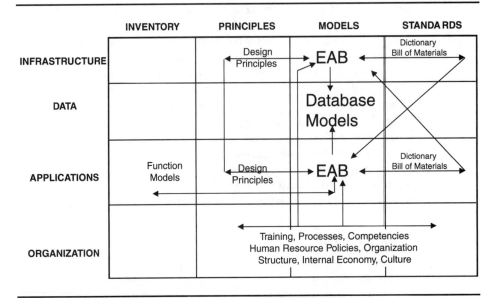

FIGURE 3.99   Reconciling EAB with the Index Architecture Framework. This figure illustrates how the EAB cells relate to the other architecture cells.

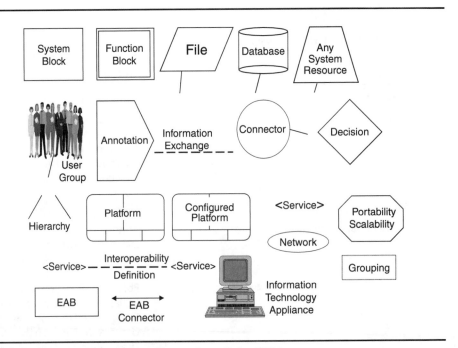

FIGURE 3.100   EAB Cheatsheet illustrating all the EAB icons.

TABLE 3.14 Subject Index to Numbered Notions

Notion Number	Notion Title	Notion Number	Notion Title
1	Overview	2	More Basic Ideas
3	Audience	4	Notational Rules
5	Cover Page	6	Page Layout
7	Logical Pages	8	Sections
9	Subsections	10	Design Definition
11	Front Matter	12	Separator Page
13	System Block Icon	14	Source and Sink System Blocks
15	System Block Nesting	16	File Icon
17	Database Icon	18	Database Functional Specification
19	Any System Resource Icon	20	User Group and Information Appliance Icons
21	User Group Functional Specification	22	Annotation Icon
23	Information Exchange Icon	24	Hierarchical Decomposition of System Blocks and Pages
25	Decorating	26	Horizontal Connectors
27	Decision Rule Icon	28	Dictionary Bill of Materials
29	Object Grouping	30	Titled Lists
31	Network Icon	32	Footnotes and Endnotes
33	Transaction Functional Specification	34	Platform Icon
35	Platform Diagram Page Numbering	36	Platform Diagram Relationships to (Sub)system Block Diagrams and Interoperability Diagrams
37	Platform Base Area Variables	38	Application Area Variables
39	Database Icon Revisited	40	Platform Diagram Use of Other EAB Icons and Notational Rules
41	Configured Platform Icon and Service Icon	42	Configured Platform Icon
43	Service Icon	44	Service Path
45	Global Application Layers	46	Interoperability Definition
47	User Group Icon Revisited	48	Scalability Functional Specifications and Portability Functional Specifications.
49	Interoperability Diagram Use of Other EAB Icons and Notational Rules	50	Function Icon
51	Cut-Out Diagrams	52	Horizontal Connecting of Objects across EABs
53	Vertical Connecting of System Block Icons or Function Block Icons across EABs	54	Vertical Connecting of Application Layers to System Block Icons across EABs
55	Core Diagram Referencing of Support Diagrams in other EABs	56	Distributed EABs
57	User-Defined Functional Specifications	58	Sketching
59	Scenarios	60	Roles and Responsibilities
61	Architecture or Design?	62	Reconciling EAB

CONCLUSION

Architecture gurus often tell eager and appreciative audiences what IT architecture is like, stating repeatedly and with great fanfare that IT architecture is like bridge design, or airplane design, or building design. Though they are absolutely right, they miss the substance of their own analogies. IT architecture is like those others mentioned, but what makes them architectures is that they all are represented through rigorous blueprinting.

The intent of this chapter was to bring rigorous blueprinting to IT architecture, so that IT architects really can be like airplane or building architects. EAB is rich in functionality and can be used to blueprint a wide variety of IT architectures from the very simple to the extremely complex. The EAB user must first customize and then standardize EAB for use within his or her IT environment.

The following chapters explain how to evolve EABs across time by the use of configuration management and how to design architectures with EAB to maximize maneuverability.

ENDNOTES

1. The fifth core diagram, cut-out, is manifestly different from the others and is fully explained in Notion 51.
2. Variables are normally defined the first time they are encountered. In subsequent encounters, they are not reexplained unless the new context demands supplementary clarification.
3. Additional system block icon variables are defined in Notion 53.
4. Additional database icon variables are defined in Notion 39.
5. The logic of atomic diagrams is fully explained when we discuss the cut-out subsection (Notion 51).
6. Cut-out diagrams, discussed in Notion 51, are a way to provide an object-centric view of an architecture.
7. Using connector icons to link across multiple EABs is explained in Notion 52.
8. See Endnote 6.
9. The business model functional decomposition is, likewise, the source of functions for the function lists that are placed on (sub)system blocks, as well as the $func variable on $all on platforms and configured platforms.

CHAPTER 4

Configuration
Management

EABs have to be created, executed, stored, and revised. To enable extreme business maneuverability, EABs must be able to go through rapid, efficient, and effective configuration management. In most IT organizations today, architecture drawings are not blueprints; they are throwaway sketches. Since they offer no persistent value, there is no need for change management. Each architectural effort is another desert start. The usual gang of suspects is gathered together again in a room to again play the game "what is the current architecture?" This is a time-consuming, expensive, and wasteful process. Architects spend most of their time in tiresome meetings during which they mull over vague sketches and debate what is, rather than crafting what will be.

EABs, to the contrary, are active models that direct the IT architecture and prescribe exactly what is to be done. They do not mirror the business systems; the business systems mirror the EABs. This is not a minor point. To enable IT agility, the blueprints must always be an accurate representation of the system reality. This means that your blueprints become your levers for hypercompetitive behavior, demanding that, for the first time, structured configuration management be applied to IT architecture drawings.

Configuration management (CM) is the well-established discipline of orderly change control. It is generally applied to complicated collections of objects that have complex interrelationships that must be evolved in synchronization to maintain the integrity of the whole. CM is routinely applied to application development release management, where a myriad of software objects must be coordinated and synchronized. CM encompasses four broad areas of change administration:

- Identification of each object that is part of the collection and its interobject relationships
- Change control of individual objects and cross-object change synchronization
- Collection status reporting
- Collection auditing

A set of objects under configuration management that are coordinated and synchronized at a point of time are said to be *baselined*. The process of configuration management is administered through a *change control board*. For an IT architecture community, the change control board would normally be a business unit architecture council.

The inevitable question that arises is, Which changes must go through the formal configuration management process? The answer is: any change that materially alters any component of an EAB. Cosmetic changes can go through an expedited process that simply maintains the EAB. Material alterations, especially material alterations that impact cross-EAB interfaces, must go through complete review and approval. Failure to do this will compromise the integrity of your blueprints and destroy the advantage to be gained through the blueprinting initiative.

In a later section of this chapter, we will argue that IT-based hypercompetition is, in its essence, a game of who can execute architecture configuration management with superior speed and accuracy. The competitor who can execute superior architecture configuration management will present his or her opponents with an ever-increasing deteriorating situation due to their inability to match architectural change cycle times.

In the following sections, we will walk through configuration management in four different and representative EAB situations. You cannot implement blueprinting without implementing configuration management. They come together, because it only makes sense to implement EAB if you are going to maintain the blueprints in a state of currency; and it only makes sense to perform configuration management on objects worth keeping current and accurate.

The purpose of this analysis is not to prescribe a specific configuration management formula but to illustrate the nuances involved in managing the evolution of EABs. The inherent complexity of IT architecture creates challenging change control problems. Understanding the subtleties will expedite the development of your own customized and comprehensive CM plan.

DEFINITIONS

In applying configuration management to EAB, we will introduce a number of new concepts. The following definitions are helpful in understanding the next four sections and analyzing Figures 4.1 through 4.4.

Change Agent

A change agent is anyone or any role in the organization that can initiate a change to the IT systems that could impact the architecture. Architecture initiatives are generally motivated by some combination of the following three atomic change drivers:

1. New business functionality cannot be satisfied within the constraints of the current IT architecture.
2. New technology or other architectural changes could be introduced into the IT architecture that would enable it to perform existing business functionality in a superior manner.
3. New technology or other architectural changes could be introduced into the IT architecture that would preposition the architecture to be able to do 1 or 2 better in the future. This equates to making an option investment.

The resulting effort to implement the initiative is referred to as an *initiative architecture project*.

Architecture of Record

The architecture of record (AOR) is the baseline of the architecture framework that you have chosen and that you use to govern your IT architecture. Though the individual objects within the AOR will be dispersed across the organization with multiple owners, this defines a point-in-time integrity for the whole AOR. For illustration purposes, Figures 4.1 through 4.4 continue the assumption that you have chosen the Index Architecture Framework (Figure 2.3).

AOR EABs

AOR EABs comprise the set of all EABs that make up the applications model cell of the AOR. Each EAB is referred as an AOR EAB.

To-Be-Built EAB

A to-be-built EAB (TBB EAB) is a proposed EAB, reflecting the changes necessary for implementing the new requirements driven by the originating business initiative. Generally, there are multiple possible solutions to the business initiative, and the TBB EAB set is packaged into a set of scenarios for evaluation and selection.

Transaction To-Be-Built EAB

The transaction to-be-built EAB (XACTION TBB EAB) is the same as the to-be-built EAB just described, except that the domain of the blueprint is limited to the impacted portion of the EAB. The resulting EAB contains only a subview of the entire EAB.

Approved TBB EAB

This is a complete replacement TBB EAB; it is the "finalist" from the scenario evaluation and selection process. An approved TBB EAB exists in one of two states:

1. **To implement.** The approved TBB EAB has been handed off to the development organization for construction.
2. **Implemented.** The approved TBB EAB has completed the construction process and has been completed.

Approved TransactionTBB EAB

An approved transaction (XACTION) TBB EAB is the subview TBB EAB that was the finalist from the scenario evaluation and selection process. An approved XACTION TBB EAB exists in one of two states:

1. **To implement.** The approved XACTION TBB EAB has been handed off to the development organization for construction.
2. **Implemented.** The approved XACTION TBB EAB has completed the construction process and thus has been completed.

SIMPLE CONFIGURATION MANAGEMENT

In the four change management cases that are examined in the following sections, it is assumed that a baselined AOR EAB already exists. The change management process executes against established AOR EABs. If that is not the case, a one-time start-up process (not illustrated) would have to be executed to establish the AOR EAB baseline.

Figure 4.1 presents a relatively simple configuration management case. What distinguishes this case are the following attributes:

- The impact of the initiative is constrained to a single AOR EAB.
- The impacted AOR EAB is completely self-contained. It is not loosely coupled, it does not use reference EABs, and it is not a component in a distributed EAB.
- The change process is single-threaded. Only one initiative at a time goes though the change management process from start to finish.
- The AOR EAB is revised in its entirety. The final approved and implemented TBB EAB will completely replace the exiting AOR EAB.

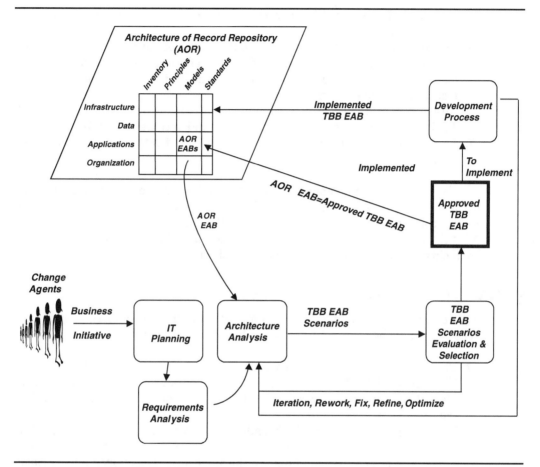

FIGURE 4.1 Simple EAB configuration management. This figure illustrates the evolution of an EAB in the simplest case.

Read Figure 4.1 as follows:

1. Change agents submit business initiatives to the IT planning process.
2. A requirements analysis is made to define the needs that must be fulfilled.
3. Architecture analysis is performed to define the changes that must be made to the AOR EAB. A set of scenario TBB EABs are developed. Each TBB EAB is a complete replacement to the AOR EAB.
4. An architecture evaluation and selection process is executed to choose the finalist TBB EAB. Problems discovered during evaluation will send the TBB EAB back to the architecture analysis step for rework. (Architecture

evaluation is discussed later in this chapter in the section entitled Architecture Evaluation.)

5. The finalist TBB EAB is promoted to the status of approved TBB EAB and turned over to the development organization for implementation. Problems discovered during development will send the TBB EAB back to the architecture analysis step for rework.

6. After completion of the development construction process, the approved TBB EAB replaces the current AOR EAB and becomes the AOR EAB.

7. The next business initiative is taken off the input work queue; the process continues ad infinitum.

Configuration management in this situation is considered relatively simple because the change management and control process is single-threaded; the EAB of concern is isolated; and the TBB EAB is a complete replacement for the AOR EAB. Though this situation is rarely the case, it serves the purpose of introducing key ideas and framing the basic change management process.

MODERATE CONFIGURATION MANAGEMENT

Figure 4.2 presents a moderately complex configuration management case. What distinguishes this case are the following attributes:

- The impact of the initiative is constrained to a single AOR EAB.
- The impacted AOR EAB is completely self-contained. It is not loosely coupled, it does not use reference EABs, and it is not a component in a distributed EAB.
- The change process is multithreaded. Multiple initiatives go though the change management process concurrently from start to finish. Initiative projects do not necessarily finish in the same order that they started. Each initiative project must be fully aware and cognizant of all the others.
- Each finalist TBB EAB is only an update to the AOR EAB; it is not a complete replacement. Each initiative TBB EAB equates to a transaction that encompasses only a subview of the AOR EAB about which it is concerned.

Read Figure 4.2 as follows:

1. Change agents submit business initiatives to the IT planning process.
2. A requirements analysis is made to define the needs that must be fulfilled.
3. Architecture analysis is performed to identify the changes that must be made to the AOR EAB. The requirements are applied to the AOR EAB, and a relevant subview of the AOR EAB, with the initiative changes, is developed. A set of scenario TBB EABs are developed but are constrained to the subviews. Only the portions of the AOR EAB that are impacted are in-

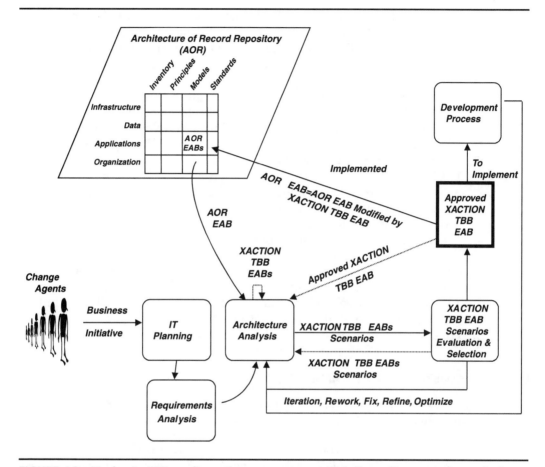

FIGURE 4.2   Moderate EAB configuration management. This figure illustrates the evolution of an EAB when multiple architectural changes occur simultaneously.

cluded. The approved TBB EAB will eventually become an update transaction against the AOR EAB.

Since multithreading occurs against the same AOR EAB, the architecture analysis must be aware of all other initiative projects going through the process so that their impact can be assessed. This is illustrated in Figure 4.2 by the dotted arrow lines. To restate, while doing architecture analysis for Initiative N, it is necessary to be fully aware of all other initiatives in all other steps of the process, in particular: other initiatives currently in architecture analysis; other initiatives going through evaluation and selection; and other initiatives that are in implementation.

1. An architecture evaluation and selection process is executed to choose the finalist TBB EAB. Problems discovered during evaluation will send the TBB EAB back to the architecture analysis step for rework. (Architecture evaluation is discussed later in this chapter in the section entitled Architecture Evaluation.)
2. The finalist TBB EAB is promoted to the status of approved Transaction (XACTION) TBB EAB and turned over to the development organization for implementation. Problems discovered during development will send the XACTION TBB EAB back to the architecture analysis step for rework.
3. After completion of the development construction process, the approved XACTION TBB EAB updates the current AOR EAB. It does not replace the AOR in its entirely. It is an update transaction against the AOR EAB that has taken into account all the other initiatives in progress and the anticipated order of completion.
4. The process continues ad infinitum.

Configuration management in this situation is considered moderately complex because: the change management and control process is multithreaded; the EAB of concern is isolated but must have full knowledge of all other initiatives against the same AOR EAB; and the TBB EAB is an update to the AOR EAB that is ordered relative to all other initiative projects.

COMPLEX CONFIGURATION MANAGEMENT

Figure 4.3 presents a complex configuration management case. What distinguishes this case are the following attributes:

- The impact of the initiative is across multiple AOR EABs.
- The set of impacted AOR EABs includes both loosely coupled and reference EABs.
- The change process is multithreaded. Multiple initiatives against each AOR EAB go though the change management process concurrently from start to finish. Initiative projects will not necessarily finish in the same order that they started. Each initiative project must be fully aware and cognizant of all the others.
- Each finalist TBB EAB is only an update to the AOR EAB; it is not a complete replacement. Each TBB EAB equates to a transaction that encompasses only a subview of the AOR EAB about which it is concerned.

Read Figure 4.3 as follows:

1. Change agents submit business initiatives to the IT planning process.
2. A requirements analysis is made to identify the needs that must be fulfilled.

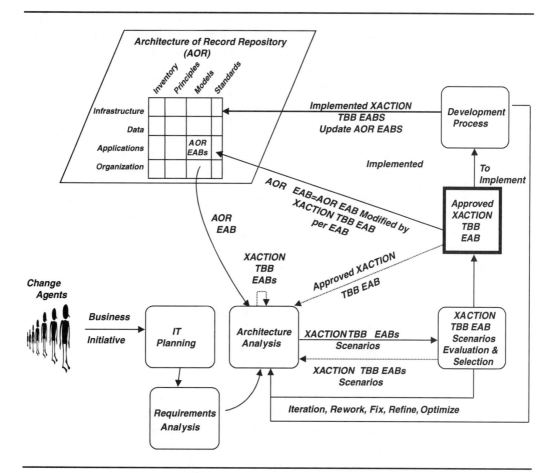

FIGURE 4.3 Complex EAB configuration management. This figure illustrates the evolution of an EAB when configuration management is applied to loosely coupled EABs.

3. Architecture analysis is performed to identify the changes that must be made to the set of AOR EABs. The requirements are applied to the AOR EAB; a relevant subview of each impacted AOR EAB, with the initiative changes, is developed. A set of scenario TBB EABs are developed for each impacted AOR EAB but are constrained to the subview. Only the portions of the AOR EAB that are impacted are included. The approved TBB EAB will eventually become an update transaction against the AOR EAB.

Since multithreading occurs against each participating AOR EAB, the architecture analysis must be aware of all other initiative projects going through the process so that their impact can be assessed. This is illustrated in Figure 4.3

by the dotted arrow lines. To restate, while doing architecture analysis for Initiative N, it is necessary to be fully aware of all other initiatives in all other steps of the process, in particular: other initiatives currently in architecture analysis; other initiatives going through evaluation and selection; and other initiatives that are in implementation for each impacted AOR EAB.

4. An architecture evaluation and selection process is executed to choose the finalist TBB EABs. Problems discovered during evaluation will send the TBB EABs back to the architecture analysis step for rework. (Architecture evaluation is discussed later in this chapter in the section entitled Architecture Evaluation.)

5. The finalist TBB EABs are promoted to the status of approved Transaction (XACTION) TBB EABs and turned over to the development organization for implementation. Problems discovered during development will send the XACTION TBB EABs back to the architecture analysis step for rework.

6. After completion of the development construction process, each approved XACTION TBB EAB updates its current AOR EAB. It does not replace its AOR in its entirety. It is an update transaction against the AOR EAB that has taken into account all the other initiatives in progress and the anticipated order of completion. Whether the updates will need to be queued for a concomitant update depends on the nature of the changes.

7. The process continues ad infinitum.

Configuration management in this situation is considered complex because: the change management and control process is multithreaded; there are multiple EABs that must have coordinated changes made, and each must have full knowledge of all other initiatives against its baseline AOR EAB and any impacted reference EABs; and each XACTION TBB EAB is an update to an AOR EAB that must be ordered relative to all other initiative projects.

VERY COMPLEX CONFIGURATION MANAGEMENT

Figure 4.4 presents a very complex configuration management case. What distinguishes this case are the following attributes:

- The impact of the initiative is across a distributed EAB (Figure 4.5).
- The set of impacted AOR EABs includes both loosely coupled and reference EABs.
- The change process is multithreaded. Multiple initiatives against the distributed EAB go through the change management process concurrently from start to finish. Initiative projects will not necessarily finish in the same order that they started. Each initiative project must be fully aware and cognizant of all the others.

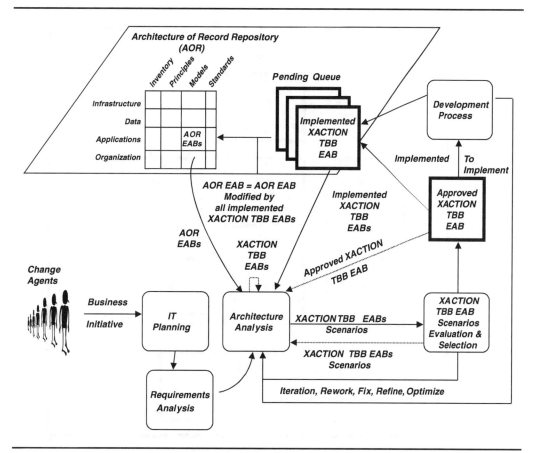

FIGURE 4.4   Very complex EAB configuration management. This figure illustrates the evolution of an EAB when configuration management is applied to distributed EABs.

- Each finalist TBB EAB is only an update to the AOR EAB; it is not a complete replacement. Each TBB EAB equates to a transaction that only encompasses a subview of the AOR EAB about which it is concerned.

Read Figure 4.4 as follows:

1. Change agents submit business initiatives to the IT planning process.
2. A requirements analysis is made to identify the needs that must be fulfilled.
3. Architecture analysis is performed to understand the changes that must be made to the distributed AOR EABs, as well as completed changes that have not yet been posted to the distributed AOR EAB. The requirements are ap-

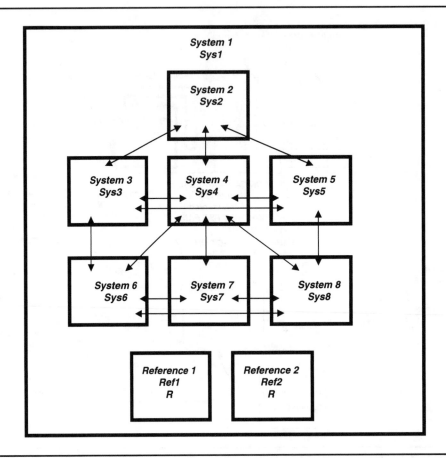

FIGURE 4.5   Distributed EAB. This figure illustrates a distributed EAB with reference EABs.

plied to the distributed AOR EAB and a relevant composite subview of the distributed AOR EAB, with the initiative changes, is developed. A set of scenario TBB EABs are developed that are constrained to the subschema view. Only the impacted portions of the AOR EAB are included. In essence, the approved TBB EAB will eventually become an update transaction against the distributed AOR EAB.

Since multithreading occurs against each participating AOR EAB, the architecture analysis step must be aware of all other initiative projects going through the process so that their impact can be assessed. To restate, while doing architecture analysis for Initiative N, it is necessary to be fully aware of all other initiatives in all other steps of the process, in particular: other initiatives currently in architecture analysis; other initiatives going through evaluation and selection; and other initiatives that are in implementation.

1. An architecture evaluation and selection process is executed to choose the finalist TBB EAB. Problems discovered during evaluation will send the TBB EAB back to the architecture analysis step for rework. (Architecture evaluation is discussed later in this chapter in the section entitled Architecture Evaluation.)
2. The finalist TBB EAB is promoted to the status of approved Transaction (XACTION) TBB EAB and turned over to the development organization for implementation. Problems discovered during development will send the XACTION TBB EAB back to the architecture analysis step for rework.
3. After completion of the development construction process, the approved XACTION TBB EAB is placed in a pending queue for a synchronized update to the distributed EAB. It is an update transaction against the distributed AOR EAB that has taken into account all the other initiatives in progress and the anticipated order of completion.
4. The process continues ad infinitum.

Configuration management in this situation is considered complex because: the change management and control process is multithreaded; there are multiple EABs that must have coordinated changes made, and each must have full knowledge of all other initiatives against its baseline distributed AOR EAB; the XACTION TBB EAB is an update to a distributed AOR EAB that must be ordered relative to all other initiative projects.

IMPLICATIONS FOR CONFIGURATION MANAGEMENT DESIGN

An analysis of the preceding four examples would indicate the following implications for the design of your architecture configuration management system:

1. Configuration management is a sophisticated process that requires thoughtful design and planning. All EAB evolution is managed through the change management process. Change management must therefore be implemented concurrently with EAB.
2. Visibility of the status of all EABs is fundamental to configuration management success. Status reporting, status tracking, and access to work-in-progress blueprints must be easily accessible to all members of the architecture community. Configuration management must manage the dependency relationships among all TBB EABs.
3. Just as the architecture of each system has to be rigorously defined, the architecture for your set of EABs has to be defined. The change control board has the responsibility for defining the set of blueprints for the domain of the

board and the evolution of that domain as changes occur to the system set. This implies that the change control board defines the meta-architecture; that is, the definition of each EAB, the definition of each reference EAB, the definition of loosely coupled EABs, and the definition of distributed EABs.

4. The strategic value of the blueprints is directly proportional to the accuracy and currency of their representations. Auditing procedures must be put in place to statistically validate the accuracy of the blueprints.

In the preceeding examples a blueprint was developed (subject to revision) in one step. An alternative model and more typical approach is to have the blueprint developed in stages, in which case, a quality gate would exist at the completion of each level of the drawings. For example, if you were following a structured development life cycle, a conceptual model may be completed at the end of the business requirements phase, a function model at the completion of the system requirements phase, and logical/physical models during the design phase. Each level of the blueprint would not be started until the prior level was approved. This staggered approach would match the movement of the initiative through the development process. Obviously, you would have to create a different configuration process to manage this alternate architecture development process.

In summary, what is required is a configuration management process that defines the set of architecture drawings that will be controlled; assures currency and accuracy of all drawings; and assures visibility of all drawings as they move between the various change management states. If you fail to do this, the quality of your drawings will rapidly deteriorate to the point at which they become useless.

Perhaps, most important is that you must address a very difficult question: Are you even doing IT architecture? Many companies use the word architecture to describe some of their IT activities, which under scrutiny, reveal that nowhere in the development process do they create and document a directive and prescriptive statement of what the architecture for the infrastructure or applications will be. Rather than an architecture being explicitly designed, it just emerges as an application bumps it way through the development process. If you are currently engaging in emergent architecture, implementing EAB will be a much more difficult task. Not only will you have to replace sketches with blueprints and implement configuration management, you will first have to teach the organization what a directive and prescriptive architecture is and develop a process that creates directive architectures to replace haphazard emergence.

CONFIGURATION MANAGEMENT AND ORGANIZATION STRUCTURE

Within a company, architecture groups can be organized and governed in one of three basic structures:

1. **Centralized.** All architecture groups report to one central management structure.
2. **Dispersed.** Architecture groups are dispersed across business units and operate independently.
3. **Integrated.** Architecture groups are dispersed across business units but engage in extensive cooperation with each other through shared governance.

Figure 4.6 illustrates an integrated structure from an organizational hierarchy perspective. Each business unit has its own development groups with architecture teams that support them. A business unit architecture council governs the business unit architecture work and serves as the change control board for the business unit. A central architecture group provides corporate leadership in architecture governance.

Figure 4.7 illustrates the interlocking governance structure. The corporate architecture group interlocks with the business unit architecture council that interlocks with the architecture groups that interlock with the development groups. Architecture is therefore both vertically and horizontally coordinated across the enterprise, and change management can be coordinated within and across business units as required.

Of particular importance is the interlocking of the architecture groups with the development groups. During the implementation phase of architecture, an on-site architect must be assigned to the development team to manage daily interpretations and approve minor changes. Major changes proposed during implementation require recycling through the formal configuration management process.

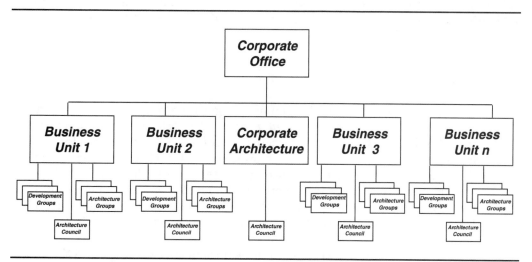

FIGURE 4.6   Organization structure. This figure illustrates an integrated organization structure for architecture groups that are spread across a multibusiness unit enterprise.

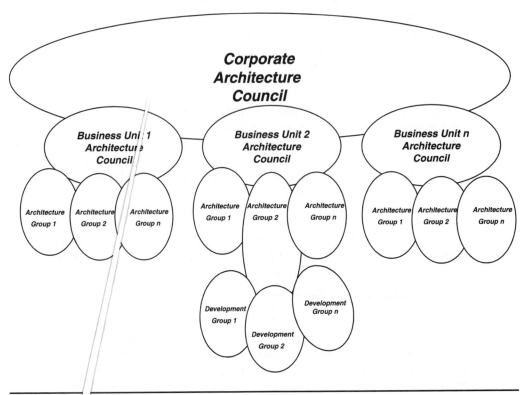

FIGURE 4.7 Interlocking governance structure. Change control can be managed vertically and horizontally through the enterprise by virtue of interlocking architecture councils.

ARCHITECTURE EVALUATION

The evaluation and selection step of configuration management is often referred to as the *architecture review process*. The focal point for the review is the EAB. Failure to provide a structurally correct EAB is grounds for canceling the review and is evidence of architecture malpractice. Criticism of candidate architectures is performed by proposing changes to the TBB EAB. It is not sufficient just to criticize the blueprint; you must propose a superior alternative to the presented blueprint. Table 4.1 summarizes typical criteria for TBB EAB evaluation and the primary organizational reviewer for each domain of review.

Fundamental to a successful architectural evaluation process is the definition and enforcement of a compliance process. A compliance process most importantly defines:

TABLE 4.1 Architecture Review Criteria

Evaluation Criteria	Definition	Primary Reviewer
Meets business requirements.	TBB EAB meets all stated business requirements.	Application and Architecture Subject Matter Experts
Will it work?	TBB EAB will technically work.	Technical Evaluation Teams and Systems Engineering Groups
Enterprise architecture fit/impact	TBB EAB fit with other EABs.	Architecture Council
Cost efficiency and cost performance	TBB EAB meets cost objectives.	Architecture Council System Engineering Groups
OA&M	TBB EAB meets operational management requirements.	Systems Operations
Maneuverability	TBB EAB will provide life cycle agility.	Architecture Council
Network impact	TBB EAB can be handled by communications networks.	Network Engineering
Architecture compliance	TBB EAB is in compliance with other architecture framework cells.	Architecture Council
Design elegance	TBB EAB is well designed.	Architecture Council
Portability, scalability, and reconfigurability	TBB EAB can be evolved.	Architecture council
Competencies/processes	Necessary competencies and processes exist to deploy and operate architecture.	Architecture Council
Adherence to vision architecture	TBB architecture moves the organization closer to its vision architecture.	Architecture Council

1. The circumstances and scheduling of reviews
2. The review criteria
3. Approval documentation
4. Rejection documentation
5. Executive exception override process for rejections
6. Enforcement methodology

Demanding particular attention is the enforcement methodology. If the compliance process has no teeth, it will have no adherence. While voluntary adherence is, of course, best of all, the universal experience of trying to introduce rigor into IT organizations is that necessity and economic penalties have a positive impact in motivating adherence.

I would therefore recommend that you consider in your compliance design:

1. Development stage building permits. Funding is released only upon the successful completion of a stage review for the next stage.
2. Organizations that ignore, circumvent or otherwise violate the review/approval process should be slapped with an architecture environment pollution tax. One way to implement this would be to apply the tax against the annual salary increase/bonus budget for the offending management team.

The simple truth is that your architecture rules deserve the same level and seriousness of compliance that your financial rules enjoy. You do not permit people to violate your financial control and integrity procedures and, with the exact same seriousness, you should not permit them to violate your architecture procedures.

Consolidated Time-Lapse TBBs

In a hypercompetitive environment, the architecture area is a beehive of activity. Therefore, it is necessary to assure that the onslaught of TBB architectures does not lead to the disintegration of the environment. It is recommended that the architecture review staff maintain time-lapse views (every six months) of the collective impact of approved but not yet implemented TBBs. This answers the critical question, What will our future AIB AOR look like once all the TBB changes are applied? In this way, the architecture community can envision the future AOR and assess the favorable or unfavorable impacts of pending TBBs. Advantage in a hypercompetitive environment is a function of coordination, not of individuality. The periodic creation of consolidated time-lapsed future views will facilitate high-quality evaluations and minimize inconsistencies, contradictions, incompleteness, inefficiencies, redundancies, and gaps.

Vision Architecture and TBB Architecture Evaluation

Most organizations have a *vision architecture,* which depicts a highly desirable future state, a target for all architectural efforts. Each TBB architecture should move the organization closer to that vision state. Of particular importance in appraising each scenario TBB blueprint, then, is an assessment of the degree to which the scenario TBB architecture yields progress toward that vision architecture.

Vision architectures are normally depicted in one of three flavors:

1. **Conceptual (sketch) vision architecture.** The desired future state is portrayed in the format of a sketch.
2. **Functional vision architecture.** The desired future state is portrayed in the format of a functional architecture.

3. **Logical vision architecture.** The desired future state is portrayed in the format of a logical architecture.

   Vision architectures are rarely portrayed as physical architectures, because of the practical problem of making specific technological commitments to an architecture that will not be implemented for years.

   Regardless of the format of presentation, of particular importance is an analysis of the TBB architecture for adherence to the architectural principles. The logic of architecture principles is that by adhering to the principles, new architectures will be developed that better meet organizational objectives. If TBB architectures are ignoring the architectural principles, then either the principles are poor and irrelevant and need to be revised or the TBB architecture should be rejected because it will detour you from your principle-driven vision state.

CONFIGURATION MANAGEMENT AS HYPERCOMPETITIVE STRATEGY

As surprising as it may seem, mundane and unexciting architecture configuration management is the battlefield of Information Age-based hypercompetition. Who will win and who will lose reduces to who can perform architecture configuration management process with superior speed, efficiency, and effectiveness. To accept this unexpected assertion, it is necessary to understand the military strategy concept called "disrupting the OODA." Figure 4.8 illustrates what a military strategist would call an OODA. When you take a military action against your opponent, to react, your opponent must execute four steps:

1. He or she must observe (O) what you have done.
2. He or she must orient (O) him or herself to what you have done. He or she must decide its implications and the degree and manner of response.
3. He or she must design (D) a response.
4. He or she must act (A); that is, execute the designed response.

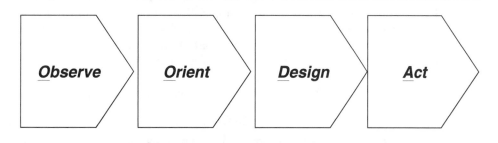

FIGURE 4.8   OODA. A military strategist takes actions to win by disrupting his or her opponent's OODA.

Military strategy often focuses on disrupting the opponent's OODA. This means answering the following questions:

1. Can I execute my initiatives so fast that my opponent is overwhelmed with a series of initiatives to respond to before he or she has even responded to the first? In other words, can I overwhelm him or her with superior cycle time?
2. Can I present my opponent with a staggered set of initiatives so that his or her partial response through his or her OODA is invalidated? In other words, can I make my opponent continually restart him- or herself without ever completing the OODA process? Obviously, in this case, the opponent loops without ever delivering a valid response.
3. Can I present my opponent with a staggered or overlapping set of initiatives so that each one tempts him or her to rework his or her in-progress OODA? In other words, can I cause him or her to thrash and never deliver any response?

So, in military strategy, disruption of an opponent's OODA means understanding the process an opponent goes through to respond to turbulence; and executing a carefully coordinated and purposefully staggered and overlapping series of actions to disrupt the response capability. If done successfully, the opponent is confronted with a hopelessly deteriorating situation. Worst of all in this situation is the psychological impact of recognizing his or her inability to cope due to the crafted dismantling of his or her OODA process. As Sun Tzu taught:

> *Overcome your opponents by dispiriting them rather than by battling with them. Overcome the opponent psychologically—cause them to lose spirit and direction so that even if the opponent's army is intact, it is useless.*

The architecture configuration management process is equivalent to the OODA. It is the process through which the business architecturally responds to marketplace disruptions and changes. If you can fundamentally execute the configuration management process better (faster, more accurately, cheaper, with greater agility, etc.), you can use that ability to disrupt your opponent's architecture configuration management process and leave him or her looping and drifting rather than responding.

Configuration management as hyper-competitor strategy means:

1. Can I execute my architectural initiatives so fast that my opponent is overwhelmed with a series of initiatives to respond to before he or she has even responded to the first? In other words, can I overwhelm him or her with superior cycle time?

2. Can I present him or her with a staggered set of initiatives so that his or her partial response through his or her architectural configuration management process is invalidated? In other words, can I make him or her continually restart him- or herself without ever completing the configuration management process? Obviously in this case, he or she loops without ever delivering a valid response.

3. Can I present him or her with a staggered or overlapping set of initiatives where each one tempts him or her to rework his or her in-progress process? In other words, can I cause him or her to thrash and never deliver any response?

You could view configuration management as merely an after-the-fact add-on to blueprinting, but actually it is a critical partner, because it is the process that puts blueprinting into motion. It is the process that permits you to use IT to disrupt not only the marketplace, but your opponent's ability to respond to your disruption. It is the process that destroys the collective adaptive capacity of your opponent.

By commanding the initiative in the OODA war of thrust and counterthrust configuration management, you command choice and you can manipulate uncertainty. By executing configuration management in a superior manner, your choices are:

1. Perform rapid experiments.
2. Implement big bets within timeframes hopelessly unachievable by your opponents.
3. Engage in a daily war of disruptive movement.
4. Reserve the right to play later; that is, let others undertake risky initiatives and have to play catch-up when and if they prove desirable.

By executing configuration management in a superior manner, you cause incredible uncertainty for your opponents. What will you do? When will you do it? How will I respond? This effectively repositions your opponent's planning view for the future from predictable to hopelessly ambiguous. It places your opponents on the horns of insoluble and friction-creating dilemmas.

Confronted with uncertainty, as a natural response, most people will automatically choose to wait. They will yearn for greater clarity before they will act. This is exactly what you want them to do. You want your opponents to put their OODA into idle while you proceed. You want them to stand still while you purposefully and aggressively maneuver.

As an alternative to waiting, to resolve the dilemmas that have been presented to them, your opponents will have to disperse their resources and efforts to cope with the puzzling set of possibilities. Since you know what you will do and they do not, you will be focused at the time and place of marketplace confrontation that you have chosen, whereas they will be dispersed. By virtue of being able to command choice, you maximize your concentration by scattering their resources to nonmaterial (secondary) activities.

CONCLUSION

By studying hypercompetition and the environmental turbulence routinely associated with it, one of the most interesting realizations is that turbulence is a very unevenly experienced phenomenon. Turbulence is an attribute of the recipient of an event, as opposed to being an attribute of the event. Whether something is disruptive, causes dislocation, upsets processes, causes friction, or in any other way is detrimental to the orderly processes of a business is entirely dependent on the reaction of the business to the event, as opposed to the inherent nature of the event.

The same initiative by a hypercompetitor can generate entirely different reactions by its opponents. One opponent, rigid and inflexible in its architecture change control process, is unable to respond; tremendous organizational friction emerges as everyone blames each other for the failure. Another competitor, agile and flexible, takes the initiative in stride and responds promptly and ruins the advantage period anticipated by the initiator. Thus, turbulence or nonturbulence is something within you, not something done to you. An event or an environment is not turbulent to you as long as you have the ability to promptly meet the new demands it presents to you.

By virtue of your architecture design processes and configuration management processes, the actions of your hyper-competitors can be matched or surpassed and you can reposition yourself from being the hyper-competitor's prey to being the hyper-competitive predator. In a hyper-competitive business world where information technology is the weaponry of combat, IT architecture configuration management is to business strategy as disruption of OODA is too military strategy. This is a most surprising and important insight that cannot be ignored and must be acted upon. An insight that will ultimately *separate the winners from the losers, the successes from the failures, the acquiring from the acquired, and the survivors from the rest.*

CHAPTER 5

Architecture Design for Extreme Maneuverability

The only reason to adopt blueprinting and to grant the blueprints a persistent life through configuration management is to enable your business to command the initiative on the hypercompetitive battlefield through extraordinary systems malleability. Unfortunately, blueprinting (Chapter 3) and configuration management (Chapter 4) are not all that's necessary to enable maximum malleability. You must add to the equation an architecture-design methodology that explicitly focuses on maneuverability, and integrates it with blueprinting and configuration management. Thus, blueprinting, configuration management, and design for extreme maneuverability form the trinity that assures that applications are built with the absolute maximum adaptive capabilities.

Blueprints will make inflexible designs obvious, but they can't prevent them from being created. The blueprinting technique is an abstract representation of your design decisions and so will represent poor design choices as well as good ones. Similarly, though configuration management efficiently moves an architecture through the change process (and during the review procedure makes poor designs apparent), it does not assure that an inflexible blueprint is not, a priori, being created. The malleability of architecture is ultimately a function of its design; therefore, you must select and integrate a design methodology that ensures architecture adaptability to create or react to turbulence.

This chapter presents a specific way to conduct the subset of the design steps that focus on maneuverability. It assumes that the design team has gathered all the requirements and that all team members have a clear understanding of what needs to be done. The design methodology focuses on how to make specific interoperability diagram choices to maximize adaptability for change.

ARCHITECTURE DESIGN FOR MANEUVERABILITY

As in Chapter 3, the unit of instruction here is a notion, used to convey an important idea or method. Notions are serially additive in meaning and thus should be read in sequential order. The notion set should be viewed as a methodology module that is plugged into your overall architecture design methodology. It assumes that EAB is used as the blueprinting system and that configuration management is used to oversee the evolution of the blueprints.

Notion 1. What Does Maneuverability Really Mean?

Extreme architecture maneuverability is the objective of hypercompetitive architecture design. Maneuverability (also called adaptability, flexibility, agility, and malleability) is a rich concept and conveys the following design imagery:

- It is the quality of a system that enables it to easily respond to change and variety.
- It is the robust capability of the architecture to deal with emerging variances from the as-is state.
- It is the capacity to take new and novel actions in response to new and novel circumstances in a timely and cost-efficient manner.
- It is the ability to respond to environmental disruption without collapse or disorganization.
- It is the ability to add, modify, and delete without causing disruption.
- It is the ability to be agile and nimble in response to fluctuations.
- It is the ability to alter form while maintaining stability and predictability of operations.

Maneuverability is a relative state; that is, an architecture, A_1, is more maneuverable than an alternative architecture, A_2, if the set of architectural choices available following A_1 includes the set of choices following A_2. In other words, A_1 permits all the moves that A_2 permits and more. Alternatively, we can say that architecture A_1 is more maneuverable than architecture A_2, even though it offers the same, different, or a fewer number of architectural moves, if the set of moves following A_1 have a greater probability of being needed and they offer superior robustness. So, relative maneuverability is not only a function of which comparative architecture permits more moves, it is a function of which architecture permits more highly valued and expected moves.

Maneuverability is not a single event, but an endless series of change events. To fully appreciate the concept of maneuverability, you must also take into account the ability of the architecture to repeatedly maneuver; this is called *architectural degrees of freedom*. For example, given that we are at architectural state A_0, the set of alternative moves we can make is called our *first degree of freedom.* Having made that move to architectural state A_1, we now have a second set of alternative moves, which represent our second degree of freedom. In summary, from a starting architectural position, there are n degrees of freedom for each possible architecture change path (Figure 5.1). To maximize maneuverability over time, you have to strike a balance between the immediate move that yields the best next architectural position to solve the immediate problem and the one that balances coping with the current problem and positioning for the best future degrees of freedom from which to choose.

Therefore, we suggest that IT architecture's maneuverability is both a very simple and a very complex concept: It is simple in that it meets the intuitive notion of the ability to change; it is complex in that it means balancing current move optimizations against future options. A design methodology for extreme maneuverability must provide mechanisms to make these trade-offs.

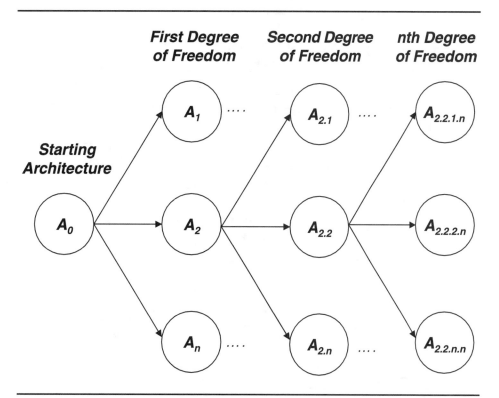

FIGURE 5.1   Degrees of architectural freedom. An architecture has n future degrees of freedom.

Notion 2. Interoperability Diagram Normalized Entity-Relationship Model

Figure 5.2 is a partial, normalized entity-relationship model that portrays the architectural relationships embodied in interoperability diagrams (Chapter 3: Notions 41 to 49). The figure illustrates the real-world complexity of designing for maneuverability. Every relationship is a joint that could be changed to enable maneuverability. Design for maneuverability is developed relative to this model. Figure 5.3 illustrates the notation used to represent relationships between entities in Figure 5.2, as follows:

1. An entity name within a box (Figure 5.3A) names an entity, or equivalently, a relational table.
2. An arrow connector between the two entities (Figure 5.3B) illustrates a one-to-many relationship between entities. The entity at the tail of the connector is the one in the relationship, and the entity at the arrow tip is the many.

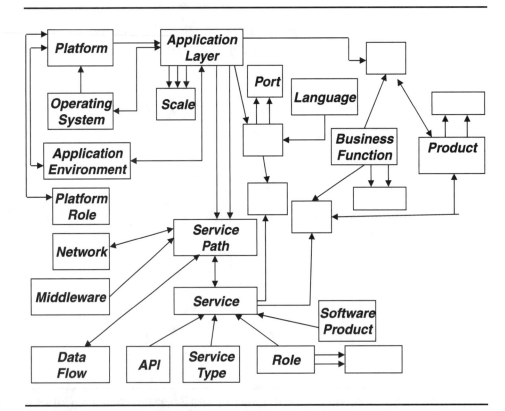

FIGURE 5.2 Interoperability diagram entity-relationship model illustrates the most important architectural relationships maintained in an interoperability diagram.

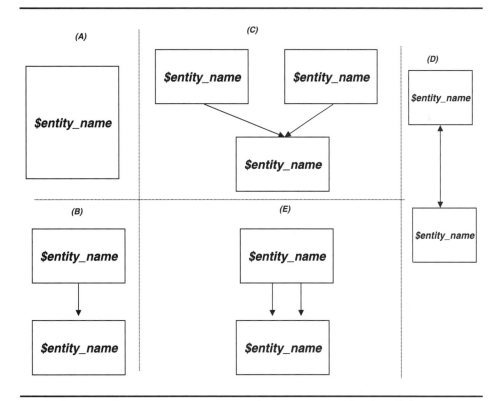

FIGURE 5.3   Entity relationship notations. The illustrated notational rules are applied in Figure 5.2.

3. A many-to-many relationship between entities is illustrated by multiple entities that engage in a one-to-many relationship with a junction record. Figure 5.3C illustrates a many-to-many relationship. The entity at the tips of the arrows is called a *junction record*. Alternatively, when the junction record does not store material data, a many-to-many relationship is illustrated with a connector line between two entities that has an arrow at each end (Figure 5.3D).

4. A special case of a many-to-many relationship is a recursive structure, where an entity engages in a many-to-many relationship with another entity of the same type. This is illustrated in Figure 5.3E.

Notion 3. Marriages and Spouses

The basic unit of maneuverability design is called a *marriage* (Figure 5.4). A marriage represents a single instance of interoperability between two applica-

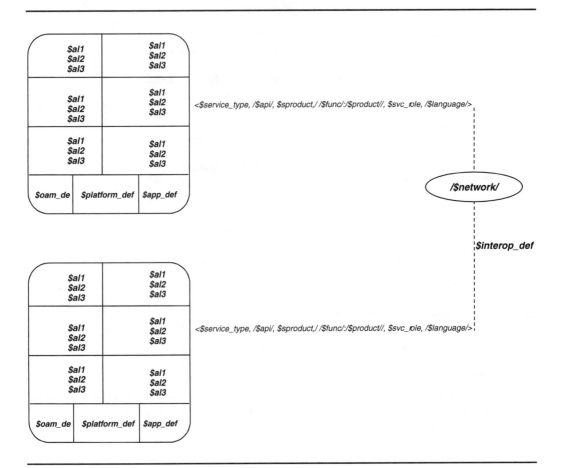

FIGURE 5.4   The basic unit of architecture design is a marriage.

tion layers on the same or different configured platforms. Each application layer involved in the marriage is called a *spouse*. Application layers may be polygamous. An application layer may be married in the following ways:

1. Multiple times to another application layer on the same or different platform.
2. Multiple times to different application layers on the same platform.
3. Multiple times to different application layers on different platforms.
4. Any combination of the three at the same time.

These marriages are defined in EAB through end-to-end service paths (Chapter 3: Notion 44). In defining these polygamous marriages, service and interoperability definitions may be completely different or used repeatedly. When two platforms have at least one end-to-end service path between them, we say that the platforms are *coupled*.

Design for extreme maneuverability equates to choosing a set of marriages that solves the immediate business problem, while balancing that solution with the maximum degrees of freedom for the architecture. Architecture design for maneuverability is therefore quite different and much more difficult than architecture design for a point-in-time problem. When solving a point-in-time problem, architecture design reduces to the selection of a set of marriages that optimally meet the business problem at a minimum lifetime cost of ownership. In contrast, when solving an architecture problem for maneuverability, you want a solution that solves the current problem but provides for maximum, net-present maneuver (see Notion 7).

Notion 4. Starting Point of Design for Extreme Maneuverability

In performing a design for extreme maneuverability, we assume the following:

- A set of design principles that promote maneuverability are in place.
- The business requirements have been identified and are understood.
- The standard components that may be used to create marriages are understood.
- Sketches have been completed that communicate the basic ways you intend to partition the application across platforms, allocate functions to platforms, and need to interoperate between application layers.
- The impacted AIB environment is understood.

Notion 5. Architecture Design for Extreme Maneuverability: Desert Start

To build a brand new application, a *desert start*, follow this process:

1. Choose a partition of an application and assign it to a platform that can serve in the necessary roles for that partition, such as a processing server, portable workstation, and so on.
2. For that platform, choose an application layer whose software layer definition matches the functions performed by the application.
3. Repeat steps 1 and 2 for another application partition that needs to interoperate with the first partition.
4. Create as many marriages as necessary between the two application layers to meet functionality requirements.
5. Repeatedly assign additional partitions to these two platforms; make marriages across all accumulated partitions until all marriages are completed.
6. Repeat steps 1 and 2.

7. Engage the application partition defined in step 6 in as many marriages as necessary with all existing application partitions.
8. Repeat steps 6 and 7 until the application is partitioned across all necessary platforms and all marriages are consummated.
9. Select an application outside of the problem application to which it is interfaced.
10. For each application partition of the interface application, create as many marriages as necessary to the problem application partitions.
11. Repeat steps 9 and 10 until all interfaces are resolved.

Obviously, in performing these steps, there is a great deal of iteration; the process is more spiral than linear.

At this point, with the resolution of all entity variables, you have created a scenario TBB architecture. The next task is to repeat steps 1 through 11 n times, and create n scenario TBB architectures. To judge which one offers the maximum adaptability over its lifetime, you'll have to analyze each from the perspective of net-present maneuver (see Notion 7).

Notion 6. Architecture Design for Extreme Maneuverability: Jungle Start

To change an existing application, called a *jungle start,* the process is driven by the type of change. Consider the following examples:

Addition of a new interface to the existing application. A new set of marriages must be consummated between the existing application partitions and the interface application.

A change to a marriage. The same type of marriage is required between two application layers, but you want to change the end-to-end service path and the interoperability definition. In this case, a new marriage with the desired service capability must be defined.

A change in language and API. You want to add a new language to an application partition and to have this language engage in interoperability. It is necessary to establish that this language is suitable for the platform and to establish a marriage for it with the required other application partitions.

For a jungle start, as for the desert start, you complete the design with a scenario TBB architecture, which you then evaluate against other scenario TBB architectures for net-present maneuver.

Notion 7. Net-Present Maneuver

The selection problem between scenario TBB architectures reduces to which architecture offers you a satisfactory solution to the current problem and positions you with the maximum *net-present maneuver*. In financial analysis, there is the concept of net-present value. In making investment decisions, you are confronted with alternatives that have very different cash flows over time. To compare them, it is necessary to discount the cash flows to the present using a weighted-average cost-of-capital, cost of money, and adjusting for risk. The result is that initially incomparable investments are normalized to the present and can be compared.

The same problem confronts the architect who wants to choose among multiple, scenario designs. Each design has to be evaluated not only for solving the immediate problem, but for the degrees of architectural freedom it will enable in the future. Given a set of satisfactory scenario architectures, the problem migrates to the decision of which one offers the best future-option values for the business. To accomplish this, the architect has to assign to each candidate scenario architecture a net-present value that reflects the cost, speed, and quality of changes that may be made to it in the future.

This is not an easy exercise. The following is a summary of the process:

1. Select a candidate TBB architecture.
2. Using this architecture as A_0, develop a set of plausible degrees-of-freedom architectures that can emanate from it. (You can use Figure 5.2 to understand which changes are made to the architecture when developing the future degrees of freedom.) To each degree-of-freedom architecture assign a maneuver value equal to its probability of occurring, multiplied by its utility, multiplied by the effort to implement it from the prior architecture state. In other words, Maneuver Value = Probability (Degree of Freedom Architecture) × Utility(Degree of Freedom Architecture) × Effort (Degree of Freedom Architecture). The net-present maneuver of this architecture is then equal to the sum of each maneuver value. In doing this, note the following:

   - A_0 is only counted once.
   - Differences in cost are accounted for in effort.
   - Differences in quality and functionality are accounted for in utility.
   - Differences in likelihood are accounted for in probability.
   - If the presence of certain architectural components is deemed especially desirable, additional weighting factors may be assigned to the calculation of the maneuver value.

3. Repeat steps 1 and 2 for each scenario TBB architecture.
4. Compare the net-present maneuver for each architecture. Select the architecture that has the highest net-present maneuver. (It is assumed that all scenario TBB architectures have been deemed acceptable, or they would have been eliminated from the candidate set.)

This is a very exacting and difficult process to execute. It is no wonder then, that in spite of endless rhetoric about maneuverability, most architects are too overwhelmed to develop a set of workable scenarios let alone a complete set of degrees-of-freedom architectures for each scenario.

From a productivity viewpoint, designing for maneuverability one marriage at a time is hopelessly inefficient. It is necessary to provide application architects with partial assemblies, subassemblies, and complete assemblies that have been preevaluated for degrees of freedom. To be maneuverable, architecture design has to be elevated from assembling elementary components to fabricating established assemblies.

Notion 8. The Work of Infrastructure Architects

It is time-consuming to do detailed and exacting design for extreme maneuverability at the element level; therefore, it is necessary to change the unit of design from elementary components to *assemblies*. An assembly is an established and standardized "couple" that is engaged in one or more marriages. Infrastructure architects should create five kinds of assembled architectures that enable application architects to snap architectures together rather than build them from scratch.[1] These preassembled architectures must also take into account the issue of degrees of freedom. The five types of architectures are:

1. **Grand infrastructure architectures.** Represent the set of all permissible marriages. Given the technology components that exist as standards, the grand infrastructure architecture defines the complete set of marriages that are permitted. This architecture is the visualization of Figure 5.2 for the enterprise. Any other architecture is a subview of this architecture.
2. **Component architectures.** Cut-outs, or views, of the grand infrastructure architecture, which focus on how a particular class of applications may be architected. A component architecture embodies those marriages that are appropriate for the component view. Typical component architectures include high-volume transaction processing, office automation, data warehousing, data markets, electronic commerce, e-mail, and the Web. There may be multiple instances of each type of component architecture because of variations in solution suitability, such as total number of users, typical number of concurrent users, reliability, performance, size of databases, and so on. Since all these component architectures originate in the same grand architecture, they can be made interoperable by instituting marriages.
3. **Subassembly architectures.** Incomplete architectures that serve as building blocks for customized application architectures. Rather than starting with raw components, in subassembly architectures, application architects snap together subassemblies that support preferred marriage configurations.
4. **Reference architectures.** Complete solutions for a given type of application. Business applications are viewed as a marketplace in need of *n* generic types of solutions. Reference architectures represent finished sets of marriages for each type of application, such as transaction processing, office au-

tomation, datamarts, and so on. The reference architecture is further distinguished by its solution suitability. An application architect views the reference architecture as an environment on top of which only application-specific variables maybe allocated. The reference architecture includes a complete OA&M architecture; has a high net-present maneuver; and is extended through additional marriages. Reference architectures are normally developed in direct collaboration with application architects.

5. **Standard architectures.** Represent application architecture subsystems with which all applications of a certain class must interface. In this case, certain functional capabilities such as e-mail services, a specific database server, or electronic-commerce interfacing are standardized. The standard architectures document each of the architectures and the marriages required to interface to it. These architectures are often done in tight collaboration with application architects.

In all these cases, maneuverability is accomplished through leverage. Higher-level, reusable building blocks replace elementary components as the unit of architectural construction. Application architects can therefore inherit from the design of each one the preparation and analysis for maneuverability, rather than perform those steps over and over. EAB drawings are used to represent each of the five types of architectures that facilitate communication.

Infrastructure architects focus on the development and maintenance of these architectures. As members of evaluation teams, they select new technologies, and it is their responsibility to analyze which new marriages are possible and how the five types of architectures will be changed by adoption of the new technologies. In essence, the infrastructure architects evaluate all new technologies in light of Figure 5.2, then alter Figure 5.2 based on the adoption of a new technology to reflect the new possible configurations. These new marriages must then be rippled through all five architectures.

Certain key insights into architecture design for extreme adaptability result from this:

1. The grand architecture should be conceptualized as a schema of permitted marriages. All other architectures are subschema views of the grand architecture schema.
2. Maneuverability is an inherited trait. Business applications inherit maneuverability from the set of marriages permitted by the grand architecture schema. In essence, a given application is a subschema of the grand architecture. Its ultimate maneuverability rests on which of the marriages it hasn't yet availed itself are available to it from the grand schema. Therefore, adaptability is not built application by application; it is inherited by the applications.
3. Application architects focus on choosing a subschema view of the grand architecture that meets their current needs and positions them for maximum

net-present maneuverability. They also focus on altering the grand architecture to create a grand architecture schema that yields the greatest net-present maneuverability while balancing total life-cycle cost.

Notion 9. Principles for Extreme Maneuverability

The principles you choose as rules and guidelines will have a profound influence on the net-present maneuverability of your architecture (Chapter 2 and Appendix C). Certainly, all principles are important, but the following should be considered a starter set to maximize net-present maneuverability:

- Open systems standards are orders of magnitude preferable to internal or proprietary standards.
- Applications should be constructed from assemblies, as opposed to raw parts.
- To be complete, application architectures must include the OA&M component.
- Technologies should be selected based on their ability to port and scale.
- Information exchange between applications should be message-based.
- To minimize the exponential growth of pairwise information exchanges, batch information exchanges must use a hub(s) structure.
- Applications are divided into discrete software layers.
- Datastores are partitioned into operational subject databases that run the business and data warehouse (datamart) databases, which are used to analyze the business.
- Databases are positioned as open servers that are accessible to all applications that need them.
- The failure to provide proper EAB documentation on an ongoing basis is, prima facie evidence of architectural malpractice and incompetence.

Since extreme maneuverability is the desired outcome of Information Age architecture, to enable coping with hypercompetition, it may be worth highlighting which principles in your set were included specifically to win this prize.

Notion 10. Revised Architecture Framework

Based on the analysis done in this chapter, the preceding chapters, and in Appendix C (where we discuss a methodology for developing principles), Figure 5.5 provides a richer architecture framework than the original framework shown in Figure 2.3. This illustration takes into account the different types of principles, the perspectives and time views of the architecture, and the allocation of different types of architectures to the framework cells. The five types of architectures just discussed have been placed in the infrastructure Models' cell. Application EABs and application distributed EABs are placed in the applications Models' cell.

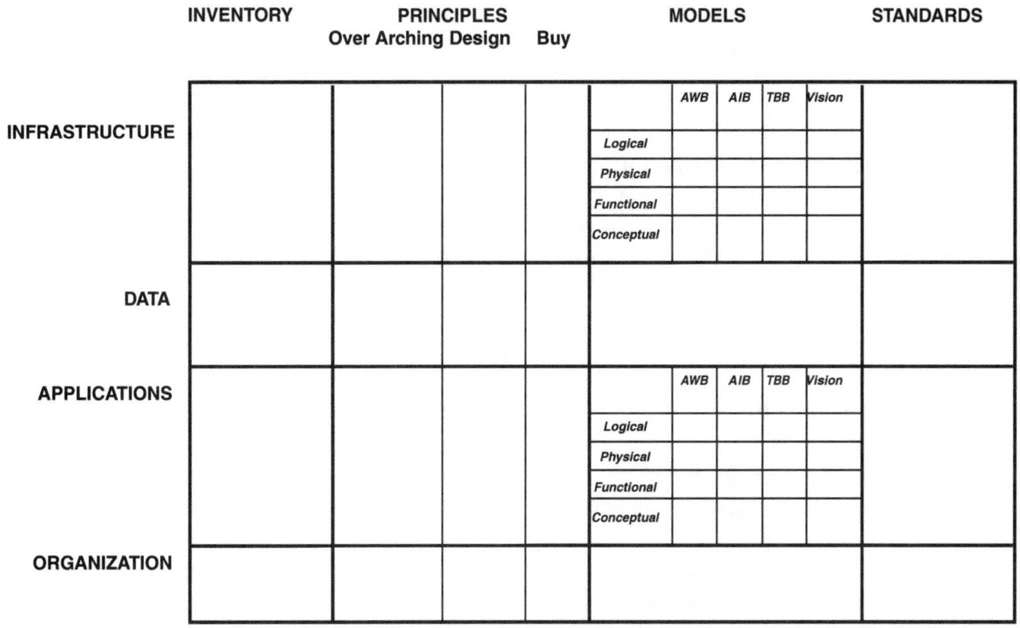

	INVENTORY	PRINCIPLES Over Arching Design	Buy	MODELS				STANDARDS
				AWB	AIB	TBB	Vision	
INFRASTRUCTURE				Logical				
				Physical				
				Functional				
				Conceptual				
DATA								
				AWB	AIB	TBB	Vision	
APPLICATIONS				Logical				
				Physical				
				Functional				
				Conceptual				
ORGANIZATION								

FIGURE 5.5 Revised architecture framework. The original framework has been revised to take into account the ideas developed throughout the book.

Summary

Designing for adaptability is easy to talk about but difficult to implement because of the numerous combinations and permutations of elements and unknown but inevitable future needs. To effectively engage in design for maneuverability, an IT organization must migrate to component architectures. It is simply too complicated and time-consuming to test architectures for degrees of freedom one at a time. It is only through aggressive reuse of established subassemblies that maneuverability can be achieved.

UNDERSTANDING THE TRINITY

The three actions—EAB, configuration management, and design for maneuverability—presented to address the issue of architecture maneuverability may be comprehended at two very different levels. At a straightforward and pragmatic level, this trio of actions offer just another three tools in the IT manager's toolbox, whereby they offer day-to-day assistance and dramatically improve the utility of architectural efforts.

Understanding the three actions at a strategic level will, in contrast, offer benefits far in excess of those enjoyed by dulled pragmatists. In developing and executing strategy, always be prepared to address two vital questions that will crystallize your intent:

1. What is the worthy outcome that I am struggling to achieve?
2. Why am I so compelled to try to achieve it?

Driven by a deep and far-reaching strategic intent, what to many may be just a set of pragmatic tools to manage architecture can be elevated to extreme advantage.

Strategic Intent: Desired Outcome

The desired outcome of your architectural initiatives is to create an IT architecture based on *strategic configuration of power* for the business. Sun Tzu taught that the mandatory capability to cope with hypercompetition was a strategic configuration of power (author paraphrase in brackets):

> A victorious strategy is not repeated, the configurations of responses to the enemy are inexhaustible [the configurations of responses to the marketplace are inexhaustible]. . . . Water configures its flow in accord with the terrain; the army controls its victory in accord with the enemy [the business controls its victory in accord with the competition]. Thus, the army does not maintain any constant STRATEGIC CONFIGURA-TION OF POWER. [Thus, an IT architecture does not maintain any fixed configuration of its components]; water has no constant shape [an IT architecture has no constant shape]. The end of an army's form is formlessness [the end of an IT architecture's form is the ability to end-lessly morph its form]. One who is able to change and transform in accord with the enemy and wrest victory is termed genius [one who is able to change and transform in accord with the marketplace and wrest success is termed genius].

By creating architectural-based strategic configurations of power, your responses to the marketplace become inexhaustible.

A strategic configuration of power has four attributes:

1. It permits an endless variety of actions.
2. It permits you to adapt expeditiously to the actions of others.
3. Its only form is temporary; it is continuously self-adaptive.
4. It is a critical contributor to advantage.

We can further understand the nature of a strategic configuration of power by deconstructing it: Strategic means advantage; configuration means elements and the relationships between those elements; power means maneuverability where maneuverability means speed plus flexibility. A strategic configuration of power, therefore, is the ability to create advantage by being able to craft the components and relationships of the components of the source of power to enable unparalleled maneuverability.

This is exactly the strategic outcome you want from your IT architecture, which is the source of Information Age hypercompetitive power. Your architecture is not merely a collection of IT components; it is a crafted collection of IT components that enable you to transform and change in accord with the marketplace in a dramatically superior manner. It gives you inexhaustible responses to the marketplace. Isn't this an outcome worth struggling to achieve? Isn't this an image that drives actions, commitment, and trade-offs differently from simply implementing just another set of IT tools? While others act to implement another tool, you struggle to implement a strategic configuration of power. They strive for mediocrity while you strive to achieve the apex of strategic acumen.

Strategic Intent: Compelling Reason

The compelling justification for suffering the hardships of creating an architecture-based strategic configuration of power is that to win the hypercompetitive wars, you must be able to execute the essence of strategy. Miyamoto Musashi, in his great classic work of strategy, *The Five Rings*, said:

> *An attack must be executed with quickness, not speed. Attack with power, not strength. There is a great difference between speed and quickness, power and strength. It is the essence of strategy.*

This aphorism may seem confusing. Most readers would think, contrary to what Musashi states, that those pairs are the same. What does he mean? As interpreted here it means there is a difference between a strategy of readiness and a strategy of actuality, but that by intent they flow into each other. A strategy of actuality is a specific set of actions taken to achieve a specific known set of objectives. You know exactly what it is that you want to achieve. A strategy of readiness is a nonspecific set of actions that position you to strike. Because you don't know exactly what will have to be done, or because events are in a state of constant flux, like a tight spring, you are ready and able to uncoil in any direction with tremendous force and quickness when you decide it is time to do so.

Speed and strength are attributes of readiness; they represent generic capabilities in a state of extreme preparation. Quickness and force are attributes of actuality; they are speed- and strength-focused and concentrated for a specific purpose. Speed, when focused and concentrated, becomes actual quickness. Strength, when focused and concentrated, becomes actual force. Readiness flows into actuality. The essence of strategy, according to Musashi, is to create an infrastructure of readiness that can swiftly transform itself into actuality at the moment and place of opportunity.

Musashi goes on to say:

> *Falling on the enemy is attacking without preconceived ideas as to how to conclude the battle.*

Musashi's advice, for an environment of extreme conflict, is to enter conflict with a strategy of readiness, and as events unfold and opportunity emerges, switch with power and quickness to a strategy of actuality.

This is the core of IT-based hypercompetitive fighting. An IT organization must position itself in a state of readiness that can on-demand switch to a state of actuality. This means putting in place a nimble architectural infrastructure that stands, coiled like a tight spring, ready to strike where, when, and how needed.

Consequently, in periods of turbulence, the essence of strategy is to achieve a state of readiness that enables you to turn speed into quickness and strength into power. This is what a hypercompetitor must be able to do. The compelling reason for creating a strategic configuration of power that lets your architecture become formless is to enable the business to continuously change its form in prompt response to whatever.

Summary

The basic principles of strategic behavior are well documented in the classical works of the discipline. What changes over time is the manner of realization and execution of the principles in harmony with the times and circumstances. The strategic logic of coping with hypercompetitors is no different today from 5,000 years ago. What is different is the need to craft the response with the technologies and tools that are currently available.

To command a war of hypercompetition, you must institute a strategic configuration of power. This is an eternal strategic principle. In this day and circumstance, the selected instrument of implementation is IT architecture. You must implement a strategic configuration of power because during periods of hypercompetition, you have to be able to execute the essence of strategy, to change speed into quickness and power into strength. This, too, is an eternal principle of strategy and provides the impetus to create the architecture-based strategic configuration of power.

When you implement the ideas in this book, you are implementing heavy-duty strategy. You are not merely implementing blueprints, configuration management, and a design methodology; you are crafting a configuration of power so that the business can execute the essence of strategy. You are implementing the timeless strategic principles of Sun Tzu and Miyamoto Musashi, but adjusted for the time and circumstance.

USING THE TRINITY AS SUSTAINABLE COMPETITIVE ADVANTAGE

Though this assertion will initially appear to contradict a basic premise of hyper-competition, that is, sustainable competitive advantages are no longer sustainable, I would suggest that the trinity of architecture actions that have been suggested can serve as the basis for a sustainable competitive advantage for the business. While it is true that EAB, configuration management, and design methods for extreme maneuverability are available to all, there is much more to advantage then simply broad and raw availability. When one studies the nature of sustainable competitive advantage, one discovers that sustainable advantages often have their roots, not in a unique specific skill or know-how, but in the difficult and subtle coordination of multiple skills or know-how.

Sustainable advantages frequently are built upon complex networks of coordination and collaboration that are extremely difficult to replicate even though the components of the coordination are available to all. It is not individual skills or know-how that generates the durable advantage; it is the web of intricate and intertwined actions that coordinate them. This is precisely the situation with regard to EAB, configuration management, and design for extreme maneuverability. The basis for architecture as a sustainable competitive advantage is not grounded in each one, but in the web of intertwined activities that must be undertaken to execute them collectively in an optimum manner.

A sustainable competitive advantage is defined as a resource, capability, asset, process, and so on that gives the enterprise a distinct attraction to its customers, a unique advantage over its competitors, and is durable over time. A sustainable competitive advantage must sustain a consistent difference to be a critical buying factor for the customer. The difference in customer perception must be directly attributable to the sustainable competitive advantage and satisfy customer key buying factors.

For an advantage to be durable, it must satisfy one or more of the following attributes:

Nontransparency. The mechanics or details of the advantage are difficult to understand. Competitors are able to see the outcome of your advantage but do not understand the specifics of how you achieve it. Your advantage is built on proprietary knowledge.

Nonaccessibility. Competitors have unequal access to the required resources to duplicate the advantage. Though they understand what you are doing, contractual, legal, or other arrangements prevent them from accessing the building blocks of the advantage. Your advantage is built upon proprietary access.

Replication. Competitors have difficulty replicating the advantage. They do not have the know-how to do it.

Coordination. The advantage requires difficult and subtle coordination of multiple resources and activities. The advantage is rooted in a perplexing web of know-how and process that competitors are unable to decipher or imitate.

As argued in the earlier chapters, in the hypercompetitive Information Age, it is through your IT architecture that you create value for your customers, that you parry your competitors. More frequently, as the world moves toward a digital economy, the software that is delivered over your architecture is the actual product that your customers receive. Thus, there is no question that architecture meets the basic requirements for becoming a sustainable competitive advantage.

The more intriguing question remains: Is it durable? Having struggled to implement EAB, configuration management, and design for extreme maneuverability, do your hypercompetitors quickly copy or leapfrog you, or can you maintain the architecture as a sustainable advantage? Can architecture meet the tests for durability, or does it simply become more ante to play the game?

The answer is that the trinity of actions fail the first three tests but pass the last one. The methods are certainly transparent. There is no secret as to what is done; the methods have open accessibility. Anyone and everyone can learn about them. The methods are superficially replicable. It is certainly within the realm of possibility to replicate a configuration management process. What is extremely difficult to copy, however, is the subtle coordination of all three activities in dynamic motion. It is not that the performance of any one of the activities is impossible to replicate; it's the coordinated orchestration of them all in a tight and mutually reinforcing manner that is difficult to duplicate. Once you have all three of them up, running, humming, and tuned, you have a beehive of graceful architectural activity. Each of the activities engages in complex interactions with the others. It is out of this unique coordination, your idiosyncratic implementation, that your architecture creates advantage.

So, though there are no secrets as to *what* is done, there is the opportunity for tremendous difference in the subtleties of *how* it is done. That is why the strategic understanding of the architecture is so important. The energy expended and the desire to perfect are quite different depending on how you appreciate your circumstance. By taking the approach that you're going to use architecture to impress your attitude on the marketplace, your beehive of architecture actions generates processes that are very distinct from a competitor who simply sees the trinity of actions as no more than the drawing and evolving of schematics. Everyone has access to the same raw architectural materials, but not everyone implements them with equal passion and insight. There is sustainable advantage to be found here for those who implement architecture with a profound understanding and appreciation of the possibilities. Architecture can pass the last test for sustainability, but passing that test is something you must do by yourself for yourself. In the business world, where the perpetual struggle is for advantage, you could do much worse then struggle to make architecture a sustainable competitive advantage.

CONCLUSION

When all is said and done, the problem of hypercompetitive business strategy reduces to being able to continuously turn the "front." Recall from the military analogies drawn earlier that armies line up against each other across a front (Figure 5.6). Then, as shown in Figure 5.7, the trick is to turn the front. The obvious reason is to permit your front-line forces to proceed unopposed, but the more compelling reason is that it disrupts the support infrastructure behind the front and displaces all the support systems from their positions. Turning the front ruins the plans of the opponent and causes tremendous friction for them as they try to reestablish order between the new front and their support infrastructure.

As shown in Figure 5.8, the same logic applies to business strategy. In a hypercompetitive business environment, it is necessary to be able to turn the front to create new value propositions for customers or to devalue the initiatives of your opponents. In the Information Age, turning the front equates to being able to turn your IT architecture. The competitor who has a deeper and more far-reaching strategy for commanding IT architecture will have the definitive advantage in an endless war of turning the fronts.

Sun Tzu said:

When your strategy is deep and far-reaching, you gain much so you can win even before you fight. When your strategy is shallow and near-sighted, you gain little, so you lose even before you do battle. Much strat-

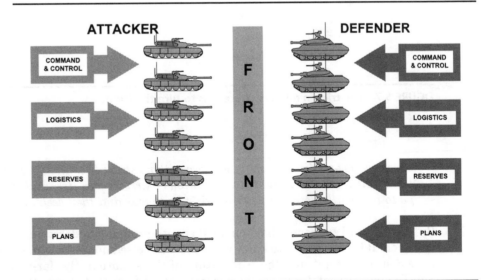

FIGURE 5.6 Opponents line up against each other across a front.

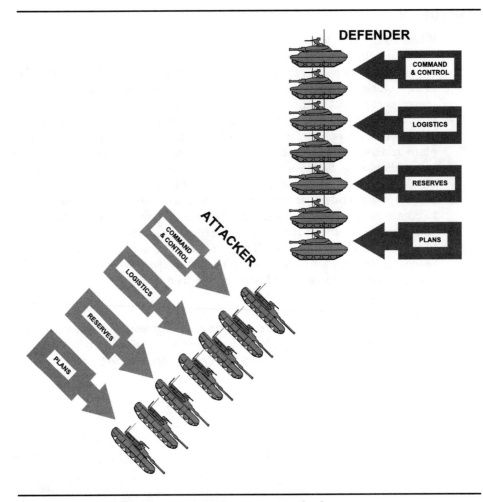

FIGURE 5.7   The trick in military strategy is to turn the front.

egy prevails over little strategy so those with no strategy cannot help but be defeated. So it is taught that victorious warriors win first and then go to war while defeated warriors first go to war and then seek to win.

By "deep," Sun Tzu means that you must enjoy a profound understanding of the situation. It is not enough to know what everyone else knows. To win, you must have distinct insight into the true nature of the situation. By "far-reaching," Sun Tzu means that it must make a momentous difference to have struggled to execute your strategy and to have succeeded. The outcome must be so unques-

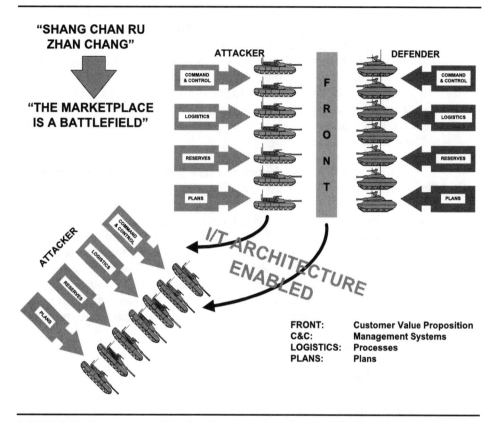

FIGURE 5.8 Hypercompetitive business strategy. Turning the front in business strategy in the Information Age equates to the ability to turn the IT architecture.

tionably positive that it justifies the arduous struggle necessary to accomplish it.

The deep and far-reaching strategy prescribed in this book is as follows:

- Industries are confronting global hypercompetition.
- An endless stream of temporary advantages must replace sustainable advantage as the means to win.
- The ability to build temporary advantages is a function of the ability of the business to maneuver.
- In the Information Age, the ability to maneuver the business is a function of the malleability of information technology. What must be maneuvered are your information systems.
- The malleability of your information technology is built upon your information technology architecture.

- To be effective, an information technology architecture framework must be selected and deployed with a shared community understanding of architecture governance and architecture strategy.
- The key architecture framework cells to enable hypercompetitive behavior are the infrastructure models and the application models.
- Infrastructure models and application models, to be effective, must be drawn using a rigorous blueprinting methodology, evolved through structured configuration management, and crafted using the design mechanism of extreme maneuverability.

This is a strategy that describes perfect alignment of IT with the business. The syllogism starts with the most pressing problem confronting the business and ends with the IT actions that resolve the problem. What could be more pressing then a hypercompetitive battle for business survival?

We are not interested in blueprinting because it is fun to play with icons or because we want to mimic the methods of our accomplished sibling engineering disciplines. We are interested in architecture blueprinting because it is the path to victory. It is the path to victory because value creation through continuous innovation has become the ante to play the game; and information technology is the predominant instrument used to implement and realize that stream of infinite innovation.

Sun Tzu said:

In ancient times, great warriors prevailed when it was easy to prevail. Their victories were not flukes. Their victories were not flukes because they positioned themselves where they would surely win; prevailing over those who have already lost.

In a hypercompetitive environment, the winning position is one that allows you to quickly gain any other position. The position that permits you to prevail over your opponents, who have already lost, is an IT architecture that enables the IT assets to quickly and efficiently morph themselves into the endless fleeting positions needed by the business. All business positions are but momentary and ephemeral positions. You will never be able to move between positions with alacrity if you do not have detailed and accurate blueprints of your architecture.

Water has no constant shape; it takes the transient shape of its container. This is the goal of an IT architecture in the hypercompetitive Information Age. Over time, you must evolve your architecture to become formless. Formless does not mean without form; it refers to the capability, on demand, to assume any form. You visualize, realize, and manage this through your representation of your architecture as embodied in your blueprints, blueprints that were shrewdly crafted using the subassembly concepts of extreme maneuverability.

From this analysis comes an important insight into the nature of information technology-based advantage. With the advent of hypercompetition, a transposition of roles occurs. What becomes strategic are the models of the IT architecture, and what becomes tactical are the business applications. The reason is that applications and their functionality are innately transitory. Hypercompetition makes them obsolete almost as fast as they are deployed. The architecture models, however, provide persistent strategic value because the knowledge they represent and impart transcends the tactical competitive interactions embodied in application functionality, and permits the business to effectively and efficiently maneuver.

In a game of ceaseless thrust and counterthrust, winning migrates from doing the same thing cheaper and faster to doing things better and different and then doing it again and again and again. That which is tactical is that which commands a point in time; that which is strategic is that which transcends time; so that which is tactical are business applications and that which is strategic are architecture models. Advantage emanates not from what you do, however beneficial, but from being able to rapidly and accurately change what you do.

Table 5.1 shows a strategic action map. The rows represent the economic factors of production; the columns represent the five types of advantage. A cell is populated with a factor of production action that creates the corresponding form of advantage for the business. As you can see, EAB is a rich strategy that utilizes all the factors of production to create three types of advantage for the business. This beneficial outcome concentrates its merit on the most critical advantage of maneuverability.

No doubt, some people will wail, But we don't have time. How can we do architecture work if we spend our precious time drawing and maintaining formal blueprints? We'll never get the work done! These are people who do not "get it." Their thinking is shallow and nearsighted. If you follow their advice, they will surely bring you to ruin.

The prescription of this book—rigorous IT architecture blueprinting leveraged with configuration management and optimized through design for extreme maneuverability—is not tangential to the work; nor is it add-on work, extra work, make work, supplementary work, throw-away work, peripheral work, or secondary work. It's the precise definition of the work of IT architects.

TABLE 5.1 EAB Advantage

	Forms of Advantage				
Factors of Production	*Cost*	*Differentiation*	*Focus*	*Execution*	*Maneuverability*
Effort Employee Zeal)					EAB
Methods (Process)	EAB			EAB	EAB
Factors (Technology)					EAB

In most companies, what architects are currently engaged in is tangential to the work; it's add-on, extra, supplementary, peripheral, secondary, and throwaway work. As is true in all other engineering disciplines, structured architecture blueprinting is the heart and essence of the work; it is the focal point, the locus, around which all engineering and architecture work revolves.

Yes, drawing and maintaining rigorous blueprints and coordinating their delivery across multiple business domains is hard work. That is why it is called a struggle for advantage. If it were easy and everyone could do it effortlessly, there would be no advantage to derive from it. To the contrary, in the challenge of the blueprinting process lie the seeds for IT architecture to become sustainable competitive advantage.

The advice here is simple: Let other architects continue doing their shallow and nearsighted view of architecture work. Let them attend the endless meetings; let them continue to pontificate, to deliver thousands of foot-high sketches, to posture, to engage in endless debates about everything, to navigate

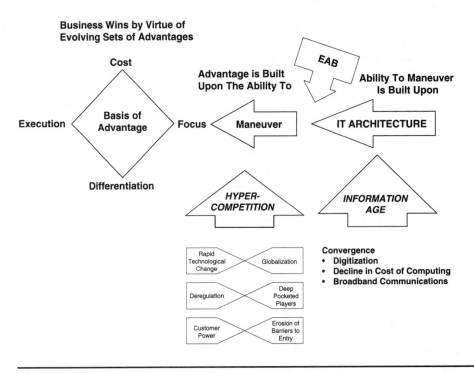

FIGURE 5.9 EAB insertion point. EAB is inserted at the juncture of hypercompetition and information architecture to enable maneuverability.

the maze, and to confuse ambiguous presentation sketches with blueprints. You have a strategy that is worth the struggle. Tell your architects, Don't show me the money, show me the drawings! Show me the means to disruption and exploitation. Show me my beautiful architecture of maneuverability

Your strategic intent should be to use IT architecture to create a strategic configuration of power. IT architecture sits at the nexus between the Information Age and hypercompetition (Figure 5.9). Crafted with the methods of extreme maneuverability, architecture blueprints become the visualization of IT-based hypercompetitive maneuverability. With this capability, the business will be able to go forth where others do not expect it, and attack where others are unprepared. This is the deep and far-reaching strategy of Enterprise IT Architecture Blueprinting, configuration management, and design for extreme maneuverability.

ENDNOTES

1. An EAB core page may be thought of as a sub-assembly drawing: an entire core diagram may be thought of as an assembly drawing.

CHAPTER 6

EAB Miscellany

The ultimate success of implementing any methodology (or information technology) involves issues beyond the methodology itself. The purpose of this chapter is to address four adjunct and important nontechnical issues that surround the successful implementation of EAB:

1. **Cost justification.** How do you cost-justify EAB to a skeptical audience?
2. **Implementation plan.** How do you structure an implementation plan to minimize friction and resistance?
3. **Commitment planning.** How do you build and sustain commitment to a blueprinting initiative in a business world marked by short attention spans and extreme cynicism?
4. **Frequently asked questions.** What are some typical questions that you will be asked as you try to move the organization from personal sketching to engineering blueprinting?

By taking these issues into account during your planning deliberations, you can dramatically raise your prospects for success. We take them into account here, one by one.

COST JUSTIFICATION

The first, and final, refuge of those who oppose the migration to formal blueprinting is the demand that you cost-justify the initiative. Though it may seem that the strategic logic of EAB (as explained in the preceding chapters), supplemented by common and business sense, is more than sufficient, sooner or later, someone will demand to see numbers that unquestionably *prove* that blueprinting makes economic sense. Any or all of the following methods, individually or in combination, can be used to meet this requirement.

Ante to Play the Game

In a marketplace where the players continually revise the value proposition, the ante to play the game also continues to mutate. The minimum technological know-how sufficient to compete yesterday is insufficient today. Architectural methods that worked for slow wars of attrition are simply inappropriate for wars of movement. EAB is an approach to architecture that becomes the ante to play the game. As discussed in Chapter 4, if your opponent is able to execute configuration management more quickly than you, you are confronted with an ever-increasing deteriorating situation. The adoption of professional blueprinting methods is not an economic choice; it is a mandatory choice. If you do not take preemptive actions to ensure competence in rigorous architecture blueprinting, you will discover, to your dismay and chagrin, that you made a poor choice as your competitors come to control and dictate the battle of the OODAs. If you can't afford to perform blueprinting, you will eventually discover that you can't afford to compete. And that is something you can't afford at all.

Cost/Value Comparison

Sketching, which is currently done, and blueprinting not only have different costs, but they also offer very different value propositions. As itemized in Table 2.4, with blueprinting dollars, you buy a very different set of value points than with your current method. Even if we were to concede that blueprinting is more expensive (to be argued in the Hidden Costs section later in this chapter), you get an entirely different set of value benefits for your dollars. What needs to be compared is cost-per-value received, not only absolute cost. When you compare costs this way, the value-per-cost unit of blueprinting is extraordinarily superior to personal sketching.

Two-Phase Strategy

When confronted with the need to radically change a strategic position, a common path is to reach the new position in two phases: The objective of phase 1 is to achieve the new capability; the objective of phase 2 is to optimize the new capability. Phase 1 positions you to do the right thing, then Phase 2 positions you to do the right thing as efficiently as possible.

Figure 6.1 illustrates this idea. The objective is to move from a low-cost/low-value position to a low-cost/high-value position. It's best to follow path A, but in practice, companies often follow path B, a pragmatic approach that throttles the complicated learning that must be mastered at a given time.

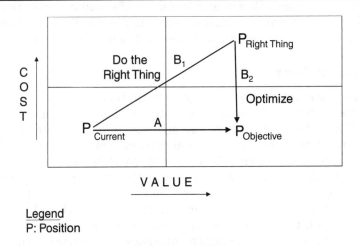

FIGURE 6.1 **Two-phase strategy. Changes in strategic positions are often accomplished in two phases.**

Even if we concede that EAB is initially more expensive, we can apply two-phase strategy to deal with it: First do the right thing, then optimize it. As CAD tools and the learning curve take effect, the costs drop dramatically. The actual two-phase strategy looks like Figure 6.2, not Figure 6.1, due to the hidden costs in the current methods of performing architecture sketching.

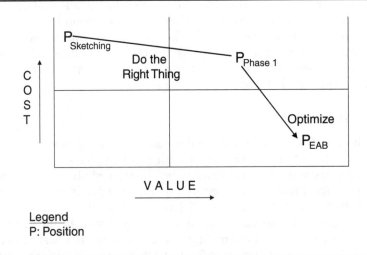

FIGURE 6.2 **Actual two-phase strategy.**

Hidden Costs

When you begin to analyze the costs associated with personal sketching, you will discover that there are many hidden costs, centering on the absence of drawing persistence and rework to correct errors or incompleteness. Since sketches are generally not maintained, the process executed is often as follows:

1. An architecture initiative begins.
2. The usual gang of suspects is rounded up and herded into a room for an extended period of time to understand the as-is-built architecture for the domain of interest; they draw a sketch of it, and resolve disagreements about the sketch.
3. The changes to the architecture are debated and documented to define the to-be-built architecture. This documentation is a combination of ambiguous sketches and text.
4. The approved to-be-built architecture is handed off to development for construction.
5. The developers, with the pragmatic need for specificity, either ignore the to-be-built sketches and do their own thing, or loop back to the architecture team for clarification. This is time-consuming and requires a large amount of rework to develop the specificity necessity to transform a sketch into an implementable architecture. Sketches are the fodder for good management conceptual presentations, but are fairly useless for developers who require precision detail.
6. The architecture is implemented and the sketches become nonmaintained shelfware.
7. The next architecture initiative is received and the process starts over again, without the ability or intent to leverage the dated and incorrect sketches.

To appreciate these hidden costs, compare the process that was just described with an EAB process:

1. An architecture initiative begins.
2. An EAB team is formed; they extract the as-is-built architecture from the relevant AOR EABs.
3. The changes to the architecture are debated and documented to define the to-be-built architecture. This is documented as an XACTION TBB EAB.
4. The approved to-be-built architecture is handed off to the development team for construction.
5. The developers, with the assistance of a construction-site architect, implement the architecture.
6. The AOR EAB is updated.
7. The next architecture initiative is received and the process starts over again with the ability and intent to leverage the existing blueprints.

It is important to understand that the same information is needed to define a new architecture, regardless of process. It is through the standardization of blueprinting and the maintenance of the blueprints that the time-consuming and expensive hidden costs of the current sketching process are eliminated. The incremental costs of maintaining the blueprints pale in comparison to the reduction in cost, resulting from not having to re-create them from scratch each time and from minimizing rework during construction, thanks to the elimination of ambiguity.

This is so important that it bears repeating. Opponents of blueprinting will try to conjure up the image that you are proposing an expensive and superfluous process to replace an already highly efficient and effective process. In general, nothing could be further from the truth. There is nothing efficient or effective about a process that has the attributes described in Table 2.4. There is every reason to anticipate that replacing personal drawings with formal drawings, nonconfiguration management with configuration management, and noncommunicative documentation with communicative documentation will yield substantial savings.

Option Value

One of the more subtle benefits of blueprints is that they permit small teams of architects to develop scenario architectures in response to what-if business proposals. In a hypercompetitive business environment, business planning through scenario modeling takes on increased importance. The business leadership has to know what their options are and whether they can execute those options. Without blueprints, the time-consuming process described under Hidden Costs has to be executed. Conversely, with accurate AOR EABs available, an architecture team can model how they would change the architecture to meet the requirements of each scenario. In analyzing the cost benefits of blueprinting, you must therefore add to the plus column the value of the architecture community being able to perform accurate and timely what-if analysis in response to dynamic business scenario planning.

Value-Chain Analysis

Value-chain analysis is a framework for classifying, analyzing, and understanding the translation of resources through processes into final products or services. It is used specifically as a means to analyze how to improve cost structure (productivity) and product differentiation. The methodology of value-chain analysis applied to cost structure is as follows:

1. Disaggregate the value chain into its discrete activities.
2. Establish a relative weight of each activity.
3. Identify for each activity the cost drivers: what drives costs, productivity, and time?

4. Identify cost-reduction opportunity links between activities. Don't be interested only in how to drive down the costs of each activity by looking at them individually. Consider where an investment in one activity would be more than offset by reduction in costs in other activities.
5. Take the actions to drive down costs and, as necessary, invest in some activities to drive out higher costs in other activities.

When you apply value-chain analysis to blueprinting, you are interested in step 4, determining which other activities involved in developing, maintaining, and operating information systems would benefit by having accurate current blueprints available. You will be pleasantly surprised by the number of other subprocesses that are enabled by having blueprints available; these will provide numerous linkages to opportunities for cost savings.

Analogy

All other engineering professions have accepted that the use of blueprints is the optimum way to define, maintain, and communicate the definition of the complex objects they are concerned with. Obviously, all of these engineering disciplines, too, are concerned about costs, yet have universally chosen blueprints as an integral component of their engineering methodology. If, as the pundits and gurus like to say, IT architecture is like building, airplane, or boat architecture why would IT architecture be unique and not require rigorous blueprints like its sibling disciplines? The only answer is that IT architecture is different because it undergoes so much change that it doesn't make sense to exert the effort to draw and maintain precision drawings, whereas the objects of the other engineering disciplines are relatively stable making it worth the effort. This evaluation doesn't qualify as even good nonsense. In fact, just the opposite is the conclusion to the argument. If something rarely changes, then sketches would be quite sufficient. If, however, something changes frequently, then precision definition is required to react quickly and eliminate the need to repetitively redefine the as-is-built model.

The truth is, there is no difference between the need for IT architecture blueprints and the need for blueprints in other engineering disciplines. If anything, due to the increasing complexity of distributed IT architectures and the impact of hypercompetition, the need for blueprints in this arena may even be greater. The same concerns for cost and quality that drove other engineering disciplines to adopt blueprinting have the same impact on the logic and economics of blueprinting and IT architecture.

Investment Center

A business can manage IT from four basic and overlapping perspectives:

1. **Cost center.** IT is an expense that is to be ruthlessly and continually pruned with a cost-reduction scythe. When viewed as a cost center, the

focus of IT management is operational efficiency, risk minimization, and unit-cost reduction.

2. **Service center.** IT is a service-to-business-driven initiative. The focus of IT management is responsiveness to business needs, development of business capabilities, execution, and cost.

3. **Investment center.** IT is a focal point of strategic business investment. The focus of IT management is to use IT to create advantage, to create/exploit marketplace opportunities, enable business growth, and respond to marketplace adversities.

4. **Profit center.** The purpose of IT is an external profit center and an internal investment center.

In an Information Age hypercompetitive business environment, IT should be viewed as an investment center. The costs associated with implementing and maintaining blueprints are investments in advantage, not in mandatory but valueless costs. When viewed from this perspective, EAB cost justification should focus on the change in revenue opportunities to the business by having current and accurate blueprints rather then solely on the costs of creating them. The higher purpose of blueprints is to enable you to make money, not to save money.

Summary

Cost justification need not be an obstacle to implementation. Cost savings do not have an exclusive monopoly on justifying strategic logic. When you apply your selected subset of the techniques from the preceding, you will discover that blueprinting not only can offer cost savings, but more important, provide business benefits that far exceed the costs, even if there is a cost increase in a particular environment.

IMPLEMENTATION MODEL

The implementation of EAB can be conceptualized as a change in strategic positions, as illustrated in Figure 6.3.

Strategic Repositioning Approach

The process called *strategic repositioning*[1] is a generic technique that provides an overarching framework for the design and migration of strategic change. The root notions of strategic repositioning are as follows:

- The state of a business at any time can be modeled as a set of strategic positions. Each position illustrates the state of the selected business area. You position those elements of the business that are crucial to your problem and that will need to be changed.

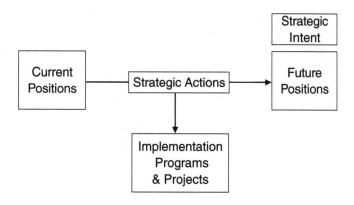

FIGURE 6.3   Implementation model. Implementing EAB can be conceptualized as a change in strategic positions.

- The position of the business (P_B at time t is equal to the set of selected positions, such as: $P_B = (P_{Competencies}, P_{Architecture}, P_{Processes}, P_{Human\ Resource\ Policies}, P_{Supplier\ Relationships}, P_{Etc.})$.
- A position may be very difficult or complicated to model. Therefore, a position may itself be defined as a set of positions. Position definition is a recursive concept.
- If you can accept that $P_{Current\ Business\ Positions}$ models the state of the business today, then you can imagine and design a desired future state for the business as $P_{Future\ Business\ Positions}$. Strategic actions (also called strategic moves, strategic acts, or strategic initiatives) must be defined and executed to move the business between the two position definitions.
- These actions are implemented through implementation programs with associated projects.
- Strategic repositioning then is the definition of:
  - $P_{Current\ Business\ Positions}$
  - $P_{Future\ Business\ Positions}$
  - Strategic actions that move you between the positions in the most efficient and effective manner

In this way, you define where you are, where you want to be, and how you will get there. If we apply this framework to EAB and use Figure 6.3 as a reference model, the essence of developing an implementation plan is as follows:

1. **Define your current positions.** This equates to understanding the current architecture framework and governance system. Which architecture frame-

work are you using? How are the cells completed? Who completes which cells? How is evolution of the cells managed? How is governance evolved?

2. **Define a strategic future intent for your efforts.** A strategic intent is a long-term stable objective for the repositioning effort. It provides a long-term anchor for the bumpy road of change. Is your intent to implement an entire architecture framework, just EAB, EAB and configuration management, or EAB, configuration management, and design for extreme maneuverability?

3. **Define your desired future positions.** How do you want them to be? Are you going to just implement EAB with configuration management or are you going to reposition your entire architecture? Which support capabilities, such as competencies training processes, need to change to support your future positions?

4. **Define your actions.** Which actions, in what order, and with what dependencies need to be taken to move you from your current position to your desired future position?

5. **Define your implementation programs.** Which implementation programs are required to execute the strategic actions? Who are the owners of the programs and who are the executive champions?

A strategic management council representing all the key stakeholders oversees the entire process.

A More Subversive Approach

The strategic repositioning approach just described only works when you have the support and endorsement of the management team. Often, strategic change, rather than coming from above, has to percolate up from below. It may be the case that you have little support for your blueprinting initiative. To be blunt, not only might managers not "get it," they might not want it. Strategic repositioning as the framework for action won't work because they won't give you a chance. Most people are just too busy or too inflexible in the way they work to change. The forces of inertia and loyalty to what *is* are so strong and entrenched that you have no choice but to form a rebel alliance. You need to disrupt business as usual to coerce their attention and interest.

In such a situation, you need to become a hypercompetitor. Your own hypercompetitive approach (which is actually much more fun) has to disrupt the inertial status quo and win them to your side. This basically consists of three steps:

1. **Establish a beachhead.** The first step is to find someone who has a compelling need to improve his or her architecture work, is in command of architect resources, and is willing to take a prudent risk. Such an individual

generally is more entrepreneurially oriented, has a knack for strategic thinking, and most of all, likes to disrupt the status quo. Working with this individual and his or her team, develop a set of drawings and publicize your accomplishments. Demonstrate without fear of contradiction that you can do it. This will negate the arguments that it won't work.

2. **Go "bowling."** Having established and solidified your beachhead, it is time to move out from the beachhead and go bowling. By bowling, we mean finding additional groups willing to experiment with EAB. Rather then trying to change the whole world at once, which is the characteristic of strategic repositioning, you are simply trying to change the world one bowling pin at a time. There are at least two ways to go bowling. You can bowl for more architecture groups, or you can pull a flanking maneuver and find nonarchitecture groups that have a compelling need for the blueprints and would be willing to put pressure on their architects. You can find these people through the previously mentioned value-chain analysis methodology. You will discover that once the entrepreneurial ice has been broken, there are many others who will be willing to take a chance, once given a successful example.

3. **Institutionalize.** In one of his books on guerrilla warfare, Mao Tse Tung said that a guerrilla army could disrupt and disspirit a conventional army, but that the defeat of a conventional army would ultimately require a conventional army. You can only get as far as the leader of your rebel alliance. As your bowling succeeds, you will develop two important ingredients for convincing the management team of the value of EAB. You will have irrefutable evidence that it works, and more important, you will have allies who will testify to its value. At this point, hopefully, they will "get it," and you can move on to strategic repositioning to institutionalize EAB.

When you execute the three-step process, remember these few points of hard-earned advice:

- Try to find an executive who will help you discreetly. Though the executive may not be willing to publicly support you yet, he or she may be quite sympathetic and willing to do a little work behind the scenes to help you along and offer some political protection.
- Don't worry that you are not following the rules to the letter. You and your allies can justify your actions as experiments, and nobody can argue with the merit of small experiments. In any case, in a perverse sort of logic, you *are* following the status quo, which states that everyone is free to diagram architecture as they please. You and your colleagues are simply pleased to do it with EAB. Since the incumbent methodology defended is complete freedom of choice, you choose rigor and precision.
- Choose your beachhead and early bowling pins wisely. It is critical to have early and visible successes. Most important in choosing the early projects

is the attitude of the teams. Commitment and willingness to expend tremendous effort will compensate for every other shortcoming.

- Specificity is your strongest ally. Once you have the demonstration blueprints done, argue from your strength. When you have to defend your actions, insist that the opponents bring examples of their sketches and methodology for comparison. Ask them to explain how they have improved their drawing methodology over the last 10 years. Ask them in what ways they are more productive today than they were three years ago.

- You will prevail if you make architecture visible and lift the fog that normally engulfs it. Remember that you have blueprints; they only have sketches. A clear comparison is not something that favors their position, and many will back off when they fully appreciate that you are serious about blueprinting.

- Keep moving. If you disrupt successfully, you will have established a beachhead and have some bowling pins in progress before the opposition forms. Speed and surprise are your friends. While your opponents argue about what to do, you are doing; and the more you have done, the harder it will be to stop your efforts.

- Engage in duels. You are the weak. Pick and focus your fights so that the advantage of the established order is weakened. By carefully supplementing your efforts with sympathetic early adopters, you can move the debate to more friendly ground.

Though it is a great deal of fun to be a rebel for a while, ultimately you can only be successful if you become the status quo. Your objective in taking this approach is not to embarrass anyone but to provide the necessary evidence to prove your point and win support for blueprinting. The sooner you can join the mainstream, the sooner your business will enjoy the full benefits of EAB. Remember, you can disrupt, win internal market share, and surprise by being an internal hypercompetitor, but to win, you will need to become the institution. Once you win, always remember your experience and remain open to innovation; else you will become what you had to overcome, and that is not winning at all.

COMMITMENT PLANNING

As you would expect, much of the focus on implementing blueprinting is directed at the blueprints. As a consequence, implementation team members routinely focus almost exclusively on the blueprinting methodology, integration of the blueprinting with the selected framework, and teaching configuration management. What they do not focus on, but is often the deciding variable in implementation success, are the human elements of strategy, and in particular, the issue of building and sustaining organizational commitment to the initiative. Though exaggerated, but only slightly so, we would assert that blueprinting strategy may need to focus on blueprints, the non-human, but its ultimate execution success is more tightly dependent on its ability to manage the human issues of organizational and individual commitment. In fact, a mediocre strategy implemented with a deep and far-reaching organizational resolve more often will be a brilliant success, while an exceptional strategy implemented with apathy will be a failure.

The absence of commitment creates friction to agility and maneuverability, and retards speed. Friction is the onerous counterforce that pushes back on effort; it saps the strength from initiatives. A commitment to blueprinting strategy means that you understand that the strategy must be concerned with the nonhuman issues; but for the nonhuman to succeed, the human issues of building and sustaining commitment must be addressed to minimize friction.

A *commitment plan* is a specific set of actions taken to establish and sustain credibility, to alter beliefs and redirect the actions of others in support of your strategy. It demonstrates the commitment of the leadership team to the strategy; and by doing so, it influences and shapes the commitment levels of the staff to the strategy. A commitment plan complements the blueprinting implementation plan.

Commitment is the willingness of individuals and organizational entities to expend high levels of effort and make sacrifices over an extended period of time to overcome obstacles and meet challenges on behalf of a shared agenda. The strategic logic of commitment is that it yields trust; trust yields belief; belief yields effort, effort that proceeds without the depleting effects of organizational friction. It is through friction-free effort that strategic performance is accelerated during commitment planning.

Ideally, no commitment planning would be necessary. If your organization clearly is going to enthusiastically and automatically embrace your initiative, you are in a very unusual and favorable situation. Unfortunately, this is usually not the case. As a result of previous half-hearted efforts, constant shifting of priorities, and a collapse of trust caused by downsizing and other "anti-people" initiatives, many IT managers find themselves with a staff who have one or more of the following attitudes:

- They are jaded, skeptical, and cynical, and regard any new initiative and strategy as the "strategic program du jour." The staff maxim is, "Don't bother, this too shall pass."
- Based on precedent, they think: "Management believes deeply in little and is committed to less." To staff, management appears to suffer from attention deficit disorder.
- Based on previous efforts to which they devoted themselves only to have their projects canceled, their feelings about management are that, "It is not that they do not have the strength of their convictions; it is that they don't even have any convictions to have strength about."

Consequently, the staff become adept at pretending to believe in a strategy and then pretending to execute it. Commitment planning is necessary to move from pretense to effort and to advance from mediocre performance to exceptional strategic performance.

Types of Commitment

Though typically presented and discussed as a nondecomposable idea, commitment can be partitioned into the three subclassifications: intellectual, emotional, and political commitment.

Intellectual Commitment

Intellectual commitment is the rationalization of an effort. It appeals to logic and reason, and is therefore normally the easiest to attain. A person who is intellectually committed is someone who understands the flow of thinking and the evidence that supports the initiative and is satisfied with that chain of thought. Due to the technical and precision nature of their work, members of an information technology community pride themselves on their reasoning abilities and usually will not support initiatives unless they have seen, critiqued, and come to satisfactory terms with the evidence.

Emotional Commitment

Emotional commitment represents how an individual feels about an initiative. An initiative may present opportunity at the same time it invokes fear. People ask themselves the loaded commitment question, "What does this mean to me?" They speculate "What will it mean to my job status, my mobility, my skills and competencies, my relationships, my personal ambition, and so on?" Emotional commitment is obviously a very personal type of commitment, thus the variety of responses to an initiative may be as varied as the number of people involved.

People who are emotionally uncomfortable with a strategy will often engage in desperate logic in an attempt to find any and all possible refutations to group together as a rebuttal. Though normally covert, an overt example of desperate logic is the following:

> Person A loans person B her car. When B returns it, Person A tells her that it has a new dent, to which person B replies, "The car had the dent when I borrowed it, and I did not return the car with a dent; and, in any case, I did not borrow your car."

A person who engages in desperate logic is very uncomfortable with a situation and will grope for any means to reduce that discomfort; certainly, such a person will not commit.

Political Commitment

Political commitment is the willingness of individuals to use their organizational power to make something happen. Organizations divide, as do all social institutions, into political interest groups based on factors such as division of work, resource allocations, shared mental models, training and skills, shared experiences, career aspirations, and job levels. Strategic change will, by definition, alter status, power, resource allocations, and importance of job positions in the organization. As a consequence, some political groups will perceive the strategy as a threat; some will prefer the status quo; and even those who would win by successful implementation will often be hesitant due to the risks associated with instituting a new political order. By their nature, political groups focus on the continued well-being of their makeup; that is, the group interest supersedes organizational interest. Groups are not interested in change, regardless of merit, that will have a negative impact on their standing. As a consequence, political groups will try to control discussions, the legitimacy of the proposed strategy, and the degree of commitment. Political commitment is, consequentially, the hardest to win.

In summary, consider that commitment sits on a continuum with two extremes: At one end are the fully committed, who understand and like the strategy, and are willing to use their power to implement it; at the other end of the continuum are the noncommitted, who think the strategy is nonsense, and who will use their political power to stop it. For the blueprinting strategy to succeed, you must gain a favorable position along the continuum that mobilizes *enough* commitment; that is, enough sustainable effort to overcome all the inevitable obstacles to implementing the strategy.

Commitment Design

Commitment is too important to be assumed, to be left to chance, or to be the product of wishful thinking. You must explicitly design a commitment strategy as part of your overall strategy. The objective of a commitment strategy is to build, sustain, and compound organizational and individual commitment to your overall strategy by overcoming overt and benign intellectual, emotional, and political opposition. You engage a commitment strategy to reduce friction to your efforts.

Figure 6.4 illustrates an eight-step process that can be used to integrate commitment into your efforts in an anticipatory manner, as opposed to being ill prepared to react to friction when it inevitably occurs. The methodology strings together a set of strategy frameworks that help you think about the problem. As with all strategy frameworks, the success you achieve from using it depends on your sensitivity, understanding, and imagination in applying it. The point is, don't just mechanically fill in the blanks.

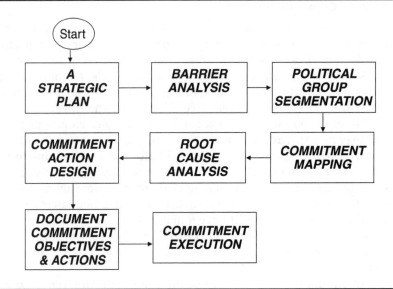

FIGURE 6.4 Commitment design methodology. An eight-step process is used to anticipate commitment problems and resolve them in an anticipatory manner.

Step 1: Strategic Plan

Any strategic initiative will require a commitment strategy if it is to have a realistic chance of altering the status quo. As illustrated in Figure 6.5, such an initiative will fall within an individual's "zone of critical evaluation." People will not commit to actions that fall within their zone of critical evaluation unless a satisfactory level of intellectual, emotional, and political commitment is achieved.

Step 2: Barrier Analysis

You should develop a barrier analysis table (Figure 6.6) that is a matrix of strategy objectives against anticipated barriers to success. The intersection of objectives with the "commitment" barrier confirms that lack of commitment will be an obstacle to address in an anticipatory manner.

Step 3: Political Groups Segmentation

As shown in Figure 6.7, segment and analyze each political group as to their potential commitment to the strategy. The questions of interest are:

- What are the defining attributes that distinguish this group of people?
- What is the group's interest? What public and private agendas are they trying to achieve?

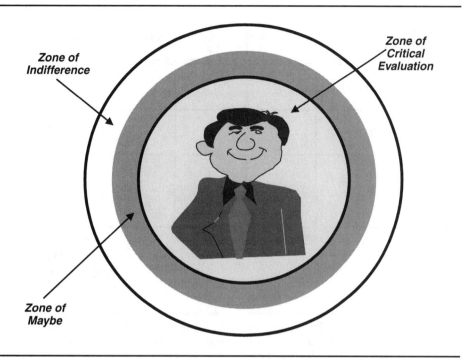

FIGURE 6.5 Zone of critical evaluation. A strategy will require a supporting commitment strategy to alter the status quo.

- What are the group commitment levels? Where do they stand on each type of commitment; what is their overall commitment reaction to the strategy?

All groups that are material to your success should be segmented and analyzed in this way.

Step 4: Commitment Map

As shown in Figure 6.8, locate each political group on a commitment map. The commitment map visualizes the initial commitment levels confronting you. For groups in supportive positions, you may want to devise commitment actions to sustain their commitment. For groups in adverse positions, you will need to undertake commitment actions to move them to more favorable positions. While a position of H, H, H would be ideal for all groups, the pragmatic objective is to reduce resistance (friction) to a manageable level; probably you will not be able to completely eliminate it. When a strategy is intended to have deep and far-reaching impact, it will of course disenfranchise some. Your goal is to win enough commitment to succeed.

	BARRIER 1	BARRIER 2	BARRIER 3	Commit- ment	BARRIER N
OBJECTIVE 1					
OBJECTIVE 2					
OBJECTIVE N					

INTERSECTION
Need commitment strategy.

FIGURE 6.6 Barrier analysis. A barrier analysis should be charted to determine whether the absence of commitment is an obstacle to achieving at least one strategic objective from the plan.

Political Group: _____

Objectives	What defines the group?	What is their agenda?	Intellectual Commitment L M H	Emotional Commitment L M H	Political Commitment L M H	Summary: Committed? Y N
OBJECTIVE 1						
OBJECTIVE 2	*N/A*	*N/A*				
OBJECTIVE N	*N/A*	*N/A*				

FIGURE 6.7 Political group segmentation. Political groups should be defined, segmented, and analyzed as to their commitment levels.

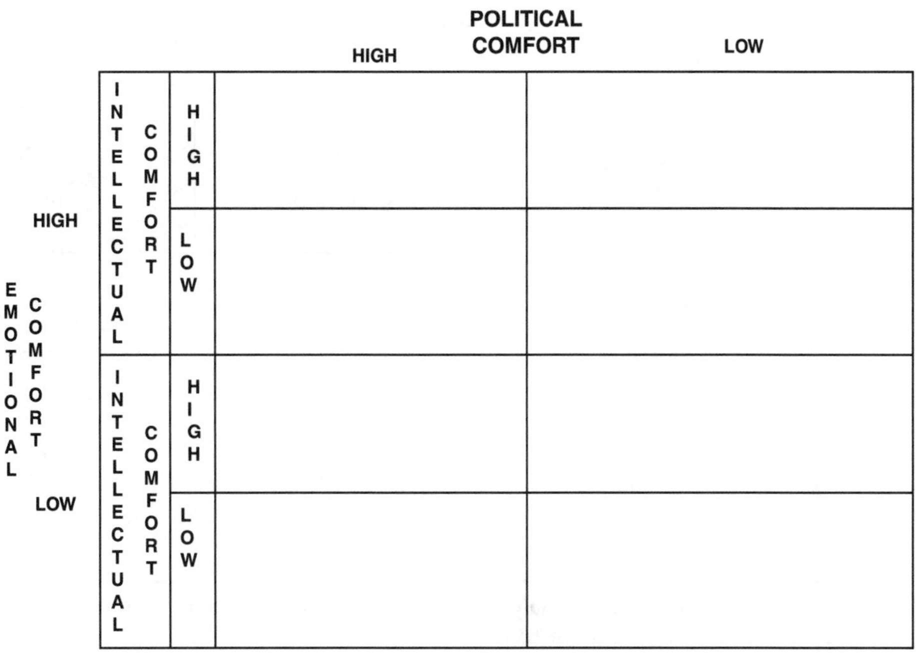

POLITICAL COMFORT

HIGH   LOW

HIGH

LOW

EMOTIONAL COMFORT

INTELLECTUAL COMFORT — HIGH

INTELLECTUAL COMFORT — LOW

INTELLECTUAL COMFORT — HIGH

INTELLECTUAL COMFORT — LOW

FIGURE 6.8 Commitment map. The commitment map visualizes the state of commitment facing you.

Step 5: Root Cause Analysis

To move nonsupportive groups to more favorable commitment positions, you must first understand why they oppose the strategy. As shown in Figure 6.9, the technique of root cause analysis can be used to perform this analysis. Root cause analysis is built on the medical model of illness diagnosis. The most discernible signs are the symptoms; these represent the external manifestations of the problem. Treatments directed at this level will provide only temporary relief. What is *causing* the symptoms is the pathology. Treatment at this level is curative, though the pathology can reoccur. Underlying the pathology is the etiology, or root cause, of the problem. Treatment at this level permanently eliminates the problem.

Conduct root cause analysis for both supportive and adverse political groups. For supportive groups, analyze the root cause of their support so that it can be sustained. For noncommitted groups, go through all three layers of analysis.

Political Group: _____

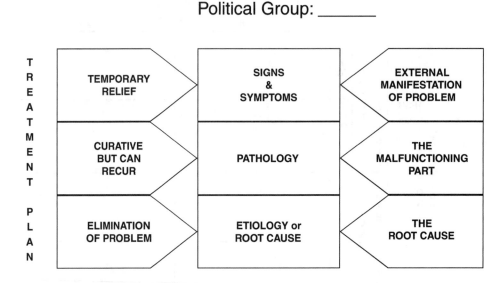

FIGURE 6.9 Root cause analysis. Root cause analysis may be used to understand the source of noncommitment to the strategy.

Step 6: Commitment Action Design

Commitment action design is the heart of the commitment design process and is the most creative activity. The first action is to draw a before-and-after commitment map (Figure 6.10), which visualizes the commitment repositioning that you want to achieve, that is, the desired future state of commitment. The figure shows the commitment positions we covet for each political group. It is good practice to itemize on the arrows that illustrate the repositioning either the influential roles and/or people that need to be persuaded to ensure that the repositioning occurs.

Having set the repositioning objectives on the before-and-after commitment map (Figure 6.10), it is now necessary to itemize the specific actions that you will take to make the change commitment positions occur. This can be documented on a root cause action map (Figure 6.11).

As shown there, for each political group, itemize the previously completed root cause analysis (Figure 6.9) and document by root cause level the treatment plan (actions) that you will take.

The actions you take are a function of your sensitivity and intimate understanding of your company, culture, and the specific situation. Typical commitment actions may include education, expert testimony, changes in the internal rewards and recognition systems, changes in the way the internal economy

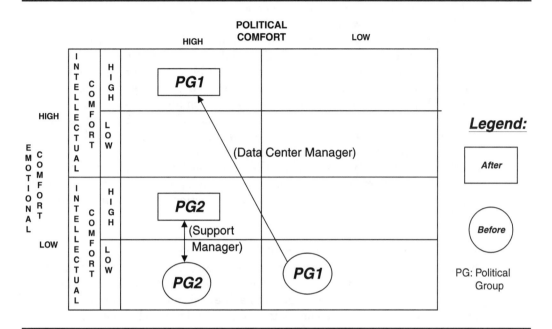

FIGURE 6.10   Before-and-after commitment map. This commitment map shows the change in commitment positions that are desired to achieve the reduced state of friction.

	Political Group 1		Political Group 2		Political Group *n*	
	Analysis	Treatment	Analysis	Treatment	Analysis	Treatment
SIGNS & SYMPTOMS						
PATHOLOGY						
ETIOLOGY						

FIGURE 6.11   Root cause action map. This framework can be used to document the treatment plan to deal with each level of the previous root cause analysis.

works, building of alliances, opening opportunities for participation, and using carrot approaches as well as bully pulpits.

Of particular importance is the development of a set of executive commitment actions that send a strong and unambiguous signal to the community that senior management supports the plan. If executive commitment begins and ends with managers just nodding their heads, the organizational proletariat will question their staying power. Senior management must take substantive commitment actions to change a skeptical staff's impression of management sincerity. Before employees will commit and extend their effort, they must believe that management will genuinely support the strategy. To establish such credibility, management must either have a reputation that has earned them respect (in which case, establishing commitment is relatively easy) or they must earn such respect by taking actions that confirm their position of commitment.

Step 7: Document Commitment Objectives and Actions

The net results of the previous six steps can be succinctly documented using the objective and action forms shown in Figure 6.12. Identify an objective for each political group and at least one action to achieve it. As is routine in documenting objectives and actions, assign a target date and method of measurement to verify that it has been achieved.

Step 8: Commitment Execution

As shown in Figure 6.13, you convert the commitment actions into implementation programs and associated projects. You also must periodically monitor these programs and projects, including updating commitment maps to adapt the commitment plan to the constantly evolving times and circumstances.

Candidate Commitment Actions

As just described in the eight-step process, implementing EAB will require a commitment plan to overcome the intellectual, emotional, and political obstacles. The following are a candidate set of representative actions that you can tailor to your management's commitment to blueprinting:

> **Architecture curriculum.** Management should fund the development of an architecture curriculum. Include EAB education in the syllabus for the application and infrastructure model cells of your architecture framework.
>
> **Executive bully pulpit.** Senior IT management should repeatedly publicize their support for blueprinting in all the various media that they use to communicate with and identify priorities to the staff.
>
> **New architect staff positions.** New IT job classifications should be developed for architecture positions. Blueprinting skills should be made a

COMMITMENT OBJECTIVE:	
DESCRIPTION:	
MEASURE:	DATE:

COMMITMENT MOVE:				
DESCRIPTION:				
OWNER:	CHAMPION :	PRIORITY :	MEASURE:	DATE:
NOTES:				

FIGURE 6.12 Commitment objectives and actions. These two forms can be used to document your commitment plan.

mandatory requirement of the IT architect classification. For imagery purposes, here are four suggested job levels (in the Information Age, your architects will prove to be your warrior class, so it's fitting to classify them in the tradition of Jedi knights):

- **Junior architect.** A novice architect who works under the direct supervision of more experienced members of the staff.
- **Jedi architect.** An experienced architect who is capable of doing all, or almost all, architecture design and documentation functions with minimum supervision.
- **Jedi master architect.** A very experienced and senior IT architect.
- **Yoda class architect.** An exceptional architect who is a rare master of the discipline.

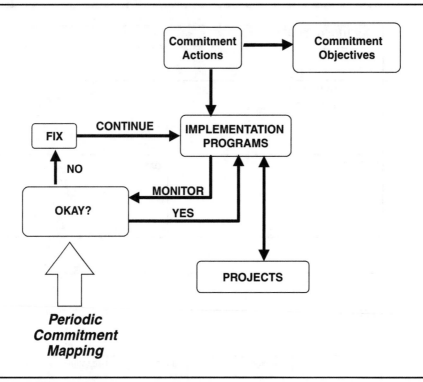

FIGURE 6.13   Commitment execution. A strategic control process must be implemented to monitor, tune, and adapt the commitment plan.

EAB presentations in lieu of sketches. IT management should insist on blueprint presentations in lieu of sketches at architecture reviews.

Staff performance reviews. Part of the performance review of architects should include an evaluation of their blueprinting skills.

Staff promotion factor. Promotion through the architect job classification levels should consider blueprinting skills.

Excellence awards. The reward and recognition program should include special public rewards and recognition for outstanding blueprinting.

Requests for proposals (RFP). Vendor system proposals must include appropriate drawings. Vendor sketches should disqualify submissions from consideration.

Value-chain partners. With the electronic bonding of the value-chain, architecture more frequently must include interfaces with value-chain partners. Efforts should be made to persuade business partners to engage in blueprinting for the systems of mutual interest.

Audit sampling tied to management bonuses. Periodic statistical auditing should be done to test the quality of the AOR EABs. A portion of annual bonuses should be tied to the results of such audits.

Consultants. Blueprinting competency should be a required skill when considering the use of professional service companies that provide architecture consulting support.

Formal architecture reviews. Formal architecture approval reviews should require that blueprints be the subject materials of the review. Architectures submitted for review that do not meet EAB standards should be failed; and repeated absence of blueprints for review should be prima facie evidence of architecture incompetence and professional malpractice.

Make tacit knowledge visible. Using your architecture framework as the context, create a Web site and make the architecture visible. Table 6.1 summarizes the contents of each architecture framework cell (Chapter 2). Because framework cells exist at different organizational levels (corporate, business unit, etc.) the design of the Web site must take into account the issues of time (as-was-built, as-is-built, to-be-built, and vision) and the partitioning of responsibilities across many architectural organization units and framework levels. This can be accomplished through a hierarchy of linked frameworks.

This list is intended to stimulate your commitment to design thinking by presenting a set of actionable examples. Remember, your custom set of commitment actions should be sensitive to your organization's culture and style.

Commitment Planning Summary

The eight-step process described in this section can guide you as you develop a commitment plan to enable your blueprinting strategy. Though the process has been illustrated as a linear process, it is, in practice, highly iterative.

As shown in Figure 6.14, your goal is to change the payoff matrix of the various political groups. Before execution of your commitment plan, the minimax (minimum-maximum lost) of their payoff matrix tells them that they have the least to lose by *not* committing. Your commitment plan changes the minimax payoff so that they have the least to lose by committing. In essence, a commitment plan works by changing the reward/lose structure for each political group so that they minimize their maximum potential lost though commitment, effort, and collaboration rather than indifference, resistance, and friction. In this way, strategic performance is enabled. The absence of commitment, not the poor selection of a blueprinting methodology, is often the primary impetus of implementation failure.

TABLE 6.1   Architecture Framework Cell Definitions

	Inventory	*Principles*	*Models*	*Standards*
Infrastructure	A structured inventory of the infrastructure IT assets.	The persistent set of rules and policies that govern the selection and utilization of information technologies.	Multiperspective (logical, physical, functional, and conceptual) diagrams, schematics, or models that illustrate the IT elements that comprise the IT infrastructure, and the interrelationships of those elements to each other. (EAB applies to this cell).	Agreed-to standards used to build and evolve the IT infrastructure.
Data	A structured inventory of the databases of record.	The persistent set of rules and policies that govern the administration, management, and utilization of the data assets.	Multiperspective (logical, physical, and conceptual) diagrams, schematics, or models (entity relationship models, multidimensional data models) that illustrate the structure and contents of the datastores.	Agreed-to standards used to build, administer, and evolve data and databases.
Applications	A structured inventory of the business applications, and the relationships of those applications to the business.	The persistent set of rules and policies that govern the design, purchasing, management, and utilization of the business applications.	Multiperspective (logical, physical, functional, and conceptual) diagrams, schematics, or models that illustrate the IT elements that comprise the business applications, and the interrelationships of those elements to each other. (EAB applies to this cell).	Agreed-to standards used to build and evolve the application portfolio.
Organization	A structured inventory of the human resources that perform architectural work.	The persistent set of rules and policies that govern the human resource.	Diagrams, schematics, or models that illustrate the management, competencies, organizational structure, and processes of the human resource.	Agreed-to standards used to manage and motivate the human resource.

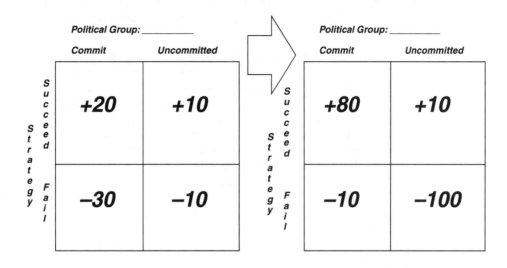

FIGURE 6.14   Minimax. A commitment plan works by changing the payoff matrix of each political group.

FREQUENTLY ASKED QUESTIONS

The introduction of EAB has generated a great deal of discussion and debate. The following are some of the more common questions whose answers have proved particularly helpful to rounding out and stimulating thought about architecture blueprinting.

Question 1. Architecture work is very creative. Won't EAB stifle creativity?

EAB focuses on how you represent and communicate IT architecture. It neither dictates nor enforces any design or development methodology. Regardless of the creative excellence of a proposed architecture, it is useless if you are the only one who can understand and appreciate it. EAB is no more stifling than the English alphabet is to a writer or the basic music notes are to a composer.

Focusing on the format of the presentation of the architecture emphasizes appearance at the cost of substance. Architecture creativity should be concerned with understanding the problem and designing an elegant solution, and doing so in a manner that maximizes net-present maneuverability and leverages standard and reference architectures. The actual presentation of the architectural solution should be a rather mundane and mechanical task.

Question 2. My customers, the developers, are perfectly happy with my current drawings and associated documentation. Why should I change?

This question assumes that a satisfactory situation is never in need of reform. If the architects are satisfied with the status quo, and the customers, the developers, are satisfied with the status quo, why fix what isn't broken? The fault with this argument is that, under scrutiny, there is often a sham. The developers may say they are very happy with the architecture sketches they are given because accepting this form leaves them ample room to do as they please. They know that sketches don't provide ample specificity to do any actual development work. Sketches are very good for talking about architecture, but not very good for implementing architecture. Developers have to do the latter.

Politically adept developers politely accept the sketches from the architect and proceed to design a solution as they choose. Since the sketches are so ambiguous, the developers know from experience that they can apply their creativity with impunity to solve the problem. They know their interpretation will be perfectly reasonable and defensible.

So your architects and developers are happy with the process because it enables each to be independent and successful. The architects sketch what they please and the developers implement what they please. The only loser in this con game is the business.

Question 3. EAB demands too much detail in some places and not enough in others. Isn't it true that you can't really standardize what needs to be expressed?

This is the Goldilocks dilemma applied to EAB: It is either too hot or too cold; it is never just right. There are two simple answers to this question:

1. If a particular icon or notation requires too much detail for a given situation, only complete it in as much detail as needed to communicate your intent. Ignore the variables that provide superfluous information.
2. If a particular icon or notation is insufficient to communicate your intent, use annotations, footnotes/endnotes, or user-defined functional specifications to elaborate the drawing with the missing information.

In the former case, you may wish to amend the methodology to eliminate the excess notation. In the latter case, you will probably want to amend the methodology with additional notation. EAB, like software or any methodology, will evolve as demanded by practical experience.

Question 4. Without an intelligent drawing tool, EAB is too labor-intensive. Shouldn't we just wait until Computer Software Engineering (CASE) or Computer-Aided Design (CAD) tools that incorporate EAB-like functionality become available?

While this argument has merit on a productivity basis, it misses the more fundamental issue. Before you can discuss how to maximize productivity, you must be doing the right thing. If sketches are inadequate, then rapidly developed sketches will only be inadequate sooner. High productivity of ambiguous architectures is not productive at all.

You first must accept that you need to adopt and implement a rigorous blueprinting system with change management and, preferably, design methods for extreme maneuverability. Given this decision, you can then work on improving productivity. Without a doubt, as CASE/CAD tools become available, formal blueprinting will be faster and easier. In the meantime, apply the available tools as best you can to do the right thing.

Question 5. We have previously tried to implement a host of software engineering practices. None of them had staying power. Why should we believe that EAB will be different?

This is a serious problem. The software industry remains in the *dawn stage*, characterized by rhetoric about methodology that far exceeds the execution of methodology. Understandably, people who are used to having complete freedom will resist the imposition of rules. EAB's staying power will only be proven if management implements it with the level of commitment discussed in this chapter.

Question 6. EAB is too much work. How can we justify the effort?

EAB is not too much work or too little work. It is the amount of work required to clearly specify an architecture. To argue reasonably that it is too much work, you must be able to demonstrate that you can communicate as much information with as much clarity to a wide audience in a simpler manner. If you can provide equal or greater amounts information with fewer icons, notations, and functional specifications, then you have a superior methodology and should share it for everybody's benefit. If you can't, then EAB is, at least for the moment, the best of the available alternatives.

Question 7. We benchmarked best architecture practices and did not find anyone doing formal blueprinting. Doesn't that indicate that many organizations are doing just fine without rigorous architecture diagramming?

Under scrutiny, benchmarking has some very undesirable attributes as the basis for making strategic decisions. If we follow the logic of this question, it would indicate that architecture strategy is pretty simple. All you have to do is benchmark best-in-class companies and mimic their procedures.

The question to ask about this approach is, which companies did the best-in-class companies mimic?

Someone has to be the innovator or nothing new worth copying happens. You have to ask yourself whether you want to be the someone others are copying or the one who copies. To be successful as a hypercompetitor, you need to be an innovator, not a follower.

Clearly then, one problem with this approach is that it is a formula for mediocrity. The logic of benchmarking is that everyone copies the leader. After a while, everyone has incorporated the same practices. Is that a formula for hypercompetitive advantage?

Another problem with this approach is that it assumes everyone is sharing his or her best practices. If you could do excellent blueprints and were engaged in a struggle for survival in a hypercompetitive marketplace, would you let your opponents know? Would you want consultants revealing to your competitors what you have struggled to achieve?

Research indicates that companies that have adopted rigorous architecture blueprinting don't talk about it; it doesn't show up in benchmarking studies because participants only share-dated methods, and they will only share-date methods because they won't give away the hard-earned basis of advantage.

Question 8. *What do we do about people who just won't change?*

Every opportunity should be given to people to learn and adapt. Unfortunately, the marketplace is a very unforgiving place. Consumers vote with their feet and dollars; they don't care that some of your architects liked it better the old way. In the end, just as there are legacy systems, there are legacy people. People who won't or can't adjust to the new methods will have to be given different opportunities in or outside the organization that are more consistent with their skills and their decision not to learn new methods.

Question 9. *The start-up effort to create a complete set of AOR EABs is too time-consuming and costly. How can we get going without establishing a complete set of AOR EABs?*

Certainly it is best to establish an AOR EAB baseline, but if you can't, do the following:

1. Have the architecture council design and publish the set of EABs that will compose the AOR.
2. As new projects are initiated, develop TBB EABs as complete replacement blueprints. The architecture team for each TBB EAB documents both an AIB blueprint and a TBB blueprint. The completed TBB EAB becomes the initial baseline EAB upon successful implementation.

As a consequence of this approach, the AOR EAB set will be created gradually as a by-product of new architecture initiatives.

In establishing an AOR EAB baseline, remember that your architecture is in motion as you try to baseline it. In addition to creating EABs for all your AIB systems, you must also take into account all the undocumented TBBs that are in progress as you do the baseline. In essence, to do a complete baseline, you must create AIB blueprints for all systems as of the baseline date, and transaction TBB blueprints for all architecture changes in progress but not implemented after that date.

Question 10. How can we make the blueprints more visible to the entire organization?

As discussed in Chapter 2, architecture is tacit knowledge, and good knowledge strategy is to spread tacit knowledge. The obvious strategy is to put the blueprints on the Web with search and browse software that permits the user to locate blueprints of interest and then navigate them both horizontally and vertically. You will be surprised to discover how easy access to the blueprints can improve productivity.

Question 11. What do you think will happen in terms of IT architecture professionalism and specialization?

IT architecture will gradually become a service that companies will buy on retainer from professional IT architecture firms. As the importance of architecture becomes clearer and the methods of doing it become more formalized, major discontinuities in the skill sets of people who are called IT architects will emerge. The delivery system for legal services, building architects, and other specialized services is based on the professional practice model. This will be the end state for IT architecture as well. Companies will have an internal staff of architects who will work on an ongoing basis with consulting firms that specialize in architecture.

Question 12. It seems impossible to learn the drawing system from just reading the book. Isn't that a limitation?

Few people learn data normalization, entity relationship modeling, object-oriented analysis, or physical database design just by reading a book. These are sophisticated and complicated methodologies that require three balanced learning experiences:

1. Didactic classroom (or equivalent) instruction.
2. Hands-on practice under the guidance of an experienced practitioner (a teacher or mentor) to accelerate the learning curve.
3. Reference materials such as books, templates, and guidelines.

Blueprinting is no different from any of these, and there is no reason to expect that it could be or would be.

Question 13: Is it true, as some architecture pundits suggest, that a comprehensive and consistent set of principles is the essence of architecture?

Principles are important and necessary but certainly not sufficient. In every engineering discipline, blueprints are the bottom line. When construction engineers huddle at a site, it is around the blueprints, not the principles. Principles are input that guides architecture work; blueprints are output. You need both.

Question 14: Isn't the Index framework missing the business view of the architecture that the Zachman framework provides?

An architect is the link between the business requirements and the developer's solution. The Index framework that we have been applying is an architect's view of the information technology architecture. As shown in Table 6.2, we can add two more columns that extend the framework to include a business view and a developer's view of the architecture. The framework is now broader in scope and should be understood to represent an information architecture framework rather than an information technology architecture framework (a subtle but important distinction). The business view provides the context for the architect's view and the architect's view provides the context for the developer's view.

It would certainly be desirable to provide a complete information architecture, and it should unquestionably be a long-term intent, but it is another order of difficulty to accomplish. Given the distressed state of IT architecture in most IT organizations today, accomplishing the Index framework would be a significant achievement. The beachhead approach is to implement the Index framework, and once that is secured, extend the framework to include the other columns.

TABLE 6.2   Information Architecture Framework

	Business	Architect's View				Developer's View
		Inventory	Principles	Models	Standards	
Infrastructure						
Data						
Applications						
Organization						

Question 15: Why can't the Unified Modeling Language (UML) be used as the drawing system for IT architecture?

This question is based on a common misunderstanding of what UML is and is not. UML is an object-oriented modeling system, with schematics and notations for application development. Thus, you could use UML as the documentation methodology for defining the requirements of an IT architecture blueprinting system, but not for the blueprinting system. To restate, UML or any other object-oriented analysis methodologies could have been used to define EAB, but in and of themselves, they are not suitable to be the blueprinting system. If you doubt that this is true, develop a complicated AIB blueprint with EAB and then try to use UML notation to express the same information. This is not a criticism of UML. Methodologies and associated drawing systems are developed with expressed purposes, and UML's purpose is the analysis and design of software applications. EAB would be as bad an analysis/design tool as UML is an architecture-blueprinting tool.

Question 16: Even if we concede that we should adopt rigorous architecture blueprinting, EAB is immature and imperfect. Why shouldn't we just wait until blueprinting is perfected?

The question is not should you wait for maturity; the question is, can you afford to wait for perfection? If the arguments in this book regarding the nexus of hypercompetition, the Information Age, and blueprinting are correct, waiting will provide temporary risk avoidance but at the cost of falling behind more risk-oriented hypercompetitors who don't share your hesitation to accept something until it is "perfect." Keep in mind that all innovation is born incomplete. The question is not whether an innovation like blueprinting is perfect; it certainly is not and never will be. The question is whether, with all its imperfections, it is clearly better than the incumbent method, sketching; and it certainly is that.

Advantage is a relative, not an absolute, concept; and it is the unquestionable relative superiority of architecture diagramming over sketching that should motivate you to adopt it as soon as possible. Presentation gurus who make their living by lamenting the absence of this feature or that feature in a new product or methodology make a living by discovering what is wrong with something. As an individual responsible for enabling your business to survive in extraordinarily challenging times, it is your challenge to find out what is right about something. The pundits and gurus talk about architecture; you have to do architecture. If you wait, you will buy some time, but eventually you will find yourself in a worse situation than the one you originally sought to avoid because those less trepidatious than you will be using blueprinting and OODA disruption against you, and you will have to then implement blueprinting with less time, preparation, and care.

Question 17: If we use EAB to draw physical architectures, would multiple drawing of a given system always result in the same schematic as the output?

The answer is yes and no. Since systems may be decomposed differently by different people, the system block hierarchical decomposition may be different, but it should terminate with the same set of application lists. The platform diagrams and interoperability diagrams should demonstrate equivalence. Though they might not be identical, it should be possible to show that they are equivalent to each other, meaning that by making different notation choices, you could map one drawing into the other. Equivalence is an important attribute of EAB that contributes to the formality of the technique. If two interoperability diagrams are supposed to represent the same domain of systems, and they are not equivalent, then one of the drawings is wrong.

Question 18: We agree with the need for rigorous blueprints, a high net-present maneuver, and an architecture that meets all review and evaluation criteria. Nevertheless, at a practical level, management is always in a frantic state to get something done. What can we do?

As stated in Chapter 5, to accelerate speed, improve quality, and maximize net-present maneuver, organizations have to move from constructing architectures from elementary components to subassemblies, component architectures, reference architectures, and standard architectures. To further expedite speed, you can use "pontoon bridge architectures." A pontoon bridge is a temporary structure used in an emergency to bridge a river or other obstacle. It trades speed in construction for short-term efficacy. Pontoon bridges are a temporary solution to be used only until the permanent structure is built to replace them.

A pontoon bridge architecture then is an entry into a specific reference architecture. It is relatively simple to construct, and the necessary construction elements are inventoried. It can function for some period of time under low or moderate utilization, but it is never intended to be the final architecture. By virtue of its net-present maneuverability, it is designed to rapidly evolve into a more stable and complete member of a reference architecture. The pontoon architecture meets the pressing need for an immediate solution, but is understood to be only a temporary solution.

Question 19: Does architecture have to be done at an enterprise level or can it be done at the business unit level?

Architecture must be governed at the enterprise level, though the execution of the architecture can be dispersed across business units. The enterprise business strategy will oscillate over time between a strong union, where all business units work tightly together, to a multistate, where business units act independently; therefore, the architecture must be resilient enough to support any point along the business unit collaboration continuum. If you govern architecture in an integrated but dispersed manner, it can provide for adaptability at any point along the continuum. If you govern it at a business unit level, it will work while the business units are independent but collapse when times and circumstances change and greater cross-business unit collaboration is required.

Question 20: How do data flow diagrams and business process flow modeling relate to EAB?

Data flow diagrams, process flow modeling, object-oriented analysis, along with a multitude of other analysis techniques may be used to analyze the business problem to determine the requirements of the architecture. As stated previously, EAB is not a design methodology; it is a system for rigorously documenting an architecture design. It complements these other methods, but does not replace them just as they don't replace it.

Question 21: When the word "application" is used as a row name in the architecture framework, does it have the same meaning as when used in the $al1 variable on a platform icon?

The confusion here is the result of the fallacy of equivocation. Equivocation occurs when the same word is used in an argument to mean two different things but the distinction is not made clear. Figure 6.15 shows the relationships that are embodied in the definition of the application row in the framework. When "application" is used to define a framework row, it means that entire figure. Within that figure the word appears again, but means a specific collection of business functions that are dispersed across IT elements. That is the meaning of "application" when used in $al1. It would be clearer to use a different name for the application framework row (system solution? function?) but a good appellation is not available.

The following will help you understand Figure 6.15:

- **System view.** A system is a coherent and ordered collection of IT objects arranged in a purposeful manner to deliver function to the business. A subsystem, a recursive concept, is a partition of a system (or subsystem) that delivers a meaningful component of the functionality of the overall system. Subsystems eventually reach a point of partitioning where further partitioning is no longer meaningful. At this point, they are apportioned into function-centric applications that are dispersed across IT elements to deliver the business functionality.
- **Process view.** A process is a coherent and ordered set of activities arranged in a purposeful manner to deliver function to the business. A subprocess, a recursive concept, is a decomposition of a process into finer detail. Subprocesses eventually reach a point where further decomposition is not meaningful and each is partitioned into multiple functions. Functions are decomposed into subfunctions (a recursive concept). Eventually, func-

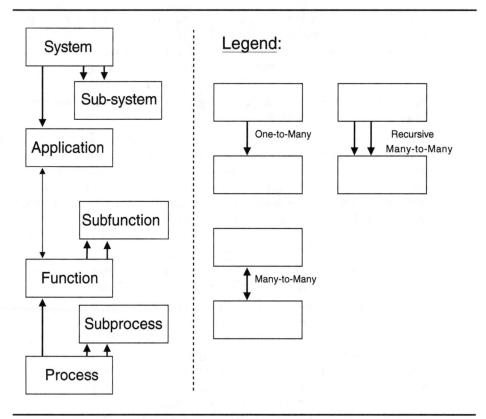

FIGURE 6.15   Definition of application row of architecture framework. The application row embodies systems, subsystems, and applications.

tion decomposition reaches a point where further decomposition is not meaningful and a final subfunction, an atomic function, is achieved. These atomic functions are allocated to function-centric applications.

An EAB diagram may then be thought of as a schematic that illustrates the crafted groupings of functions, data, and technology within the context of systems, subsystems, and applications.

Question 22: What distinguishes the relationships of system block diagrams, platform diagrams, and interoperability diagrams when they are all in the same core diagram set?

An EAB is assigned a domain that defines the boundaries of the architecture. Each of these diagram types illustrates the same domain but from different perspectives. The system block diagram illustrates the architecture, where systems are the unit of representation. The platform diagram opens up the lowest-level subsystem blocks and replaces each subsystem block by 1–n platform icons. The rest of the diagram remains whole; that is, databases, files, any system resources, and so on that appeared on the system block diagram must also appear on the platform diagram, but they now are related to a platform(s) rather than a system block. The interoperability diagrams keep the platform diagram whole, but information exchange definitions are replaced with interoperability definitions. Think of the three schematics as drawings of the same thing but at increasing levels of detail. Each schematic leverages the information from the higher-level schematic.

Any Other Questions?

The preceding questions and answers probably resolved many questions you may have had about EAB. But if you have any additional questions on IT strategy, IT architecture, or EAB, please feel free to submit them to bboar@rcgit.com. And note, you will find that many of your questions will resolve themselves as you use the methodology.

CONCLUSION

Implementing EAB is both simple and complex. It is simple in that once your staff surmount the learning curve and overcome all the start-up challenges, they will find drawing and maintaining structured blueprints to be natural, efficient, and effective. Given the chance, most people "get it" very quickly. They understand that blueprinting increases their architecture skills, accelerates the professionalism of their work, and enables them to do their jobs in a far superior manner. They internalize blueprinting, and it becomes the natural way for them to do the work.

Conversely, implementing EAB is complex because of people. People have prejudices, views, agendas, and questions; people are skeptical and have interests to protect; in short, people are people. These natural behaviors and reactions conspire to prevent the change from occurring. It is therefore very important to take into account the people issues that are addressed in this chapter. EAB will work only if you overcome the natural human resistance to change.

ENDNOTE

1. For a complete description of strategic repositioning see *The Art of Strategic Planning for Information Technology*, Bernard H. Boar, John Wiley & Sons, Inc., 1993; or *Cost-Effective Strategies for Client / Server Computing*, Bernard H. Boar, John Wiley & Sons, Inc., 1996.

Epilogue

Hiding behind the razor-thin facade of confidence and bravado of the typical CIO is an individual with the burdens and worries of Job:

> *For the thing which I did fear is come upon me. And that which I was afraid of has overtaken me. I was not at ease, neither was I quiet, nor had I rest. But trouble came.*

The thing feared most by the CIO is finally having the opportunity to serve as the basis of advantage for the business, but knowing at the same time that the foundation of that advantage, IT architecture, is in a state of disarray. Having been handed the torch of advantage for the enterprise, the CIO realizes that the advantage is constructed upon nothing more than a collection of haphazard and flimsy architectural sketches. He or she seeks greatness while his or her architecture teeters on the edge of collapse.

Referring back to Figure 6.9, root cause analysis, these troubles may be analyzed as follows:

Symptoms. The inability of the business to maneuver in response to escalating hypercompetition.

Pathology. The IT architecture is an unimaginable mess.

Root cause. The absence of disciplined architecture.

The solution to this problem will not emerge as long as the same people continue to do what they have been doing in the same manner. The solution will not be rooted in faster and cheaper. The solution will be rooted in fundamentally different and better.

The trinity of actions presented in this book expose an escape from this situation. Blueprinting provides a precision methodology through which you can communicate and document your IT architecture; configuration management describes a methodology for managing the evolution of complex collections of interrelated blueprints; and design for extreme maneuverability is a repeatable methodology for creating architectures with large adaptability spaces. So, though the thing you feared most may have come upon you, it need not be the cause of your ruination. Instead, it can become a fortuitous opportunity for renewal.

You have been presented with a rare opportunity to revolutionize how you do IT architecture. Implemented with energy, commitment, passion, and insight, you can create an architectural capability that will make you a marketplace predator to be feared. You will dominate the OODA wars of thrust and counterthrust by virtue of your ability to maneuver with unparalleled alacrity and be inside of your opponent's change cycle. As a consequence of your architectural acumen, the thing that your competitors feared most will come upon them; troubles will overwhelm them, they will know neither rest nor quiet, and the source of their fears and troubles will not be a questioning deity, it will be you.

APPENDIX A

Enterprise IT Architecture Blueprinting Icon Templates

This appendix supplies the templates for all the EAB icons defined in Chapter 3 of this book. These templates are also available via the Wiley Web site at www.wiley.com/compbooks/boar in .ppt format. Users should alter and re-standardize the templates to the specific needs of their organization before utilizing them. Each template is divided into icon and definition sections. Table A.1 provides an index for the templates.

TABLE A.1   Icon Templates

Figure Number	*Icon Template*
A.1	System Block Template.
A.2	System Block with Function List Template.
A.3	Function Block Template.
A.4	System Block Nesting Template.
A.5	File Icon with Connection Line Template.
A.6	Database Icon with Connection Line Template.
A.7	Any System Resource Icon with Connection Line Template.
A.8	User Group and Information Appliance Icons with Connection Line Template.
A.9	Annotation Icon Template.
A.10	Information Exchange Template.
A.11	Connector Icon Template.
A.12	Decision Rule Icon Template.
A.13	Hierarchical View Icon Template.
A.14	Platform Icon Template.
A.15	Configured Platform Icon Template.
A.16	Service Icon Template.
A.17	Service Path Icon Template.
A.18	Interoperability Definition Icon Template.
A.19	Scalability and Portability Icon Template.
A.20	Network Icon Template.
A.21	Object Grouping and Titling Icon Template.
A.22	Application List and Footnote List Templates.
A.23	Function List, Product List and OSI List Templates.
A.24	EAB Icon Template.
A.25	EAB Connector Icon Template.

```
$object_number
$system_name
$system_ acronym
$system_alias
$parent_id
/$child_id/
```

$object_number: A unique number identifying the system or subsystem of the form Sn.n.
$system_name: A unique name identifying the system or subsystem.
$system_acronym: A unique acronym identifying the system or subsystem.
$system_alias: An alias name for the system/subsystem.
$parent_id: Parent: $page_header\$parent_object_number
$parent_object_number: The object number, S number, of the parent system block.
$child_id: Child: $page_header\$child_object_number
$child_object_number: The object number, S number, of the child system block.
$page_header: $arch_acronym\$version_nbr of the parent or child EAB

FIGURE A.1   System block template.

```
$object_number
$system_name
$system_ acronym
$system_alias
$parent_id
/$child_id/

-Function List-
/$func/
```

$object_number: A unique number identifying the system or subsystem of the form Sn.n.
$system_name: A unique name identifying the system or subsystem.
$system_acronym: A unique acronym identifying the system or subsystem.
$system_alias: An alias name for the system/subsystem.
$parent_id: Parent: $page_header\$parent_object_number
$parent_object_number: The object number, S number, of the parent system block.
$child_id : Child: $page_header\$child_object_number
$child_object_number: The object number, S number, of the child system block.
$page_header: $arch_acronym\$version_nbr of the parent or child EAB
Function List: Title
$func: The name of a business function performed within this system block.

FIGURE A. 2   System block with function list template.

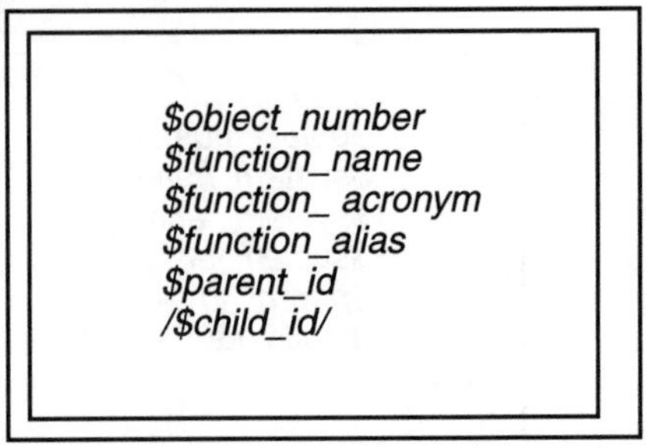

$object_number
$function_name
$function_ acronym
$function_alias
$parent_id
/$child_id/

$object_number: A unique number identifying the function or subfunction of the form Fn.n.
$function_name: A unique name identifying the function or subfunction.
$function_acronym: A unique acronym identifying the function or subfunction.
$function_alias: An alias name for the function/subfunction.
$parent_id: Parent: $page_header\$parent_object_number
$parent_object_number: The object number, F number, of the parent function block.
$child_id : Child: $page_header\$child_object_number
$child_object_number: The object number, F number, of the child function block.
$page_header: $arch_acronym\$version_nbr of the parent or child EAB

FIGURE A.3   Function block template.

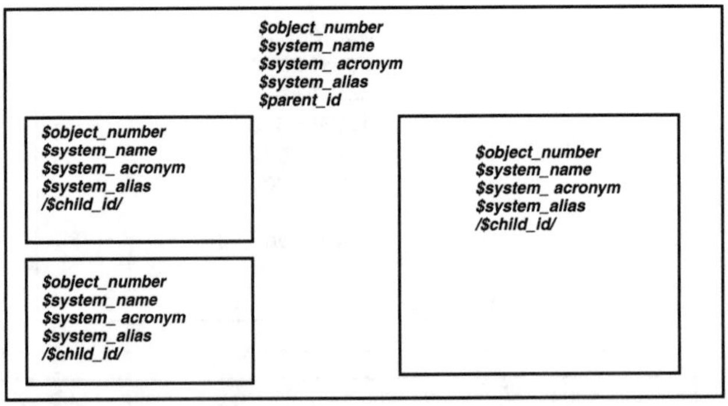

$object_number
$system_name
$system_ acronym
$system_alias
$parent_id

$object_number
$system_name
$system_ acronym
$system_alias
/$child_id/

$object_number
$system_name
$system_ acronym
$system_alias
/$child_id/

$object_number
$system_name
$system_ acronym
$system_alias
/$child_id/

$object_number: A unique number identifying the system or subsystem of the form Sn.n.
$system_name: A unique name identifying the system or subsystem.
$system_acronym: A unique acronym identifying the system or subsystem.
$system_alias: An alias name for the system/subsystem.
$parent_id: Parent: $page_header\$parent_object_number
$parent_object_number: The object number, S number, of the parent system block.
$child_id: Child: $page_header\$child_object_number
$child_object_number: The object number, S number, of the child system block.
$page_header: $arch_acronym\$version_nbr of the parent or child EAB

FIGURE A.4   System block nesting template.

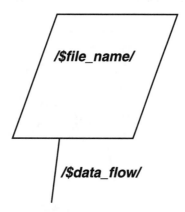

/$file_name/

/$data_flow/

$file_name: The unique name of a file.
$data_flow: The name(s) of the data item(s) being exchanged.

Note: The connector line should have a directional arrowhead.

FIGURE A.5   File icon with connection line template.

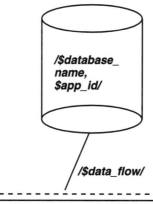

/$database_
name,
$app_id/

/$data_flow/

$database_name: The name of the database.
$app_id: The $app_id of the DT application layer that manages the database.
$data_flow: The name of the data items being exchanged.

Note: The connector line should have a directional arrowhead.

FIGURE A.6   Database icon with connection line template.

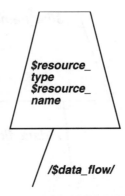

*$resource_
type
$resource_
name*

/$data_flow/

$resource_type: The type of resource: i.e., printer, plotter, etc.
$resource_name: A unique name of a resource.
$data_flow: The name of the data items being exchanged.

Note: The connector line should have a directional arrowhead

FIGURE A.7   Any system resource icon with connection line template.

/$user_group/**   **/$user_group/

                                    <UI, /$api/, $sproduct>
                                    /$data_flow $concurrent_user /

/$data_flow
$concurrent_users/

$user_group: $user_group_name, $geo, $total_users
$user_group_name: The functional title of the user group.
$total_users: Total number of users.
$concurrent_users: Concurrent users.
$geo: The geographical location of the user group.
$data_flow: The name of the data items being exchanged
$api: Defines the API or protocol that is invoked to interface with the service.
$sproduct: Defines the software product that delivers the service.
$itd: Either a generic type of information technology device or a specific information technology device.

Note: The connector line(s) should have a directional arrowhead.

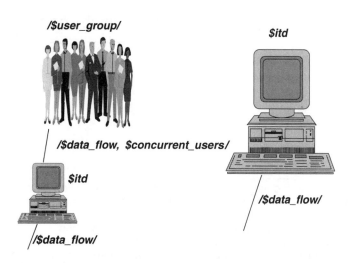

/$user_group/**   **$itd

/$data_flow, $concurrent_users/

$itd

/$data_flow/

/$data_flow/

FIGURE A.8 User group and information appliance icons with connection line template.

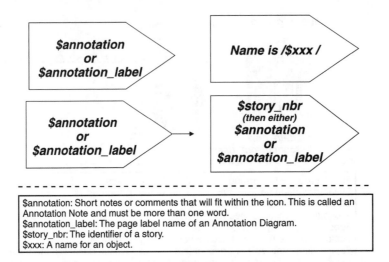

$annotation
or
$annotation_label

Name is /$xxx /

$annotation
or
$annotation_label

$story_nbr
(then either)
$annotation
or
$annotation_label

$annotation: Short notes or comments that will fit within the icon. This is called an Annotation Note and must be more than one word.
$annotation_label: The page label name of an Annotation Diagram.
$story_nbr: The identifier of a story.
$xxx: A name for an object.

FIGURE A.9   Annotation icon template.

$information_exchange

$information exchange: Defines the information that is flowing between objects. An information exchange is defined by an ordered set of the form
/$data_flow, $frequency, $ onoffline, middleware_def/.
$data_flow: The name of the data items being exchanged.
$frequency: The frequency of the exchange; i.e, real-time, daily, on-demand, etc.
$onoffline: Indicates whether the exchange is done online or batch.
$middleware_def: The name of the middleware that governs the exchange.

Note: The connector line should have a directional arrowhead.

FIGURE A.10   Information exchange template.

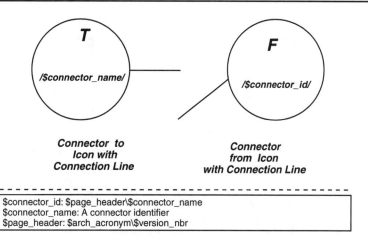

Connector to
Icon with
Connection Line

Connector
from Icon
with Connection Line

```
$connector_id: $page_header\$connector_name
$connector_name: A connector identifier
$page_header: $arch_acronym\$version_nbr
```

FIGURE A.11 Connector icon template.

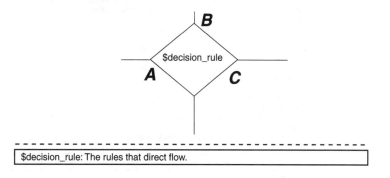

```
$decision_rule: The rules that direct flow.
```

FIGURE A.12 Decision rule icon template.

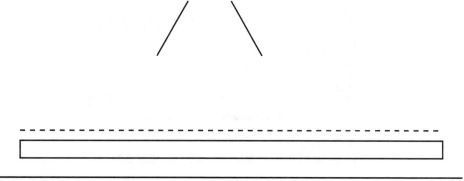

FIGURE A.13 Hierarchical view icon template.

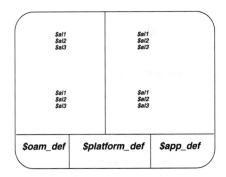

$al1 $al2 $al3	$al1 $al2 $al3
$al1 $al2 $al3	$al1 $al2 $al3

| $oam_def | $platform_def | $app_def |

$platform_def: Defines global attributes of the platform.
$platform_def: $object_nbr, $platform_name,$itd,/$role/,$os,$spec,$geo,
$machine_id
$object_nbr: An EAB unique number for this object of the form Pn.
$platform_name: A unique name for the platform.
$itd: Either a generic type of information technology device or a specific
information technology device.
$role: The role of the platform; i.e., Web server, enterprise server, desktop client, etc.

$os: The OS that runs on this platform. For dumb devices, this is left null.
$spec: A $page_label that points to a Detail Specification diagram.
$geo: The location of the ITD.
$machine-id: The physical identifier of the platform.

$app_def: Defines application attributes of the platform.
$app_def: /$appenv/
$app_env: The name of an application environment that all business applications
run under.

$oam_def: Defines OA&M attributes of the platform.
$oam_def: $support_domain, /$oam_env/
$oam_env: The name of an OA&M environment that all OA&M applications run
under.
$support_domain: Defines the organizational unit that is responsible for supporting
this device.

$al1: Defines application area identity.
$al1: ($app_id, $app_name, $app_type, $app_env,
$page_header\$system_block_object_nbr, //$func/:/$product//)
$app_id: A unique identifier number assigned to identify the application in the
format Pn.
$app_layer: The type of application layer; i.e., PN, PR, DT, etc.
$app_type: Identifies whether the application is an OA&M application or business
APP (default).
$app_name: The name of the application.
$page_header\$system_block_object_nbr: The number of a parent system block
preceded by the EAB acronym and version number that the system block is on.
$func: A business function performed by this application.
$product: A business product supported by this application.

$al2: defines OS an application or OA&M environments in sync with the
$app_env.
$al2: ((/$os/, /$env/))
$os: The OS that runs on top of previously defined OS for this platform.
$env (either $appenv or $oamenv): The application or OAM environment that runs
on top of the previously defined $app_ def or oam_def.

$al3: defines the software languages.
$al3: ((($language/)))
$languages: The languages that the associated application is written in.

FIGURE A.14 Platform icon template.

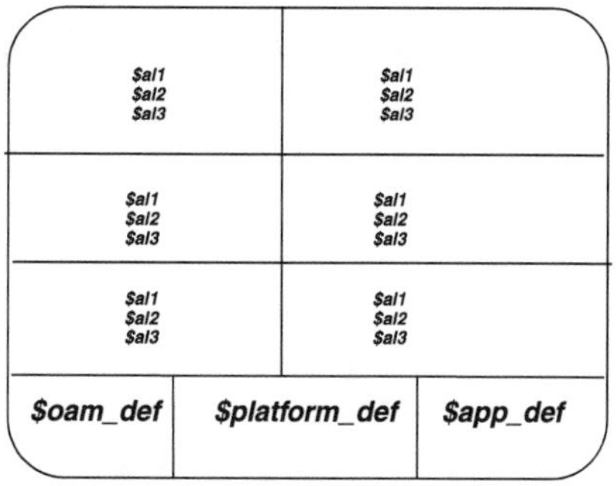

The following table/icon structure shows:

$al1 $al2 $al3	$al1 $al2 $al3
$al1 $al2 $al3	$al1 $al2 $al3
$al1 $al2 $al3	$al1 $al2 $al3

| $oam_def | $platform_def | $app_def |

$platform_def: Defines global attributes of the platform.
$platform_def: $object_nbr, $platform_name,$itd,/$role/,$os,$spec,$geo,
$machine_id
$object_nbr: A unique number for this object of the form In.
$platform_name: A unique name for the platform.
$itd: Either the generic type of information technology device or the specific type of
information technology device.
$role: The role of the platform, i.e., Web server, enterprise server, desktop client, etc.

$os: The OS that runs on this platform. For dumb devices, this is left null.
$spec: A $page_label that points to a Detail Specification diagram.
$geo: The location of the ITD.
$machine-id: The physical identifier of the platform.

$app_def: Defines application attributes of the platform.
$app_def: /$ appenv/
$app_env: The name of an application environment that all business applications
run under.

$oam_def: Defines OA&M attributes of the platform.
$oam_def: $support_domain, /$oam_env/
$oam_env: The name of an OA&M environment that all OA&M applications run
under.
$support_domain: Defines the organizational unit that is responsible for supporting
this device.

$al1: Defines application area identity.
$al1: ($app_id, $app_name, $app_type, $app_env,
$page_header\$system_block_object_nbr, //$func/:/$product//)
$app_id: A unique identifier number assigned to identify the application in the
format Pn. If a global layer, the format is Gn.
$app_layer: The type of application layer; i.e., PN, PR, DT, etc.
$app_type: Identifies whether the application is an OA&M application or business
application (default).
$app_name: The name of the application.
$page_header\$system_block_object_nbr: The number of a parent system block
preceded by the EAB acronym and version number that the system block is on.
$func: A business function performed by this application
$product: A business product supported by this application.

$al2: defines OS and application or OAM environments in sync with the $app_ env.
$al2: ((/$os/, /$env/))
$os: The OS that runs on top of previously defined OS for this platform.
$env (either $appenv or $oamenv): The application or OAM environment that runs
 on top of the previously defined $app_ def or oam_def.

$al3: Defines the software languages.
$al3: ((((/$language/))).
$languages: The languages that the associated application is written in.

FIGURE A.15   Configured platform icon template.

<$service_type, /$api/, $sproduct, //$func/:/$product//, $svc_role, /$language/>

$service: defines a service.
$service: <$service_type, /$ api/, $product, $svc_role,$language>
$service_type: Defines a unique type of service.
$api: Defines the API or protocol that is invoked to interface with the service.
$sproduct: Defines the software product that delivers the service.
$svc_role: Defines the interoperability role of the application layer.
$language: The language that invokes the associated API(s).
$func: A business function performed by the associated application.
$product: A business product enabled by the associated $func.

FIGURE A.16   Service icon template.

<$service_type, /$api/, $sproduct, //$func/:/$product//, $svc_role,/$language><$service_type, /$api/, $sproduct>

| *or* | *and* |

$service: Defines a service.
$service: <$service_type, /$api/, $product, $svc_role>
$service_type: defines a unique type of service.
$api: Defines the API or protocol that is invoked to interface with the service.
$sproduct: Defines the product that delivers the service.
$language: The language that invokes the associated API(s).
$svc_role: Defines the interoperability role of the application layer.
$func: A business function performed by the associated application.
$product: A business product enabled by the associated $func .

FIGURE A.17   Service path icon template.

$interop_def

/$service/* --*/$service/

- -

$interop_def: Defines interoperability attributes.
$interop_def: $middleware_def, $trans_def, /$data_flow $frequency/
$middleware_def: Defines the middleware framework that governs the interoperability.
$trans_def: Defines whether the interoperability supports transactions. Codes are Y
(yes) or N (no). Default is no.
$data_flow: The name of the data items being exchanged.
$frequency: The frequency of the exchange; i.e., interactive, daily, on-demand, etc.

FIGURE A.18   Interoperability definition icon template.

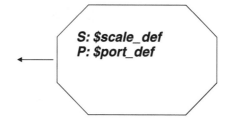

- -

$scale_def: Defines the label of a Scalability diagram.
$port_def: Defines the label of a Portability diagram.

FIGURE A.19   Scalability and portability icon template.

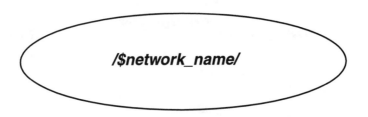

$network_name: defines the name of a physical network, a type of network or "..." for an unknown network.

FIGURE A.20   Network icon template.

$title: The title of the grouping.

FIGURE A.21   Object grouping and titling icon template.

–Application List for $system_ acronym–	–Footnote List–	–System List–
1. $app1	1. $footnote1	1. $system_name1
2. $app2	2. $footnote2	2. $system_name2
3. $app3	3. $footnote3	3. $system_name3
4. $app4	4. $footnote4	4. $system_name4
5. $app5	5. $footnote5	5. $system_name5
n. $appn	n. $footnoten	n. $system_namen

$system_acronym: A unique acronym identifying the system or subsystem.
$app: The name of a business application.
$footnote: A footnote.
$system_name: A unique name identifying the system or subsystem.

FIGURE A.22 Application, system, and footnote list templates.

–Function List–	–Product List–	–Function_Product List–	–OSIList–
			1. $layer7
1. $func1	1. $product1	1. /$func/:/$product/	2. $layer6
2. $func2	2. $product2	2. /$func/:/$product/	3. $layer5
3. $func3	3. $product3	3. /$func/:/$product/	4. $layer4
4. $func4	4. $product4	4. /$func/:/$product/	5. $layer3
5. $func5	5. $product5	5. /$func/:/$product/	6. $layer2
n. $funcn	n. $productn	n. /$func/:/$product/	7. $layer1

$func: The name of a business function.
$product: The name of a product or service that this (sub)system block supports.
$layer7: OSI layer 7 definition
$layer6: OSI layer 6 definition
$layer5: OSI layer 5 definition
$layer4: OSI layer 4 definition
$layer3: OSI layer 3 definition
$layer2: OSI layer 2 definition
$layer1: OSI layer 1 definition

FIGURE A.23 Function, product, and OSI list templates.

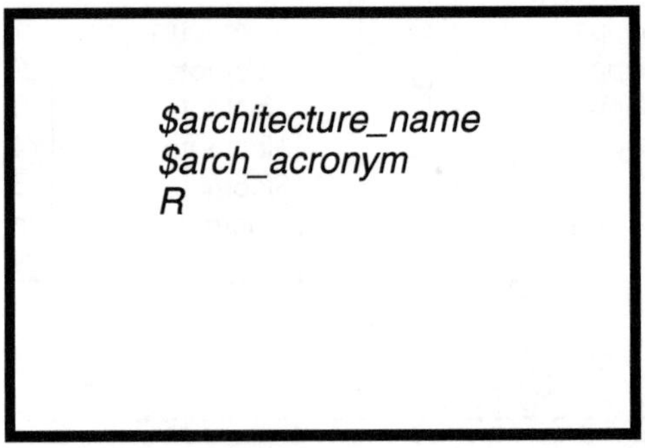

$architecture_name
$arch_acronym
R

$architecture_name: The name of an EAB architecture.
$arch_acronym: The acronym of the above architecture.
R: Reference EAB.

FIGURE A.24   EAB icon template.

FIGURE A.25   EAB linkage icon template.

Enterprise IT Architecture Blueprinting Diagram and Page Templates

This appendix supplies the page templates for all of the diagrams defined in Chapter 3. These templates are also available on the Wiley Web page at www.wiley.com/compbooks/boar in .ppt format. Users should adopt and customize the templates for the specific needs of their organization before utilizing them. Table B.1 provides an index of the page templates.

TABLE B.1 Page Templates

Figure Number	Template Name
B.1	Enterprise Architecture Blueprint Cover Page
B.2	Table of Contents
B.3	Overview
B.4	Design Definition
B.5	Legends
B.6	Change Control
B.7	Separator Page for Section Core Subsection SB
B.8	System Block Diagram
B.9	Separator Page for Section Core Subsection PL
B.10	Platform Diagram
B.11	Separator Page for Section Core Subsection Interop
B.12	Interoperability Diagram
B.13	Separator Page for Section Core Subsection Cut-Out
B.14	Cut-Out Diagram .
B.15	Separator Page for Section Core Subsection Function
B.16	Function Diagram
B.17	Separator Page for Annotation Section
B.18	Annotation Functional Specification
B.19	Separator Page for Dictionary Section
B.20	Dictionary Bill of Materials
B.21	Separator Page for Detail Section
B.22	Detail Functional Specification
B.23	Separator Page for Database Section
B.24	Database Functional Specification
B.25	Separator Page for Transaction Section
B.26	Transaction Functional Specification
B.27	Separator Page for Portability Section
B.28	Portability Functional Specification
B.29	Separator Page for Scalability Section
B.30	Scalability Functional Specification
B.31	Separator Page for User Group Section
B.32	User Group Functional Specification
B.33	Separator Page for Network Section
B.34	Network Functional Specification

ENTERPRISE ARCHITECTURE BLUEPRINT COVER PAGE

$architecture_name $parent_architecture_name
$arch_acronym $parent_arch_acronym
$version_nbr $status
$version_date $prepared_by
$architecture_preversion_number $reach_info

$architecture_purpose

$company
_logo

FIGURE B.1 Enterprise Architecture blueprint cover page.

Table of Contents

Section	Subsection	Page Label	Page Number	Page Title

$prepared_by	$page_label	Page 1.0	EAB Table of Contents	$company
--------------	-------------	----------	-----------------------	_logo
$reach_info	Front			

FIGURE B.2 Table of contents.

Overview

1. *Introduction/Purpose: $introduction*
2. *Overview: $overview*
3. *Scope: $scope*
4. *Problem Statement: $problem*
5. *Objectives: $objectives*
6. *Audience: $audience*
7. *Assumptions: &assumptions*
8. *Team and Contact List : &teamlist*
9. *Highlights: $highlights*
10. *Executive Summary: $esummary*
11. *Change Summary: $change_summary*
12. *Other: $your_choice*

$prepared_by	$page_label	Page 2.0	EAB Overview	$company _logo
$reach_info	Front			

FIGURE B.3   Overview.

Design Definition

1. *$design_option_1_ and_choice*
2. *$design_option_2_ and_choice*
n. *$design_option_n_ and_choice*

n+1. Distributed EAB Diagram

$prepared_by	$page_label	Page 3.0	EAB Design Definition	$company _logo
$reach_info	Front			

FIGURE B.4   Design definition.

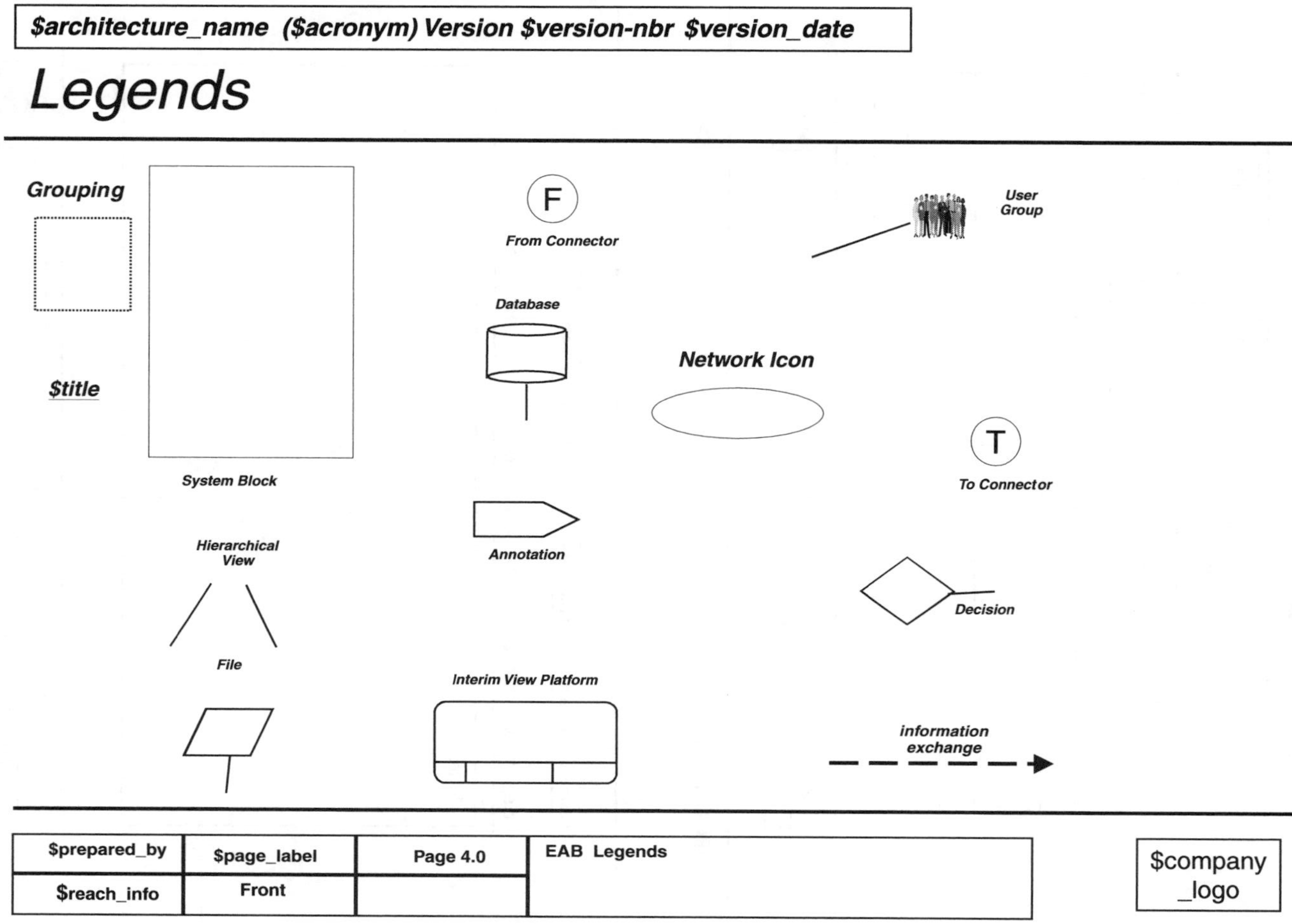

Legends

$architecture_name ($acronym) Version $version-nbr $version_date

Grouping

$title

System Block

Hierarchical
View

File

(F) From Connector

Database

Annotation

Network Icon

User
Group

(T) To Connector

Decision

Interim View Platform

information
exchange

$company
_logo

$prepared_by	$page_label	Page 4.0	EAB Legends
$reach_info	Front		

FIGURE B.5 Legends.

287

Change Control

Section	Subsection	Page Label	Page Number	Page Title

$prepared_by	$page_label	Page 5.0	EAB Change Control	$company_logo
$reach_info	Front			

FIGURE B.6   Change control.

Separator Page for Section Core$sect_suffix Subsection SB

$intro_notes

$prepared_by	$page_label	Page 0.0 $page_suffix	$page_purpose	$company_logo
$reach_info	Core$sect_suffix	SB		

FIGURE B.7   Separator page for section core subsection SB.

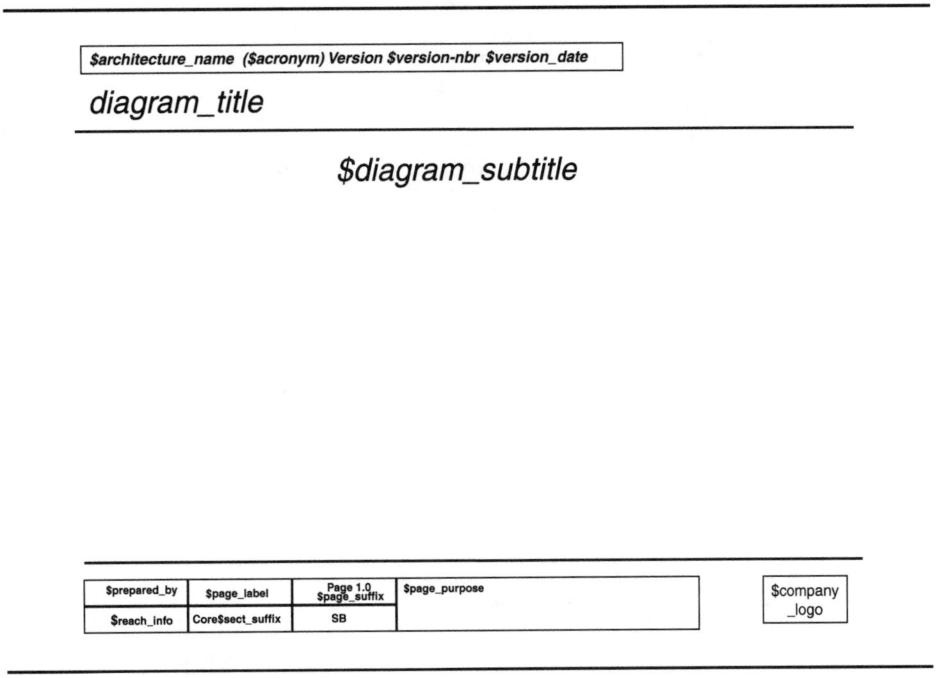
$architecture_name ($acronym) Version $version-nbr $version_date
diagram_title
$diagram_subtitle
$prepared_by
$page_label
Page 1.0
$page_suffix
$page_purpose
$reach_info
Core$sect_suffix
SB
$company _logo

FIGURE B.8 System Block diagram.

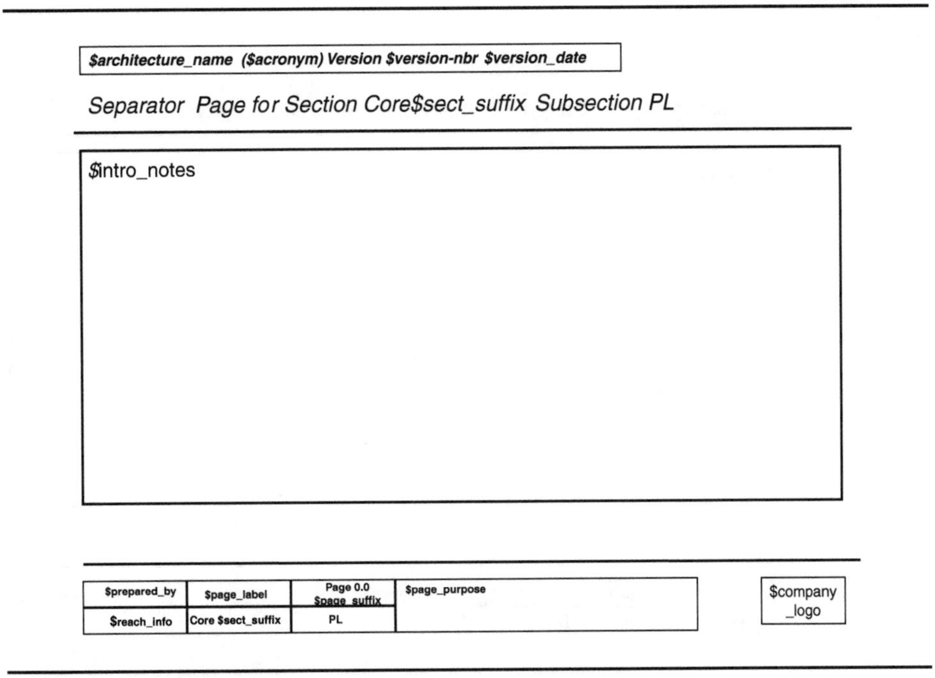
$architecture_name ($acronym) Version $version-nbr $version_date
Separator Page for Section Core$sect_suffix Subsection PL
$intro_notes
$prepared_by
$page_label
Page 0.0
$page_suffix
$page_purpose
$reach_info
Core $sect_suffix
PL
$company _logo

FIGURE B.9 Separator page for section core subsection PL.

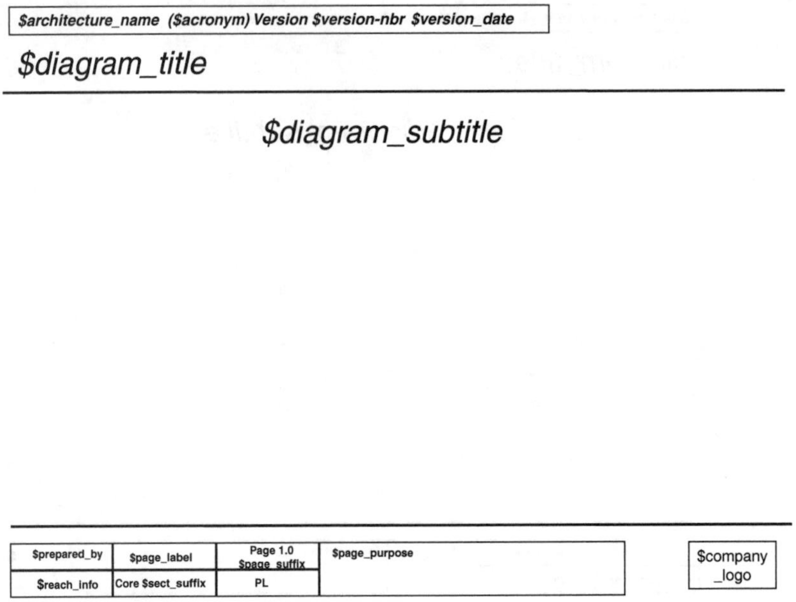

$architecture_name ($acronym) Version $version-nbr $version_date

$diagram_title

$diagram_subtitle

$prepared_by	$page_label	Page 1.0 $page_suffix	$page_purpose		$company _logo
$reach_info	Core $sect_suffix	PL			

FIGURE B.10   Platform diagram.

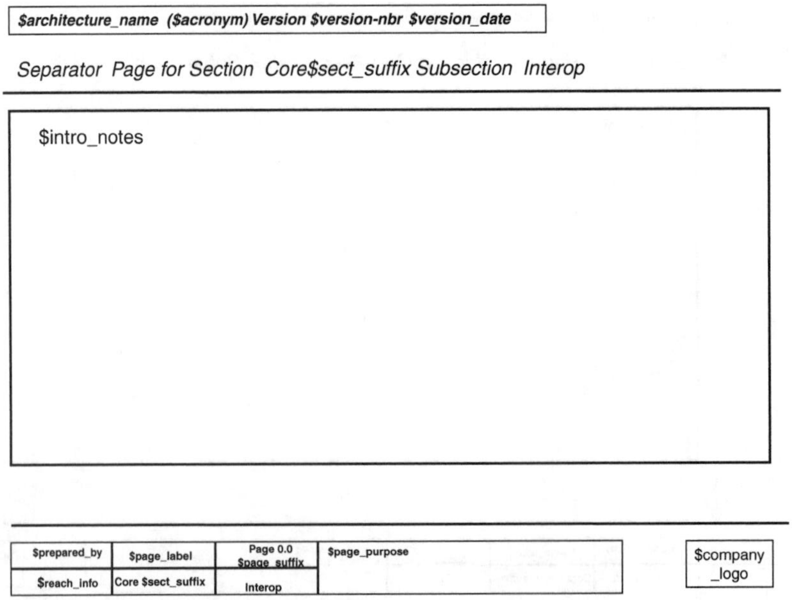

$architecture_name ($acronym) Version $version-nbr $version_date

Separator Page for Section Core$sect_suffix Subsection Interop

$intro_notes

$prepared_by	$page_label	Page 0.0 $page_suffix	$page_purpose		$company _logo
$reach_info	Core $sect_suffix	Interop			

FIGURE B.11   Separator page for section core subsection Interop.

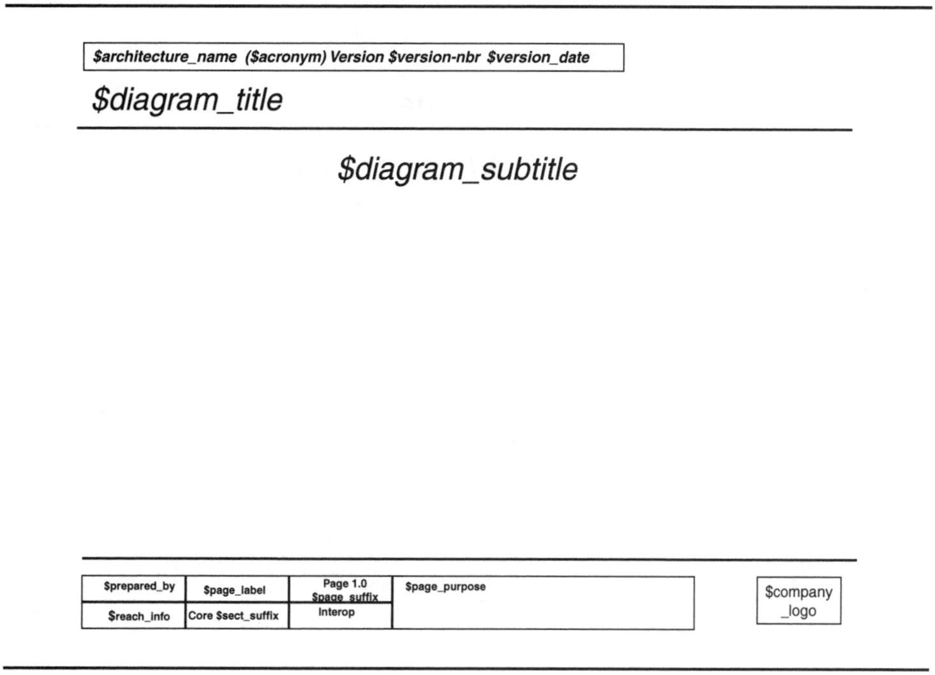

```
$architecture_name ($acronym) Version $version-nbr $version_date
```

$diagram_title

$diagram_subtitle

$prepared_by	$page_label	Page 1.0 $page_suffix	$page_purpose	$company _logo
$reach_info	Core $sect_suffix	Interop		

FIGURE B.12   Interoperability diagram.

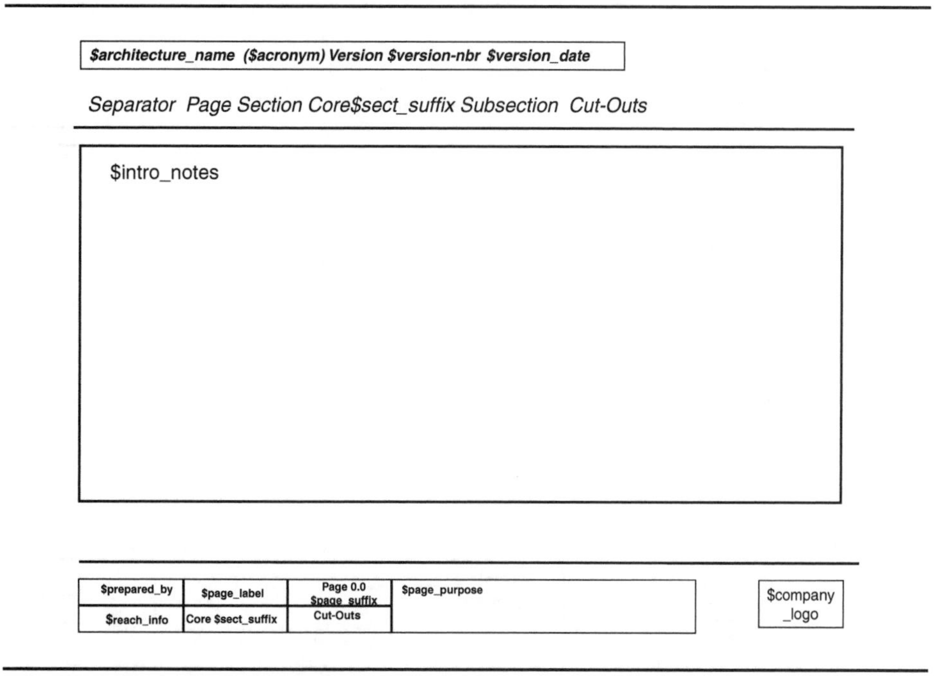

```
$architecture_name ($acronym) Version $version-nbr $version_date
```

Separator Page Section Core$sect_suffix Subsection Cut-Outs

$intro_notes

$prepared_by	$page_label	Page 0.0 $page_suffix	$page_purpose	$company _logo
$reach_info	Core $sect_suffix	Cut-Outs		

FIGURE B.13   Separator Page for section core subsection cut-out.

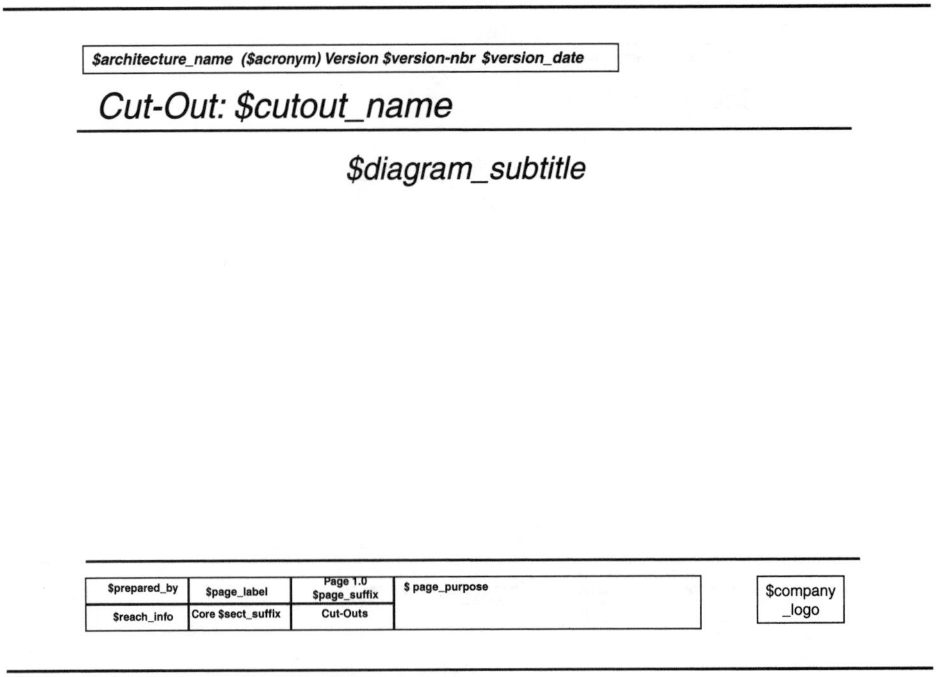

$architecture_name ($acronym) Version $version-nbr $version_date

Cut-Out: $cutout_name

$diagram_subtitle

$prepared_by	$page_label	Page 1.0 $page_suffix	$ page_purpose		$company _logo
$reach_info	Core $sect_suffix	Cut-Outs			

FIGURE B.14   Cut-out diagram.

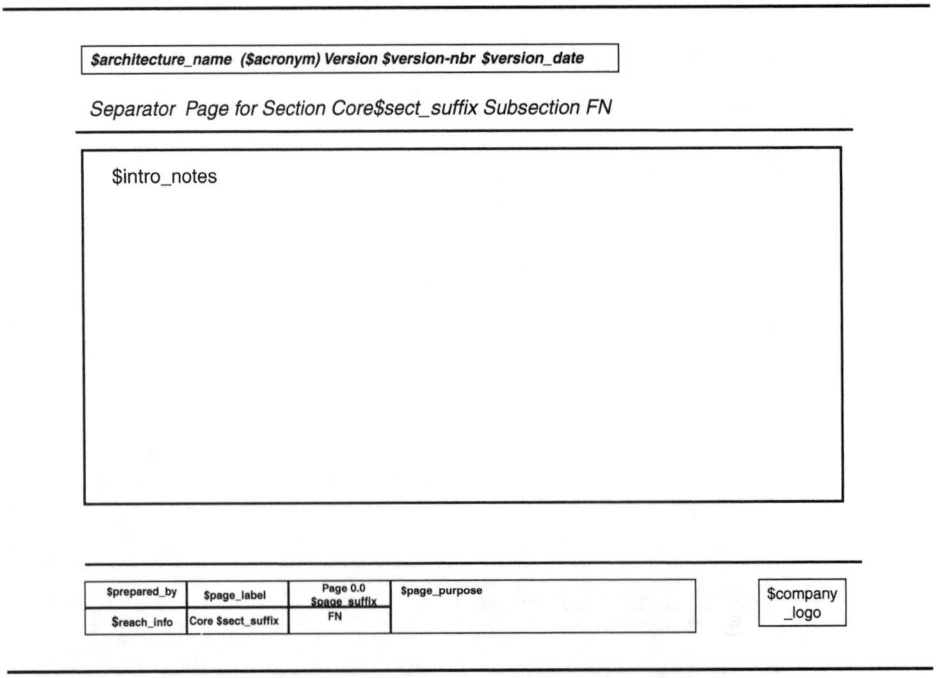

$architecture_name ($acronym) Version $version-nbr $version_date

Separator Page for Section Core$sect_suffix Subsection FN

$intro_notes

$prepared_by	$page_label	Page 0.0 $page_suffix	$page_purpose		$company _logo
$reach_info	Core $sect_suffix	FN			

FIGURE B.15   Separator page for section core subsection function.

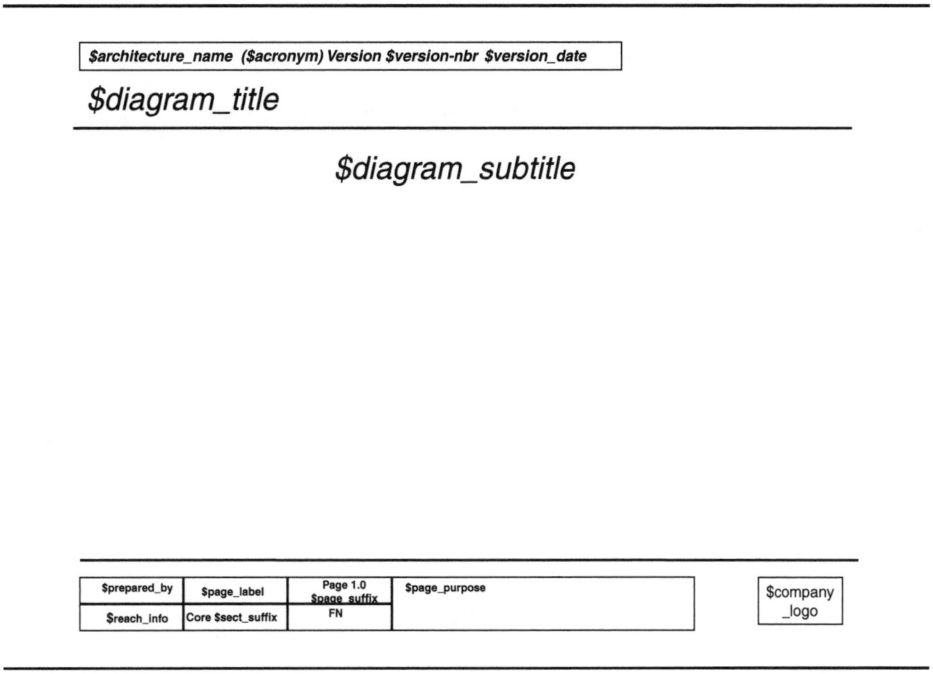

$architecture_name ($acronym) Version $version-nbr $version_date

$diagram_title

$diagram_subtitle

$prepared_by	$page_label	Page 1.0 $page_suffix	$page_purpose		$company _logo
$reach_info	Core $sect_suffix	FN			

FIGURE B.16   Function diagram.

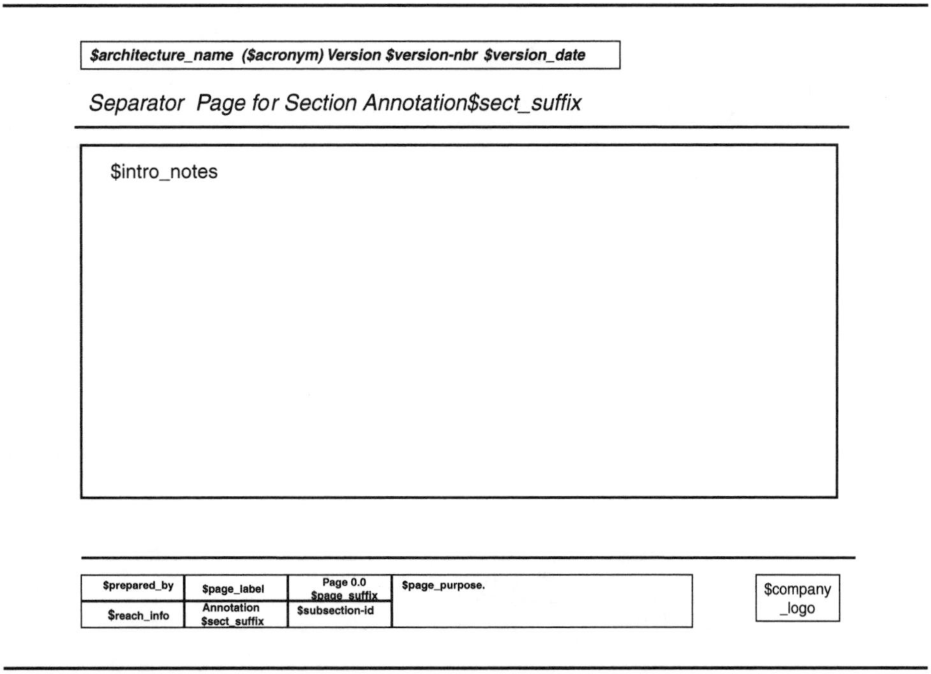

$architecture_name ($acronym) Version $version-nbr $version_date

Separator Page for Section Annotation$sect_suffix

$intro_notes

$prepared_by	$page_label	Page 0.0 $page_suffix	$page_purpose.		$company _logo
$reach_info	Annotation $sect_suffix	$subsection-id			

FIGURE B.17   Separator page for annotation section.

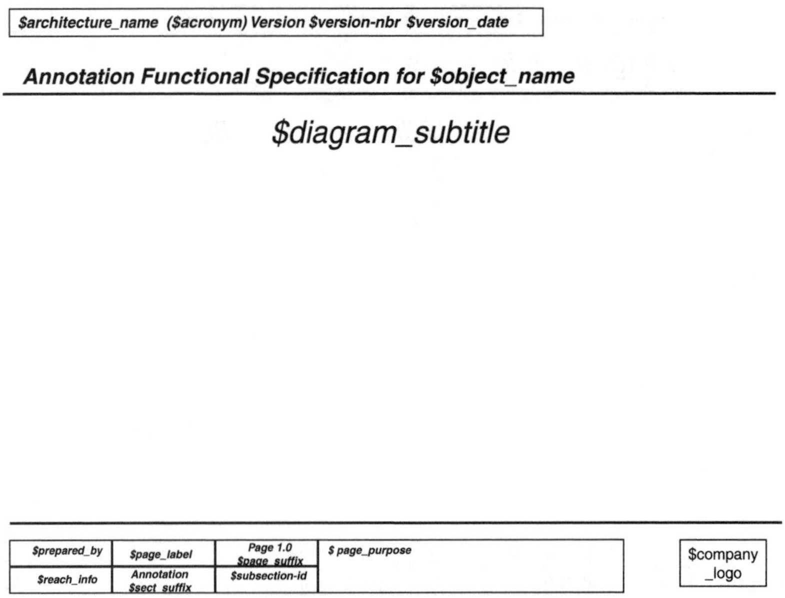

$architecture_name ($acronym) Version $version-nbr $version_date

Annotation Functional Specification for $object_name

$diagram_subtitle

$prepared_by	$page_label	Page 1.0 $page_suffix	$ page_purpose		$company _logo
$reach_info	Annotation $sect_suffix	$subsection-id			

FIGURE B.18   Annotation functional specification.

$architecture_name ($acronym) Version $version-nbr $version_date

Separator Page for Section Dictionary$sect_suffix

$intro_notes

$prepared_by	$page_label	Page 0.0 $page_suffix	$page_purpose		$company _logo
$reach_info	Dictionary $sect_suffix	$subsection-id			

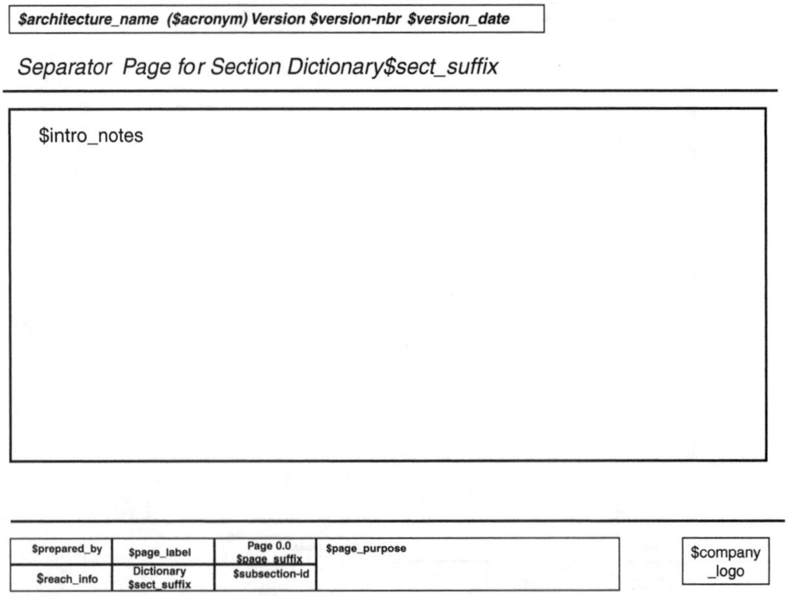

FIGURE B.19   Separator page for Dictionary section.

| $architecture_name ($acronym) Version $version-nbr $version_date |

Dictionary Bill of Materials

$diagram_subtitle

Object	Object Type	Definition	Comments

$prepared_by	$page_label	Page 1.0 $page_suffix	$ page_purpose	$company_logo
$reach_info	Dictionary $sect_suffix	$subsection-id		

FIGURE B.20   Dictionary Bill of Materials.

| $architecture_name ($acronym) Version $version-nbr $version_date |

Separator Page for Section Detail $sect_suffix

$intro_notes

$prepared_by	$page_label	Page 0.0 $page_suffix	$page_purpose	$company_logo
$reach_info	Detail $sect_suffix	$subsection-id		

FIGURE B.21   Separator page for Detail section.

Detail Functional Specification For $platform_name

Specification Class	Specification Item	Specification	Comments
Hardware			
Software			
RAS			
Other			

$prepared_by	$page_label	Page 1.0 $page_suffix	$page_purpose	$company_logo
$reach_info	Detail $sect_suffix	$subsection-id		

FIGURE B.22   Detail functional specification.

Separator Page for Database Section $sect_suffix

$intro_notes

$prepared_by	$page_label	Page 0.0 $page_suffix	$page_purpose	$company_logo
$reach_info	Database $sect_suffix	$subsection-id		

FIGURE B.23   Separator page for Database section.

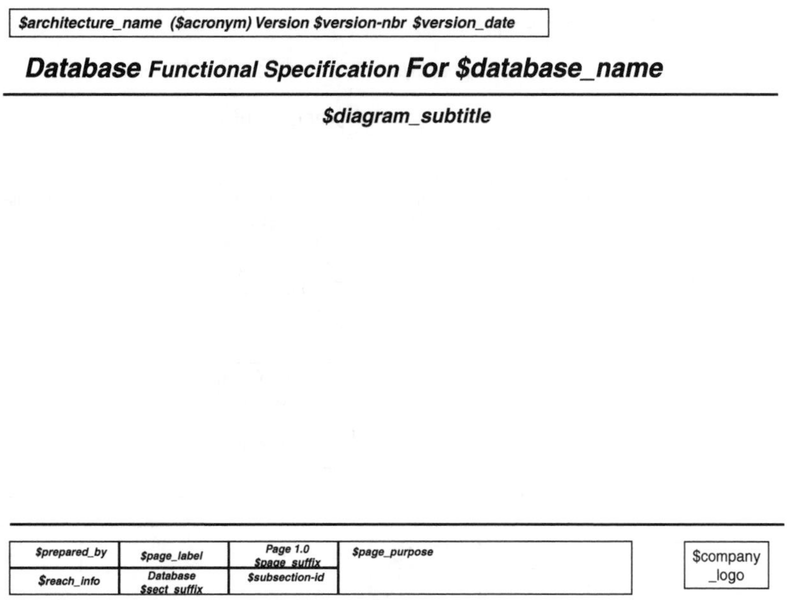

$architecture_name ($acronym) Version $version-nbr $version_date

Database Functional Specification For $database_name

$diagram_subtitle

$prepared_by	$page_label	Page 1.0 $page_suffix	$page_purpose	$company_logo
$reach_info	Database $sect_suffix	$subsection-id		

FIGURE B.24   Database functional specification.

$architecture_name ($acronym) Version $version-nbr $version_date

Separator Page for Transaction Section $sect_suffix

$intro_notes

$prepared_by	$page_label	Page 0.0 $page_suffix	$page_purpose	$company_logo
$reach_info	Transaction $sect_suffix	$subsection-id		

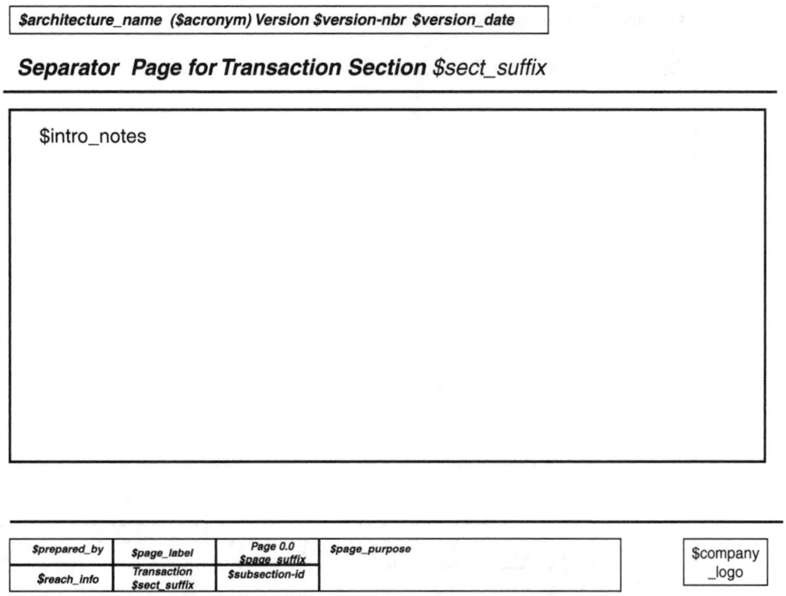

FIGURE B.25   Separator page for Transaction section.

$architecture_name ($acronym) Version $version-nbr $version_date

Transaction **Functional Specification** For *$data_flow*

$diagram_subtitle

Transaction Name	Transaction Definition	Transaction Specification	Comments
		Normal Volume: Peak Volume: Performance: Requirements: Security:	
		Normal Volume: Peak Volume: Performance: Requirements: Security:	

$prepared_by	$page_label	Page 1.0 $page_suffix	$page_purpose	$company _logo
$reach_info	Transaction $sect_suffix	$subsection-id		

FIGURE B.26 Transaction functional specification.

$architecture_name ($acronym) Version $version-nbr $version_date

Separator *Page for* **Portability Section** *$sect_suffix*

$intro_notes

$prepared_by	$page_label	Page 0.0 $page_suffix	$page_purpose	$company _logo
$reach_info	Portability $sect_suffix	$subsection-id		

FIGURE B.27 Separator page for Portability section.

$architecture_name ($acronym) Version $version-nbr $version_date

Portability Functional Specification *For $port_set*

$diagram_subtitle

Language	ITD	OS	App. Env.	OA&M Env.	Compiler	LE	DLL	Etc.

$prepared_by	$page_label	Page 1.0 $page_suffix	$page_purpose	$company _logo
$reach_info	Portability $sect_suffix	$subsection-id		

FIGURE B.28   Portability functional specification.

$architecture_name ($acronym) Version $version-nbr $version_date

Separator Page for Scalability Section $sect_suffix

$intro_notes

$prepared_by	$page_label	Page 0.0 $page suffix	$page_purpose	$company _logo
$reach_info	Scalability $sect_suffix	$subsection-id		

FIGURE B.29   Separator page for Scalability section.

$architecture_name ($acronym) Version $version-nbr $version_date

Scalability Functional Specification For $scale_set

$diagram_subtitle

ITD	OS	Application Environment	OA&M Environment	Scale Factor

$prepared_by	$page_label	Page 1.0 $page_suffix	$page_purpose	$company _logo
$reach_info	Scalability $sect_suffix	$subsection-id		

FIGURE B.30   Scalability functional specification.

$architecture_name ($acronym) Version $version-nbr $version_date

Separator Page for User Group Section $sect_suffix

$intro_notes

$prepared_by	$page_label	Page 0.0 $page_suffix	$page_purpose	$company _logo
$reach_info	User Group $sect_suffix	$subsection-id		

FIGURE B.31   Separator page for User Group section.

User Group Functional Specification

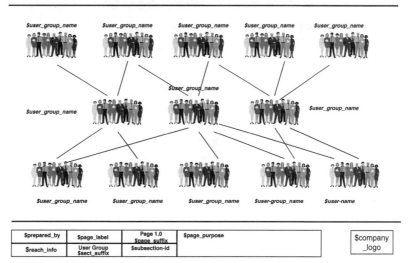

$prepared_by	$page_label	Page 1.0 $page_suffix	$page_purpose		$company _logo
$reach_info	User Group $sect_suffix	$subsection-id			

FIGURE B.32   User Group functional specification.

$architecture_name ($acronym) Version $version-nbr $version_date

Separator Page for Network Section *$sect_suffix*

$intro_notes

$prepared_by	$page_label	Page 0.0 $page_suffix	$page_purpose		$company _logo
$reach_info	Network $sect_suffix	$subsection-id			

FIGURE B.33   Separator page Network section.

$architecture_name ($acronym) Version $version-nbr $version_date

Network *Functional Specification* ***For $network_name***

$diagram_subtitle

$prepared_by	$page_label	Page 1.0 $page_suffix	$page_purpose	$company _logo
$reach_info	Network $sect_suffix	$subsection-id		

FIGURE B.34   Network functional specification.

APPENDIX C

Architecture Principle Development Methodology

As stated in Chapter 2, architecture principles define the rules and guidelines that steer the selection and deployment of information technologies. It is axiomatic that these principles must be aligned with the most pressing needs of the business. Alignment means that you can trace the selection of information technologies and the design of the IT architecture to the most pressing business drivers. A business driver is an external market force that can either materially devalue the current business model or provide an opportunity to materially improve market share, customer satisfaction, or revenue.

Alignment of the business drivers with the IT standards and architecture models is achieved by following a five-step process. In executing this process, all decisions are made independent of any specific application or temporary but pressing need. The idea is to develop a set of principles that transcend a single specific business application and serve to optimize the architecture, as a whole, over the planning horizon. You want to develop a set of principles that are not faddish, rather that have persistence over time. You want a set of principles that give clear direction to a future vision architecture that enables the business to command the business drivers. As a result, some applications may need to be suboptimized to permit an overall optimization of the architecture to the business drivers. A well-crafted set of principles is built on the maxim, "the needs of the many over the needs of the few."

STEP 1: MATRIX BUSINESS DRIVERS TO MAJOR BUSINESS INITIATIVES

An analysis matrix is created that intersects the dominant business drivers of the enterprise—for the planning horizon—against the types of major business initiatives that are required to address them (see Table C.1).

Cells are populated with an X to indicate the relationships between business drivers and business initiatives. Each business driver should be addressed by at least one business initiative and each business initiative should address at least one business driver. Examples of business drivers are:

- Rapid technological change of IT
- Industry deregulation
- Customer power—ease of substitution
- Globalization of marketplace
- Rise of multiple, deep-pocketed players
- Basic products become commodities—cost pressures
- Multiple concurrent market/product fronts
- Changing customer demographics

TABLE C.1 Matrix Major Business Drivers to Business Initiatives

Business Drivers	Major Business Initiatives							
	Initiative 1	Initiative 2	Initiative 3	Initiative 4	Initiative 5	Initiative 6	Initiative 7	Initiative n
Business Driver 1								
Business Driver 2								
Business Driver 3								
Business Driver 4								
Business Driver 5								
Business Driver 6								
Business Driver 7								
Business Driver n								

Examples of major business initiatives are:

- Become low-cost provider.
- Offer value bundles.
- Obtain new distribution channels.
- Become customer facing.
- Achieve premier customer care.
- Serve the global customer.
- Business simplification.
- Create a common IT infrastructure.
- Create more innovative products.
- Enhance revenue per customer.
- Increase customer share.
- Redefine value proposition.
- Create centers of excellence.

STEP 2: MATRIX MAJOR BUSINESS INITIATIVES TO MAJOR IT REQUIREMENTS

An analysis matrix is created that intersects the major business initiatives against the IT requirements and capabilities that are required to address them (see Table C.2).

Cells are populated with an X to indicate the relationships between business initiatives and IT requirements. Each business initiative should be ad-

TABLE C.2   Matrix Major Business Initiatives to IT Requirements

Major Business Initiative	IT Requirements							
	Requirement 1	Requirement 2	Requirement 3	Requirement 4	Requirement 5	Requirement 6	Requirement 7	Requirement n
Initiative 1								
Initiative 2								
Initiative 3								
Initiative 4								
Initiative 5								
Initiative 6								
Initiative 7								
Initiative n								

dressed by at least one IT requirement and each IT requirement should address at least one business initiative. Examples of IT requirements are:

- Maneuverability through speed and agility
- Reusability
- Standardization of technologies and processes
- Interlock systems with customers and suppliers
- Modularity
- Single view of subject data
- Ease of substitution of components
- Function-centric rather than product-centric systems
- Multilanguage support
- Adherence to industry standards
- Re-skill of workforce
- Integration—not aggregation
- Enterprise architecture
- Productivity
- Balance build versus buy
- Open interoperability

STEP 3: MATRIX MAJOR IT REQUIREMENTS TO PRINCIPLES

An analysis matrix is created that intersects the major IT requirements against principles that serve as rules or guidelines for the selection and deployment of information technologies (see Table C.3).

TABLE C.3   Matrix Major IT Requirements to Principles

IT Requirements	Principles							
	Principle 1	Principle 2	Principle 3	Principle 4	Principle 5	Principle 6	Principle 7	Principle n
Requirement 1								
Requirement 2								
Requirement 3								
Requirement 4								
Requirement 5								
Requirement 6								
Requirement 7								
Requirement n								

Cells are populated with an X to indicate the relationships between IT requirements and principles. Each IT requirement should generate at least one principle and each principle must address at least one IT requirement. Examples of principles are given in Table 2.1.

STEP 4: MATRIX PRINCIPLES TO CLASS OF PRINCIPLE

An analysis matrix is created that allocates the principles to one of three classes of principles. These classes are:

1. **Overarching Principles.** Provide broad rules or guidelines for using the IT assets.
2. **Design Principles.** Provide rules or guidelines that influence design decisions.
3. **Buy Principles.** Provide rules or guidelines for how to make purchase decisions.

Each principle is further distinguished by whether it is a rule that must be followed or a guideline that is a strong recommendation (see Table C.4).

Matrix cells are populated with an X to indicate the mapping of the principles to the class of principles. Each principle must be mapped to a class and each class should have at least one principle.

TABLE C.4   Matrix Principles to Class of Principle

| | Classes of Principles | | | | | |
| | Overarching | | Design | | Buy | |
Principles	Rule	Guideline	Rule	Guideline	Rule	Guideline
Principle 1						
Principle 2						
Principle 3						
Principle 4						
Principle 5						
Principle 6						
Principle n						

STEP 5: MAP CLASSIFIED PRINCIPLES TO ARCHITECTURE PRINCIPLE CELLS

Each classified principle is assigned to an architecture framework principle cell. Each cell in Figure C.1 is populated with a principle. Each classified principle must be explicitly designated as an infrastructure principle, a data principle, an application principle, or an organization principle cell within the architecture framework. Based on the distribution of the mapping across architecture principle cells, it may be necessary to iterate the process and return to Step 3. Iteration of steps 3 through 5 continues until a satisfactory distribution of principles is generated across all architecture principle cells.

Infrastructure Principles												Data Principles												Application Principles												Organization Principles											
Over-Arching		Design		Buy		Over-Arching		Design		Buy		Over-Arching		Design		Buy		Over-Arching		Design		Buy	
Rule	Guide Line	Rule	Guide Line	Rule	Guide Line	Rule	Guide Line	Rule	Guide Line	Rule	Guide Line	Rule	Guide Line	Rule	Guide Line	Rule	Guide Line	Rule	Guide Line	Rule	Guide Line	Rule	Guide Line

FIGURE C.1 Each principle is mapped to the appropriate cell in the architecture principle column.

SUMMARY

This process permits you to demonstrate and visualize the logical alignment of the principles with the major business drivers through forward or backward chaining through the matrices. Starting with the business drivers, you can forward-chain your way to the principles—that are enabling the business to contend with the driver. Conversely, starting with a principle, you can work your way back to the business drivers that governed the decision. In this way, business leaders can be confident that business imperatives drive the selection of information technologies, and that technology decisions are not made asynchronous to the most pressing concerns of the business.

Index

A

B

C